		Fahrenheit	Celsius
Zone 1		below -50°	below -46°
Zone 2		-50° to -40°	-46° to -40°
Zone 3		-40° to -30°	-40° to -34°
Zone 4		-30° to -20°	-34° to -29°
Zone 5		-20° to -10°	-29° to -23°
Zone 6		-10° to 0°	-23° to -18°
Zone 7		0° to 10°	-18° to -12°
Zone 8		10° to 20°	-12° to -7°
Zone 9		20° to 30°	-7° to -1°
Zone 10		30° to 40°	-1° to 4°
Zone 11		above 40°	above 4°

Hardiness Across America

Zones in the United States are based on average minimum temperatures, with Zone 11 rated warmest, and Zone 1 coldest. Plants in this book are rated according to the coldest temperatures they survive. Summer heat and humidity, and lack of winter chilling in warmer climates, may limit the ability of some plants to thrive. Because of this, and the fact that within each Zone are microclimates that can be colder or warmer, we suggest that you use the Zones as a guide—but feel free to experiment with plants rated marginally hardy.

WILD ABOUT HERBS

ROGER TABOR

Reader's
Digest

The Reader's Digest Association, Inc.
Pleasantville, New York/Montreal

Frances Lincoln Project Staff
Contributing Editors, Anne Askwith, Michael Brunström,
Serena Dilnot, Alison Freegard, Penelope Miller, Sarah Mitchell
Designer, Caroline Hillier

Reader's Digest Project Staff
Project Editor, Fred DuBose
Project Designer, Jennifer R. Tokarski
Contributing Editors, Delilah Smittle, Elizabeth P. Stell

Reader's Digest Books
Executive Editor, Dolores York
Senior Designer, George McKeon
Director, Trade Publishing, Christopher T. Reggio

Editorial Director, Christopher Cavanaugh
Senior Design Director, Elizabeth Tunnicliffe

Consultants
Ronald D. Gardner, Senior Extension Associate, Cornell
University
Jacintha Cauffield, PhD (Pharmacy)

Library of Congress Cataloging-in-Publication Data
Tabor, Roger K.
    Wild about herbs/Roger Tabor.
        p.cm.
    ISBN 0-7621-0307-8
    1.Herbs. 2.Herb gardening. 3. Herbs–Utilization
    4. Cookery (Herbs) I. Title.
    SB351.H5 T23 2002
    635'.7–dc21   2001048629

Printed in Singapore

10 9 8 7 6 5 4 3 2 1

PAGE 1 Aloe vera on a windowsill
PAGES 2–3 left: clary sage right: chives and oregano
OPPOSITE clockwise from top: winter savory, hops,
dandelion, meadowsweet and flat-leaved parsley

Contents

Introduction 6

The Use of Herbs in History 8
The use of herbs worldwide from antiquity
to the present day

Growing & Preserving Herbs 16
Expert gardening advice & tips

Useful Herbs 38
Detailed information on over 100 herbs

Herbs for Healthy Eating 114
Cooking with herbs

The Power of Herbs 136
A guide to simple, safe home remedies

Herbs at Home 150
Household & cosmetic uses

Glossary 166
Further reading 170
Index 171
Acknowledgments 176

Introduction

When is a plant an herb? To the botanist an herb is any plant that dies back down to the ground each year. The cook will immediately think of the traditional culinary herbs, such as mint and the fashionable basil. A health professional may define an herb as a plant that has a medicinal action; a beauty therapist might think of the value of herbs in skin treatments. These various descriptions illustrate a key fact about herbs: that they are useful in a wide diversity of ways.

Herbs have been useful to humanity through most of recorded history. They grace our gardens, as they have done from Roman times and earlier. Potpourris, nosegays of herbs, incense, and herb-scented candles provide sweet smells in our homes today, just as herbs strewn on the floor masked less pleasant odors in the past. From dill with its subtle tang to hot, peppery oregano, from lemony-tasting sorrel to anise-flavored tarragon, herbs have long been used to enhance food. And herbs have played a vital role as healing plants from ancient times to the present day.

The last decade has seen a spectacular resurgence of interest in herbs. In part this interest reflects a need, in an age when most people have become progressively divorced from their rural heritage, to be in touch with living plants and the soil. Growing herbs is one of the simplest means of achieving this; even those who have no garden can find space for a pot of basil or parsley. We take pleasure in nurturing herbs, and satisfaction in the usefulness of something that we have grown ourselves.

Within the medical world too there is renewed interest in herbs. As the pharmaceutical industry developed, making drugs from isolated herb components and later reproducing the isolated components synthetically, a gulf grew between traditional herbal therapies and conventional medicine. That divide is now diminishing. On one side, there is a revival of interest in medical botany. Many new drugs, including those for the treatment of devastating diseases such as cancer, are being derived from plants. Yew, for instance, is the source of some of the most potent drugs used in the treatment of ovarian and breast cancer. And on the other side, as many people turn to naturopaths and herbalists to complement or as alternatives to conventional medical treatment, herbal medicine is regaining some of the prominence it had historically.

A similarly diverse approach is at the heart of this book. Modern Western culture makes clear distinctions between medicine, botany, horticulture, and cuisine, but at one time the overlap between the concerns of the herbalist, the doctor, the apothecary, the gardener, and the cook was considerable. *Wild about Herbs* returns to the old approach, covering all aspects of the cultivation and use of herbs. Focusing on a hundred of the most useful herbs, of which individual descriptions are given in the directory on pages 38–113, it aims to show how herbs can play an integral part in our lives, and aims to help all who are interested in herbs to use them wisely, effectively, and creatively.

HERB CONSERVATION ALERT

There is a long tradition both of gathering herbs from the wild and of growing herbs in gardens. However, with the population explosion of the last two centuries and increasing commercial pressures, some wild-growing species have come under threat. The gathering of these species has by necessity become restricted. The International Union for the Conservation of Nature's Species Survival Commission has concluded that around 13 percent of the world's plants are threatened with global extinction. The 1975 Convention on International Trade in Endangered Species (CITES), an international treaty administered by the UN Environment Program and now signed by over a hundred countries, lists several

Angelica, sweet cicely, and both Russian and variegated comfrey are among the herbs that thrive in this luxuriant garden.

hundred species that cannot be commercially traded because they are endangered.

For example, wild American ginseng (*Panax quinquefolius*) has been so overharvested in eastern North America that its exploitation in international trade is regulated under CITES. A less extreme, but still troubling case is that of echinacea. It is the best-selling North American native herb, accounting for nearly 10 percent of the total herbal sales in the United States. Its popularity has led to overcollecting in the wild. Of the three common species of echinacea in North America, all of which have been used

medicinally, *Echinacea purpurea* is extensively cultivated now in many countries, so preparations are often made from cultivated plants. *E. angustifolia* and *E. pallida* are harder to germinate, so stocks in cultivation are much lower; overharvesting in the wild therefore poses a great threat.

If you are to act as a responsible herb lover, then, restrict your herb gathering to those plants that are abundant in the wild, and do not on any account dig up rootstocks. Instead, try your best to keep seed-grown plants of threatened native species alive in pots and herb gardens.

The
Use of
Herbs
in
History

Archeology has provided evidence of the use of herbs by the earliest cultures. In Iraq, a Neanderthal man was buried some 60,000 years ago surrounded by herbs including yarrow and ephedra (*Ephedra sinica*). The ancient Egyptians are known to have used herbs extensively in burials. They made offerings of incense and fragrant oils, cleansed the body with spices and herbs (including cumin, anise, marjoram, and cinnamon), and used herbs in ointments for embalming. Ancient Egyptians also used herbs in cooking and in fumigation.

The earliest known writings on the use of herbs are from Assyria, on clay tablets from around 2500 BC; these list some 250 plants. The remarkable Ebers papyrus from ancient Egypt, of about 1500 BC, describes some 700 medicinal herbs including the opium poppy, garlic, castor oil plant, elderberry, wormwood, and aloe.

The Vedas, Indian epic poems dating from about 1500 BC, contain rich material on the herbal lore of that time. The medical treatise *Charaka Samhita,* preserved by oral tradition from around 700 BC and written down in the first century AD, mentions some 350 herbal medicines. This ancient knowledge is the basis of the Ayurvedic medicine still practiced today.

In the first century BC, Pliny the Elder wrote a remarkable encyclopedia, *Naturalis Historia,* with fascinating insights into herb use in the Roman world—in ointments and perfume as well as for medicine. He recommended dill to "cause belching" (dispel gas) and anise as an aphrodisiac. Roman formal gardens, built by the fashionable elite, included herbs such as bay and rosemary and often a *hortus,* an enclosed space for the cultivation of vegetables. The Roman landowner Columella brings to life the first-century Roman herb garden:

> *Now is the time, if pickles cheap you seek,*
> *To plant the caper and harsh elecampane*
> *And threatening fennel; creeping roots of mint*
> *And fragrant dill are spaced out now,*

A fourteenth-century manuscript of the *Tacuinum Sanitatis*. This Latin version of a work by the Arab Ibn al Baytar helped bring Arab medicinal knowledge to Europe.

> *And rue, which the olive's flavor*
> *Improves, and mustard which forces tears.*

In Greece and Rome and the lands of the north Mediterranean, locally grown scented plants such as branches of dried rosemary were burned at religious festivals. The Romans would also cascade rose petals over guests at meals and use the scent of roses in the bathhouse.

During the Roman Empire, the Romans took Mediterranean herbs to Britain and the rest of northern Europe. Among the herbs they introduced, both as food and as medicine, were garlic, onions, and chives, as well as summer and winter savory, parsley, spearmint, sweet marjoram, calendula, anise, and rosemary. Trade between southern Europe, India, and the East added to the European diet exotic spices, including ginger (used for cooking and to settle the stomach), pepper, and cinnamon.

After the fall of the Roman Empire in the fifth century AD, the greatest advances in herbal medicine occurred in Arab lands. The Arabs studied the classical Greek and Roman medical texts and also researched plant medicines from India and the Far East. The excellence of Arab medicine was extended to medieval Europe early in the eighth century AD when Islamic forces conquered Spain, where they were to retain power for hundreds of years. Arab medical texts and herbals were translated into Latin, the common European language of educated men at that time. For example, versions of a work that became known as the *Tacuinum Sanitatis,* by the Spanish Arab doctor Ibn al Baytar, have been found in historic libraries across Europe. The most significant medical text of this period was the *Al Qanun fi Tibb* (the "Canon of Medicine"), written in the beginning of the eleventh century by Ibn Sina, known as Avicenna. One influential Arab contribution was the separation of essential oils from herbs by distillation. Avicenna gets partial credit, as he improved the design of the still.

During the Middle Ages and beyond, villages and communities for the most part relied on local "wise" men and women, who gathered herbs from the woods and hedgerows to use in folk remedies. Although there was much superstition attached to herbs, there was also a widespread local knowledge of their uses. Such knowledge is illustrated by the remedies of a tenth-century Saxon doctor described in the *Leech Book of Bald,* the earliest European medical herbal in the vernacular.

People could also seek medical help from monasteries, which spread across Europe with Christianity. Monasteries were the only hospitals at the time, and they grew much of their own medicine in "physic" herb gardens. These physic gardens echoed the enclosed courtyard gardens of the Romans; the cloister's rectangular area was divided by paths into four or more intensively cultivated beds. A plan that has survived in the

With distillation, a process discovered by eleventh-century Arab doctors and shown in this woodcut from Rösslin's *Kräuterbuch* ("Book of Herbs") of 1536, it became possible to separate the essential oils from herbs.

A doctor selects herbs for medicinal purposes, in an illustration from *Roman de la Rose,* about 1400. The garden is typical of the layout of "physic" gardens of the time: in an enclosed area narrow paths divide the ground into small beds, each containing different herbs.

ninth-century monastery of St. Gall, in Switzerland, shows a physic garden containing, among other herbs, mints, rosemary, rue, pennyroyal, sage, fennel, tansy, and savory, as well as a larger kitchen garden that includes chervil, coriander, dill, garlic, and onions. Fragments of medieval glass and ceramic stills that have been excavated from a number of monastic sites across England suggest that the distillation of essential oils and alcohol was quite common.

With the Crusades and the expansion of trade routes in the Middle Ages, many new seasonings became available to Europe. By the fifteenth century imported herbs and spices including cardamom, nutmeg, and turmeric were being used by those who could afford them to add flavor or mask it. Garlic, mustard, and

fennel were easy to cultivate locally and so became quite widely available. When European explorers began to reach the Americas in the late 1400s, they were excited to find a rich flora that was entirely new to them, whereupon they sent many plants back to Europe.

Apothecaries were quick to make use of any newly discovered herbs. By the end of the Middle Ages, apothecaries had become skilled professionals. They served a seven-year apprenticeship to acquire the botanical expertise to make up herbal medications and treat patients, as prescribed by a physician. Apothecaries bought ingredients from "herb women" and root gatherers; they also grew herbs in their own physic gardens. They made perfumes from flowers and herbs. These were used to overcome foul odors and deter insects and other parasites, as people rarely bathed and rarely washed their richly made garments. Apothecaries also used herbs to spice wines, to make candies such as "cumfyttes of aniseed and sweet fennel," and as ingredients in cosmetics.

Private households from great houses to small cottages used home-grown herbs for a wide range of purposes besides seasoning and medicine. Herbs such as meadowsweet were strewn on damp earth floors to release pleasant smells when walked upon; herbal scents were thought to purify a home and help keep out pests such as fleas and lice. Sweet-smelling herbs were added to straw used in mattresses and pillows. Herb mixtures including dried lavender and rose petals were hung in cupboards in small bags to perfume the contents; herbs such as wormwood or mugwort (*Artemisia vulgaris*) might be included to help deter insects. Dried herbs placed with flowers in small boxes or bags ("pomanders") or small bouquets ("tussie mussies") were carried into foul-smelling places where there might be a risk of infection. Herbal oils were used in scented candles to mask the smell of burning tallow.

Until the fifteenth century, European herbals were manuscripts written in Latin and copied by monks, and therefore available only to a narrow elite. However, with the invention of the printing press, the switch from Latin to the local vernacular in written texts, and increasing literacy, knowledge of herbs and their uses became available to a wider range of people. Women in particular used the advice in herbals to help them in their household duties.

In the sixteenth century, a physician by the name of Philippus Theophrastus Bombastus von Hohenheim, known as Paracelsus, was a significant influence in the development of Western medicine. He lauded the use of local herbs and folk remedies, while advocating the study of exact dosage and the pharmacologically active principles of plants as well as chemical cures. Paracelsus also revived interest in the Doctrine of Signatures, an ancient theory that

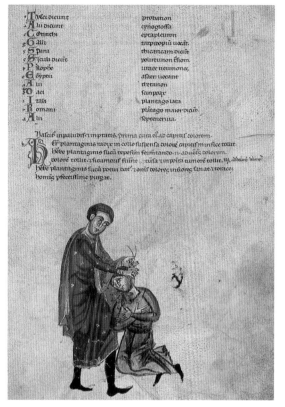

An illustration from a thirteenth-century Italian manuscript shows an apothecary wrapping a plantain root around a patient's head—an early record of a treatment for headaches and earaches.

crops up in many different eras and cultures. According to this theory, when making each species of plant, God left a sign that identified which part of the body it could treat. For instance, it was thought that the blotches on the leaves of lungwort looked like a section of lungs, indicating that the plant could be used to treat bronchial conditions.

Paracelsus' call for the close observation of plants helped inspire the golden age of English scientific herbals. These works mention many species recently brought back to Europe from the Americas by explorers and traders. The best known of these is the Culpeper herbal, originally published as *The English Physitian* in 1649 by physician and herbalist Nicholas Culpeper. He was castigated by the medical establishment because he drew upon the Doctrine of Signatures and included astrological advice. Still, he based his herbal on extensive experience, and it became one of the best-selling herbals of all time. It is still in print today.

The settlement of the Americas promoted the exchange of plants and herbal knowledge between the Old and the New Worlds. In Europe the unfamiliar herbs from abroad were studied at the new botanic gardens such as the Chelsea Physic Garden in London and the Jardin du Roi in Paris. Exotic imports like nasturtium were incorporated into existing ornamental gardens. Among the fashionable set, utilitarian herb gardens were becoming more ornamental. In Europe the seventeenth century saw the heyday of the knot garden, a pattern of low clipped hedges of scented evergreen herbs such as germander (*Teucrium chamaedrys*), lavender, hyssop, boxwood (*Buxus sempervirens*), winter savory, sweet marjoram, and thyme.

As well as sending new plant discoveries back to Europe, settlers took culinary and medicinal herbs to the Americas. For example, in 1631 John Winthrop brought and then cultivated forty-eight herbs including rosemary, thyme, and clary. Initially, through lack of knowledge of American plants, settlers relied on the tried-and-trusted herbs they had brought with them. Gradually, however, they adopted some herbs used by Native Americans. For example, bee balm became a substitute for imported black tea, fevers were treated with boneset, and bloodroot was used to produce a rich red dye.

In time Native American foods—such as the potato—and medicinal plants were introduced to Europe, Asia, and Africa. One of the many introductions from South America was Peruvian bark (*Chinchona* spp.), first recorded by a Spanish Jesuit missionary in 1633 and better known by the name of the alkaloid it contains, quinine. Used for centuries by the native peoples to treat fevers, quinine remained the most effective treatment for malaria worldwide until the First World War. Another South

American discovery was ipecacuanha (*Psychotria ipecacuanha*), taken to Europe in 1672. Better known as ipecac, this plant contains an alkaloid (emetine) that kills amoebas and formerly was a key drug in the treatment of amoebic dysentery. Ipecac is still used to induce vomiting in some cases of poisoning.

In North America popular interest in herbs, as well as reaction against orthodox medicine and its excessive use of mercury and bleedings, inspired movements to amalgamate European and Native American traditions of herbal medicine. At the end of the eighteenth century Samuel Thompson developed a therapeutic regime based on native herbs and Native American remedies, in particular the concept of using herbs that induce sweat to treat disease. The popular Eclectic School, founded in the 1830s by Dr. Wooster Beech, blended Native American herbal treatments with those of the European tradition and mainstream medicine.

Thompsonian and Eclectic medicine owed some of their popularity to the Shakers, who were responsible for making plant medicines widely available. This communal sect developed the first large-scale wholesale herb business. In the 1820s they began selling dried herbs gathered from the wild and soon gained recognition for the purity and quality of their products. To meet increasing demand, they began to propagate and cultivate herbs on a large scale. They also began to process some of the herbs as extracts, ointments, and patent medicines (including formulas specified by Samuel Thompson). By the 1830s they were shipping herbs, seeds, and herbal medicines around the world. The Shakers also sold a few culinary herbs (sage, summer savory, sweet marjoram, and creeping thyme), essential oils, and flower waters. Rose water, the best-known flower water, was popular for cosmetic purposes and also as a flavoring. In the nineteenth century, rose water was used in desserts the way that vanilla extract is used today; the Shakers used it in apple pie.

The usefulness of the opium poppy as a painkiller increased greatly when its active component, morphine, was isolated in 1803, making more exact dosages possible. Three cultivars are depicted here in an engraving from Jean-Louis Prevost's *Collection des fleurs et des fruits*, 1805.

At the end of the eighteenth century, active components from medicinal herbs began to be identified and isolated. One of the first plants to be studied in this manner was foxglove. In the second half of the eighteenth century Dr. William Withering learned of the medicinal uses of foxglove from a village woman who, to his astonishment, cured dropsy by prescribing an herbal tea. He deduced that foxglove yielded an active principle, digitalis (a glycoside), which helps the heart. Morphine was isolated from the opium poppy and identified in 1803. Other alkaloids were similarly extracted—quinine from Peruvian bark, aconite from monkshood (*Aconitum napellus*), and atropine from deadly nightshade.

In the 1830s salicylic acid was identified in willow bark and extracted from meadowsweet. It was subsequently the first active ingredient to be synthesized. In 1899 the German pharmaceutical company Bayer produced a modified form that was to become the world's first proprietary drug, aspirin. The use of isolated herbal components (principally essential oils, alkaloids, and glycosides) plus other drugs synthesized in the laboratory launched a different approach to medical treatment. Up until then exact herbal prescription had been impossible because of the varying strength of the active principles in individual plants; now it was possible to make the isolated principles, or synthetic equivalents, into exact doses.

These developments, together with significant advances in medicine such as the discovery of antibiotics, led to a decline in herbal medicine in the West during most of the twentieth century. However, recent years have seen a change in attitude. The high cost of pharmaceutical drugs, a growing awareness of potentially serious side effects, the failure of conventional medicine to combat some chronic illnesses, and health problems associated with environmental pollutants are some of the factors that have led to renewed public interest in natural treatments. Herbal medicine's popularity has been boosted by modern research, which in many cases has validated traditional uses—for instance, St.-John's-wort as a treatment for depression. Research has also shown that it is sometimes more effective to use the whole plant rather than the extracted constituents prescribed by conventional medicine. Herbal medicine of various ancient traditions—including Chinese and Ayurvedic medicine—is being sought out to complement, or to provide an alternative to, conventional medicine.

Over the past quarter century, interest in all facets of herbs has grown tremendously. Herbs are now widely available, and they are included in everything from foods and beverages to crafts and cosmetics. They are grown, in both commercial herb farms and private gardens, more widely than ever before. Herbs remain integral to our lives, as they were to those of our ancestors thousands of years ago.

Growing
&
Preserving
Herbs

Growing herbs

Any gardener can enjoy home-grown herbs and their abundant ornamental and useful qualities. When planted in the conditions they prefer, herbs are easy to grow, and they are simple to harvest and preserve for home use. Whether you have a large plot devoted to herbs, a medium-sized garden in which you intersperse herbs with other plants, or just a window box or a couple of pots, the pleasure of growing herbs can be yours.

GARDEN STYLE: FORMAL OR INFORMAL?

Broadly speaking, when planning a garden for herbs, you can choose a design that is either formal or informal. Any design is, of course, a matter of individual choice and may combine elements of the two. In a formal design, the beds are divided into sections in a clear pattern, based on geometric shapes. A formal herb garden can be square or rectangular—as was common in Roman times and later in medieval monastery gardens. Another option is a symmetrical arrangement of beds including shapes such as regular curves, triangles, and circles as well as squares and rectangles. Traditionally the beds are defined by hedges, paths, or low walls to provide ease of access and to confine the herbs. Beds are filled with herbs grown in clearly delineated and controlled clumps, or as blocks of one kind of herb.

A traditional form of herb garden that still provides inspiration today is the knot, a twining or looping pattern of clipped low hedges. While boxwood is a traditional hedging plant for knot gardens, herbs can also be used. Rosemary, lavender, and thyme tolerate the frequent pruning required; for a more relaxed look (or to eliminate clipping) try parsley or chives. The spaces between hedges can be filled with colored gravel or herbs, especially those with a contrasting leaf color or texture.

The crisscrossing lines of a knot garden make a perfect—and traditional—setting for herbs. Here, the formality of the geometric boxwood-edged beds is softened by gentle mounds of wall germander.

In this informal but carefully orchestrated design, herbs such as lavender are planted in striking drifts, while hops are grown up tepees to give height and structure to the planting. The tepees are surrounded by contrasting circles of bright calendula.

When planning a formal herb garden, you will find it easiest to plan the design on graph paper first, drawing the layout to scale. Transfer the design to the ground using stakes and string. Mark straight lines with string secured by stakes at either end. Draw curved lines on the ground as arcs, with a stake tied by string to another stake planted in the ground.

An informal design is asymmetrical, with a more natural, less controlled arrangement of plants than in a formal design. Any paths are curving or winding. In "cottage garden" style, herbs grow close together, profusely and abundantly in generous clumps, their shapes informal. Although the effect is natural looking, the herbs will have the greatest decorative effect when selected and positioned with regard to color and form (see *Selecting Herbs*, right).

There is no reason to restrict herbs to herb gardens. They can be included as part of an ornamental garden, worked into a design—a flower border, for instance—as decorative elements, so combining beauty and utility. Annual and biennial herbs—basil, dill, chervil, coriander, and summer savory, for example— are easy to incorporate into a vegetable garden. Planting herbs among vegetables or flowers can add diversity, color, and decorative effect.

SELECTING HERBS

When choosing herbs to plant, a primary consideration should be selecting the right plant for the right place (see *Growing Conditions for Some Garden Herbs*, pages 20–21). Selecting herbs that prefer sun for a corner of the garden that only offers shade, or planting an herb that likes fertile conditions in a patch of poor soil, will produce sickly plants and disappointing results. Within these parameters, whatever design you choose will be more effective if you create pleasing contrasts and combinations of color and form.

Consider choosing some herbs for their flowers: Feverfew for its full bouquet of white,

(continued on page 22)

GROWING CONDITIONS FOR SOME GARDEN HERBS

Herb	Common name	Soil fertility/ drainage	Sun/shade	Propagation	Zones	Comments
Achillea millefolium	Yarrow	moderately rich, well-drained	sun	seed or division	P 3–9	divide every couple of years to control spread
Agrimonia eupatoria	Agrimony	well-drained	sun	seed or division	P 6–9	
Alchemilla mollis	Lady's mantle	rich, moist	full sun to partial shade	seed or division	P 4–7	self-sows; deadhead to prevent unwanted seedlings
Allium cepa	Onion	rich, moist	full sun	seed or sets	B 4–9	grown as annual; onion sets (small bulbs) are readily available
Allium sativum	Garlic	light, well-drained	full sun	bulbs	P 4–9	
Allium schoenoprasum	Chives	moderately rich, well-drained	full sun to light shade	seed or division	P 3–9	benefits from division every few years
Aloe vera	Aloe	well-drained, dry to average	sun	offsets	P 10–11	easy to grow as a houseplant
Althaea officinalis	Marshmallow	moist to wet, light	full sun	seed or division	P 3–9	
Anethum graveolens	Dill	moderately rich, moist, well-drained	full sun	seed	HA	sow outdoors after last frost; does not transplant well
Angelica archangelica	Angelica	rich, moist, well-drained	partial shade	seed	B 4–9	seeds require stratification
Anthriscus cereifolium	Chervil	rich, moist	partial shade	seed	B 3–8	sow outdoors in early spring; does not transplant well. Do not cover seeds; they need light to germinate
Apium graveolens var. dulce	Celery	rich, moist, well-drained	full sun	seed	B 7–9	sow seeds 10–12 weeks before transplanting outdoors
Armoracia rusticana	Horseradish	rich, moist, well-drained	full sun	root cuttings, seed, or division	P 3–9	choose site carefully, as it is difficult to eradicate
Artemisia abrotanum	Southernwood	average, well-drained	full sun to light shade	division or cuttings	P 5–9	
Artemisia dracunculus	Tarragon	rich, well-drained	full sun	division or cuttings	P 3–9	
Calendula officinalis	Calendula	average, well-drained	full sun to light shade	seed	HA	sow seeds outdoors 4–6 weeks before last frost date
Chamaemelum nobile	Perennial chamomile	most soils	full sun to light shade	division, seed, or cuttings	P 4–8	
Cichorium intybus	Chicory	rich, well-drained	full sun	seed	P 3–9	
Convallaria majalis†	Lily-of-the-valley	rich, moist	partial shade	division	P 2–8	grows in full sun in cool climates
Coriandrum sativum	Coriander	moderately rich, well-drained	full sun to light shade	seed	HA	sow outdoors after last frost; does not transplant well
Digitalis purpurea†	Foxglove	moist, well-drained	partial shade	seed	B 4–8	self-sows; blooms second year
Echinacea spp.	Purple coneflower	most soils	full sun	seed	P 3–9	
Eupatorium perfoliatum	Boneset	rich, moist	full sun to partial shade	seed or division	P 3–9	
Eupatorium purpureum	Joe Pye weed	rich, moist to wet	full sun to light shade	division	P 3–9	can be grown from seed if stratified
Filipendula ulmaria	Meadowsweet	constantly moist to wet, fertile	full sun to partial shade	division	P 3–9	
Foeniculum vulgare	Fennel	well-drained	full sun	seed	P 5–9	short-lived but self-sows
Hamamelis virginiana	Witch hazel	rich, moist	partial shade	seed or layering	S 3–8	seeds require stratification
Humulus lupulus	Hops	rich, well-drained	full sun	cuttings	P 3–8	take cuttings in spring from female plants (or buy roots)
Hypericum perforatum	St.-John's-wort	average to poor	full sun	seed, cuttings, or division	P 3–8	
Inula helenium	Elecampane	moist, well-drained	full sun	division or seed	P 3–9	
Laurus nobilis	Bay	moderately rich, moist, well-drained	full sun to partial shade	semi-ripe cuttings	S 8–10	
Lavandula spp.	Lavender	average to dry, well-drained	full sun	semi-ripe cuttings or division	P 5–8	L. stoechas is less hardy (zone 7)
Linum usitatissimum	Flax	well-drained	full sun	seed	HA	sow outdoors in early spring
Marrubium vulgare	White horehound	well-drained to dry	full sun	seed or division	P 4–8	may self-sow
Matricaria recutita	Annual chamomile	sandy, well-drained	full sun	seed	HA	sow outdoors in early spring
Melissa officinalis	Lemon balm	well-drained, moist	full sun to partial shade	cuttings, layering, division, or seed	P 4–9	self-sows; shear back to prevent unwanted seedlings

Herb	Common name	Soil fertility/ drainage	Sun/shade	Propagation	Zones	Comments
Mentha spp.	Mints	rich, moist to wet	full sun to partial shade	cuttings, layering, or division	P 5–9	divide every couple of years to control spread
Monarda didyma	Bee balm	rich, moist	full sun to light shade	division	P 4–9	divide every couple of years to control spread
Nepeta cataria	Catnip	average, well-drained	full sun to partial shade	seed or division	P 4–9	self-sows; shear back to prevent unwanted seedlings
Ocimum basilicum	Basil	rich, moist, well-drained	full sun	seed	TA	sow indoors 8 weeks before last frost, or outdoors after last frost
Origanum majorana	Sweet marjoram	average to rich, well-drained	full sun	seed, division, or cuttings	P 9–10	usually grown as annual; sow indoors 8 weeks before last frost
Origanum onites	Pot marjoram	well-drained to dry	full sun	seed	P 8–10	sow indoors 8 weeks before last frost
Origanum vulgare	Oregano	well-drained to dry	full sun	cuttings or division	P 5–9	
Petroselinum crispum	Parsley	rich, moist, well-drained	full sun to light shade	seed	B 6–9	usually grown as an annual; presoak seeds in warm water to speed up germination
Pimpinella anisum	Anise	average to poor well-drained	full sun	seed	TA	does not transplant well; sow seeds outdoors after danger of frost has passed
Potentilla erecta	Tormentil	well-drained	full sun to partial shade	seed or division	P 4–9	
Primula veris	Cowslip	moist, rich	light to partial shade	seed or division	P 5–9	may self-sow
Rheum palmatum	Chinese rhubarb	rich, moist, well-drained	full sun to light shade	seed or division	P 5–8	
Rosa spp.	Rose	well-drained, moist, fertile	full sun	hardwood cuttings	S zones vary	seed only works for species, not cultivars
Rosmarinus officinalis	Rosemary	well-drained to dry	full sun	semi-ripe cuttings or layering	P 8–10	overwinter indoors in cold climates
Rumex acetosa	Sorrel	rich, moist	full sun to partial shade	seed or division	P 4–8	divide every couple of years to control spread
Ruta graveolens†	Rue	average, well-drained	full sun to partial shade	seed, division or cuttings	P 4–9	
Salvia officinalis	Sage	average, well-drained to dry	full sun	seed, division, cuttings, or layering	S 5–8	cultivars ('Tricolor' etc.) are less hardy and cannot be grown from seed, only cuttings
Salvia sclarea	Clary sage	well-drained	full sun	seed	B 4–9	may self-sow
Satureja hortensis	Summer savory	average, well-drained	full sun	cuttings, layering, division, or seed	HA	may self-sow
Satureja montana	Winter savory	dry to well-drained	full sun	seed	P 5–8	sow seeds indoors 1 month before last frost date
Silybum marianum	Milk thistle	well-drained	full sun	seed	HA	sow outdoors in late spring
Symphytum officinale	Comfrey	average, moist, well-drained	full sun to partial shade	seed, division, or root cuttings	P 3–8	divide frequently to control spread; hard to remove
Tanacetum balsamita	Costmary	well-drained, rich	full sun to light shade	division (produces little or no seed)	P 4–9	divide frequently to control spread
Tanacetum parthenium	Feverfew	well-drained	full sun	seed	P 4–9	self-sows; deadhead to prevent unwanted seedlings
Tanacetum vulgare†	Tansy	well-drained	full sun to partial shade	seed or division	P 4–8	divide often to control spread
Taraxacum officinale	Dandelion	any soil	full sun to partial shade	seed	P 3–10	
Thymus spp.	Thyme	light, dry, well-drained	full sun to partial shade	layering, cuttings, or division	P 4–8	
Tropaeolum majus	Nasturtium	poor to average, moist, well-drained	full sun	seed	TA	
Valeriana officinalis	Valerian	average, moist, well-drained	full sun to partial shade	seed or division	P 4–9	
Verbena officinalis	Vervain	moist, well-drained	full sun	seed, stem cuttings, division	P 4–8	
Zingiber officinale	Ginger	moist, rich, well-drained	partial shade	division	P 9–11	

Key
S Shrub
P Perennial
B Biennial
HA Hardy annual
HHA Half-hardy annual
TA Tender annual
† Toxic

The tall, flat flowerheads of yarrow (far left) add height to a sunny summer border, while the small flowers of the lower-growing sweet marjoram (left) and winter savory (above) make a pretty edging to a path or terrace.

daisylike flowers, bee balm for its bright scarlet mop-heads, yarrow for its summer-long display of flat-topped white, rose, or yellow flowers. When planning groups of herbs, look for contrasting colors for bold effects—orange calendulas with lime-green lady's mantle blossoms. If you prefer the subtle hues of similar colors, combine the gray-green leaves of sage or catnip with blue-flowered flax and silvery-leaved, purple-flowered lavender.

Some herbs make dramatic focal points. The evergreen leaves of a clipped bay or rosemary will add structure to a design throughout the year in all but the coldest climates. Tall herbs, such as angelica with its umbels of yellow-green flowers or the striking elecampane, make a less formal focal point. Some herbs add dramatic architectural shape and contrast, including Chinese rhubarb with its huge palm-shaped leaves and graceful feathery-leaved fennel. The colored leaves of many herbs provide opportunities for attractive groupings and contrasts. Herbs with dark purple leaves or pale to silvery leaves—among them purple sage, lavender, and the artemisias—provide opportunities for attractive contrasts with green leaves. Try different combinations to find plantings that you like.

Upright herbs such as thyme and neatly shaped plants like chives fit into a manicured, formal style, while willowy plants such as dill and fennel or sprawling ones such as mints, catnip, and calendula are best used in an informal or cottage-style design. Low-growing carpeting herbs such as creeping thyme or chamomile can soften the edges of paths or tumble over walls.

Generally, it is best to plant tall species at the back of a border or in the center of an island bed, and lower-growing species at the front or edge of a border or bed. Groups of plants of the same species stand out more effectively than individual plants, which may get lost. Repeating colors or clumps of the same species in different parts of the garden can create a unifying effect.

You will also, of course, choose herbs for when you want your herb garden to be in bloom. Remember to take account of whether they are annuals or biennials, which need to be sown again or replanted every year or two years. Perennials or shrubs take a permanent place in the garden. See the chart on pages 20–21 for the characteristics and entries in the directory (*Useful Herbs*, pages 38–113) for flowering times of individual herbs.

SELECTING HERBS FOR DIFFERENT USES

As well as—or rather than—choosing herbs for their visual effect, you may well wish to choose herbs to grow for particular purposes. If so, when planning your design, consider also the amounts you will require for harvesting.

HERBS FOR THE KITCHEN

angelica • anise • basil • bay • celery • chervil • chicory • chives coriander • dandelion • dill • fennel • garlic • ginger • horseradish nasturtium • onion • oregano • parsley • rosemary (left) • sage sorrel • spearmint • summer savory • sweet marjoram • tarragon thyme • winter savory

HERBS FOR FRAGRANCE

bee balm • clary sage (left) • costmary • fennel • lavender lemon balm • lily-of-the-valley • meadowsweet • pennyroyal peppermint • pot marjoram • roses • sage • southernwood • spearmint • sweet marjoram • thyme

HERBS FOR A MEDICINAL GARDEN

agrimony • bee balm • calendula (left) • chamomiles • chervil Chinese rhubarb • comfrey • cowslip • dill • fennel • flax • garlic ginger • hops • lavender • lemon balm • licorice • marshmallow meadowsweet • onion • peppermint • roses • sage • thyme valerian • white horehound • yarrow

HERBS FOR CRAFTS

bay • calendula • chamomile • costmary • dill • English lavender feverfew • French lavender (left) • hops • lady's mantle meadowsweet • nasturtium • pennyroyal • rosemary • roses southernwood • thyme • wormwood • yarrow

HERBS FOR CUT FLOWERS

angelica • apple mint • bee balm • boneset • calendula • chives costmary • cowslip • dill • fennel • feverfew • flax • foxglove (left) Joe Pye weed • lady's mantle • lavender • lily-of-the-valley meadowsweet • purple coneflower • roses • sage • St.-John's-wort tansy • valerian • yarrow

An herb garden in miniature—parsley, chives, and marjoram grow happily in two containers.

It is useful to confine the roots of invasive plants such as peppermint in a container.

GROWING HERBS IN CONTAINERS

Many herbs tolerate being grown within the confines of containers, and people have grown herbs this way for centuries all over the world. Growing herbs in containers is obviously ideal for those with little garden space. Even if you have an herb garden, you might like to have a few culinary herbs in containers as well, conveniently near the kitchen door or on a windowsill. Containers are useful for controlling spreading herbs such as mints, which can be invasive. They have the advantage of being portable, enabling you to place plants in their ideal amount of sun or shade, or to move tender plants indoors in winter. Pots also allow you to provide the right soil and water conditions for individual plants—useful for gardeners who have to cope with extremely alkaline, stony, or otherwise difficult soils. Containers offer scope for creating handsome plant combinations and for making groupings of particular herbs, such as Italian cooking herbs or herbs for teas.

Culinary herbs that do well in pots include basil, bay, chervil, chives, lemon balm, sweet marjoram, mints, parsley, rosemary, sage, savory, tarragon, and thyme. Ornamental herbs suitable for pots include bee balm, calendula, chamomile, feverfew, and lavender.

When choosing the container size, take into account the size of the mature plant and make sure that the container is deep enough to accommodate the roots. Make sure the pot has at least one hole in the bottom for drainage. Most herbs require a minimum depth of 8 inches (20 cm). Peppermint and other mints, and feverfew, which can grow up to 3 feet (1 m) high, need pots at least 1 foot (30 cm) across and 10 inches (25 cm) deep. Tall "strawberry" pots can accommodate several smaller herbs. Large herbs such as rosemary and bay look attractive when grown singly in large individual pots.

Clay pots are best for herbs that need good drainage; plastic or ceramic pots are better for plants such as mints and basil that require moisture. However, clay pots filled with soil will crack if temperatures drop much below zero. Large clay pots are extremely heavy once filled with soil (this may be an advantage in a windy spot). If planting more than one herb in a pot, use a larger pot and group plants according to their requirements for sun or shade, moisture, and soil type (see entries on pages 20–21).

Plant the herbs in potting soil (not garden soil), either a mix bought from a garden center or a home-made blend. A good potting mix is 3 parts well-rotted compost, 1 part garden soil, and 4 parts peat moss. Cover the bottom of the pot with gravel or pieces of broken clay pot to ensure good drainage.

Some herbs—basil, bay, chives, dill, ginger, marjoram, the mints, oregano, parsley, rosemary, sage, and winter savory—can be grown indoors. They need a lot of light, so place them on a sunny windowsill or on a table next to the window. Avoid putting indoor herbs above a radiator, or where they will be subjected to fluctuating temperatures or drafts.

HERBS IN RAISED BEDS

Raised beds can be a useful way of growing herbs. They provide easy access for maintaining and harvesting and also make it easier to enjoy the scents of the herbs. If you have soil that does not drain well (because it is in a low spot or contains too much clay), you can provide a suitable environment for herbs by creating raised beds. Only a couple of herbs tolerate poorly drained soil, and even those generally grow best in evenly moist but well-drained soil. All other herbs require good drainage, either evenly moist but well-drained soil or average to dry well-drained soil.

HERBS FOR BEES AND BUTTERFLIES

Growing herbs is a good way of enriching your local ecology, for herb flowers attract many bees and butterflies. Herb flowers loved by bees include bee balm, lavender, lemon balm, the mints, rosemary, and thyme. Comfrey (above) is a bee magnet, but plant it with caution—perhaps in an out-of-the-way corner—as it is invasive and difficult to get rid of. It is worth growing a large bed of oregano or Joe Pye weed just to see the color and movement of visiting butterflies. Butterflies are attracted by flowers that supply nectar; these include bee balm, boneset, lavender, mints, all types of sage, tansy, and yarrow. Herbs will be most attractive to bees and butterflies if you plant them in the sun and in a sheltered spot.

A height of 4 inches (10 cm) is usually adequate to improve drainage. Taller beds provide a more comfortable height for working—about 1–2 feet (30–60 cm) from the ground. Any raised bed more than 4 inches (10 cm) tall will need a retaining wall. An easy option is sturdy, wide boards supported by upright posts hammered firmly into the ground. Walls made of brick, stone, or concrete blocks should be laid on top of coarse sand or gravel in a foundation trench at least 4 inches (10 cm) deep. The width should be designed for easy access. If the bed can be reached from both sides, it can be up to 4 feet (125 cm) wide; if it is accessible from only one side, keep the width to 30 inches (75 cm) or less. Fill the retaining wall with good, light topsoil mixed with well-rotted compost.

Raising the soil level even a few inches by creating a raised bed can improve soil conditions for herbs.

Growing conditions for herbs

Success with growing herbs in the garden improves when you plant them in the growing conditions they prefer—that is, the soil and site of their natural habitat. Many herbs prefer well-drained to very well-drained soil. Those such as lavender that are at home in the wild on rocky Mediterranean hillsides or equivalent locations prefer sunny sites with good air circulation where the soil drains rapidly. Such plants are identifiable by common visual attributes: Gray to silvery leaves, often covered with fine hairs, are usually long and slender in shape to reduce the surface area (which helps minimize the loss of water from the plant through transpiration). These adaptations help plants survive in a hot, sunny habitat where, because of low rainfall and evaporation of water from the soil, water is not readily available to the plant.

A few herbs prefer or tolerate damp or wet positions, and often (but not always) these also tolerate partial shade. Marshmallow, Joe Pye weed, and all angelicas are herbs that in the wild grow in marshes, wetlands, and alongside streams; they are the best choices for constantly moist to wet soils and boggy areas.

Most herbs grow best in full sun, at least six hours of direct sunlight a day. A few herbs—those native to open woodland areas, scrubland, and hedgerows—are happy in partial shade. The best herbs for partial shade include angelica, bee balm, boneset, chervil, cowslip, foxglove, lady's mantle, lemon balm, meadowsweet, all of the mints, perennial chamomile, sorrel, and valerian. The ideal soil pH for most herbs is 6.3 to 7.0 (slightly acidic to neutral), although they will tolerate a slightly wider range.

For the specific cultural requirements of individual herbs, consult the chart on pages 20–21, and individual entries in *Useful Herbs*, pages 38–113.

Common and French lavender prefer well-drained, average soil in full sun.

Angelica grows best in moist soils and enjoys partially shaded positions.

If existing conditions are not ideally suited for a particular herb, it is sometimes possible to ameliorate them. In a sunny site, plant tall herbs to create a small area of partial shade. Adding organic matter such as compost to a heavy clay soil will improve drainage and please plants that require fast-draining soil. Gravel mulches around herbs help channel water from the crowns so plants dry out more quickly; this may improve survival in rainy climates. To lower the pH of a soil, add plenty of organic matter or peat moss, and mulch with pine needles. To raise pH, add lime in the form of limestone, oystershell, or dolomite lime; follow amounts recommended on the label for the pH measurement of your soil. Where soils are especially difficult (thin and stony, or extremely alkaline) the best solution is often to plant herbs in a raised bed of imported soil or in containers (see pages 24–25). Many herbs tolerate less-than-ideal conditions, so it is always worth experimenting to see what plants you can grow in your garden.

HARDINESS

You will also need to take into account a plant's frost hardiness. While hardy herbs are able to withstand low temperatures, tender herbs such as basil or nasturtiums will succumb in freezing weather. Hardiness zones show the minimum temperatures at which a plant is likely to survive. The chart on pages 20–21 includes hardiness zones in the United States based on average minimum temperatures, as illustrated on the map at the front of the book. For hardiness zones in Canada, check the map at the back.

The zones only provide a guide, however. You may be able to grow herbs that are of marginal hardiness for your area if you can protect them from extreme temperatures: For example, if you plant them in a protected microclimate, if they are insulated by nearly continuous snow cover during the winter, or if you protect them with a loose cover of evergreen boughs. You can grow tender herbs and those not hardy in your climate in containers and move them indoors in freezing weather.

Meadowsweet grows best in moist, fertile soil; it prefers full sun but tolerates some shade.

Lady's mantle is happy in most kinds of rich soil, dry or wet (but not boggy), in sun or partial shade.

Caring for herbs

The key to producing healthy herbs—or any other plants—is looking after the soil. Be sure to feed it regularly with organic matter such as compost or manure to replenish it with the nutrients it needs to feed the plants. Herbs are fairly easy to feed, since most of them need less fertilizer than other plants; spreading an inch or so (2.5 cm) of compost over the soil each year provides all the nutrients that most herbs need. Those described as needing rich soil (see pages 20–21) benefit from extra compost partway through the growing season; alternatively, feed them with fertilizer at half the strength recommended on the product label.

During the growing season, in a formal garden, herb hedges will need to be clipped. Fast-growing herbs such as costmary and tansy may need to be pruned to keep them under control. Even in an informal garden, sprawling herbs may require occasional trimming. You may need to remove any unwanted self-seeders. Deadheading flowering herbs (removing the faded blooms) will encourage fresh growth and more flowers, but do not deadhead if you want to harvest the seed heads. Invasive spreading herbs such as mints can form dense mats of roots and take over the garden, but you can contain their vigorous roots by planting the herb in a large pot and sinking the container up to rim level in the ground.

Before the first frosts, bring tender herbs indoors or into the greenhouse for winter. Cut down herbaceous perennials once frost has killed back their foliage; wait until spring to cut back silver-leaved and evergreen plants. After a couple of heavy frosts, mulch loosely with straw to protect plants from alternate freezing and thawing of the soil, which pushes them out of the ground. Where the ground freezes during the winter, provide additional protection for marginally hardy herbs by covering with extra straw or a couple of evergreen branches. If you experience problems with winter survival of herbs that are supposed to be hardy in your climate, try improving soil drainage—for example, by building a raised bed. Many herbs do well in dry conditions, and even those that like moist soil usually prefer it to be well-drained. In fact, poor drainage over winter is fatal to many herbs, especially those that have gray to silver leaves.

LOOKING AFTER HERBS IN CONTAINERS

Confined to a pot, herbs exhaust the nutrients in the soil very quickly, particularly when they are harvested frequently (which encourages regrowth). They will benefit from the application of a liquid fertilizer every six weeks. You can buy a commercial fertilizer, but use at half the rate recommended for vegetables or flowers. You can also make your own from compost or well-rotted manure, suspended in a burlap sack and allowed to steep in water for a few days; before use dilute with water until it is the color of weak tea.

Pot-grown herbs benefit from frequent trimming to keep them compact. Taller plants may need staking.

Growing herbs indoors on even a sunny windowsill cuts the light by up to half compared with growing herbs outdoors. Reduced light produces taller, floppier growth. Also, the light only comes from one side, so it is important to rotate the pots regularly to give plants as much light as possible and keep them from becoming lopsided. An optimal temperature for the indoor herb garden is 60–70°F (15–21°C), though cooler temperatures work well also.

With all herbs in containers it is important to monitor watering, as pots can dry out rapidly both indoors and out. However, particularly with indoor pots, it is also important not to overwater, as that encourages root rot fungus, which can kill plants. Check pots an hour or so after watering; any water remaining in the tray or saucer below the pot should be dumped out.

Controlling pests and diseases

SELF-DEFENSE

Generally herbs seem to be more resistant to disease and insect attack than many garden plants. This may be because most garden herbs are little changed from their wild ancestors, while many other garden plants have been selected or hybridized. Herbs also often have chemical components that provide protection.

Horseradish and other plants of the mustard family (Cruciferae), for instance, release hot-flavored mustard oil (allyl isothiocyanate). When attacked, its strong taste repels many pests. Cultivated brassicas, on the other hand, tend to have been bred or selected for milder flavors and therefore will have less allyl isothiocyanate and correspondingly lower resistance to pests.

The most widespread anti-insect compounds found in plants are tannins. In midsummer the leaves of some oak trees increase their tannin content and it has been shown that the numbers of insect species feeding suddenly drops. Many plants in the rose family (Rosaceae)—including agrimony, tormentil, blackberries, and raspberries—have in their leaves high levels of tannins, which act as an insect deterrent.

There can be a downside to this, however. Although many herb plants can similarly persuade a range of insect and animal attackers to stay away, if one insect species is not harmed by the toxin produced by the plant, it can take advantage of the lack of competition and specialize in that type of plant. Such insects then may become dependent on, and a particular pest to, that otherwise protected plant. In the case of the Cruciferae, that is what has happened with the cabbage worm (*Pieris brassicae*). The mustard oil entices it to lay its eggs on cabbage plants and their relatives.

PROTECTING HERBS

However hard herbs work to defend themselves, they are not immune to pests and diseases, and it is likely that you will need to take measures to protect them.

The healthier plants and their environment are, the less likely they will be to succumb to attack. To this end, the herb gardener will be wise to maintain the quality of the soil by regularly incorporating organic matter; to buy plants in good condition; and to plant the right plant in the right place (see the chart on pages 20–21 and *Growing Conditions for Herbs* on pages 26–27). All these measures contribute to the growth of strong plants.

Including a wide range of plants helps prevent pests from taking control, because a diversity of plants encourages a diversity of wildlife; for example, birds as well as ladybugs and other beneficial insects that feed on pests. Good drainage and good air circulation (avoiding overcrowding of plants) are crucial to prevent root rot and many other diseases. Keep beds free from plant debris, and remove any diseased or damaged parts of plants as soon as possible. With vigilance, you can pick off pests such as beetles or slugs before too much damage is done.

The charts overleaf list common pests and diseases affecting herbs and some simple organic controls that will help prevent or control them. Insecticidal soap can be purchased at most garden centers; while not harmful to animals, it must be used as directed to avoid burning plants. Diatomaceous earth, also available at garden centers, is the fossilized shell remains of algae; the microscopic sharp edges cut into soft-bodied pests such as slugs, killing them. When handling diatomaceous earth always wear a dust mask, to protect the lungs.

A simple garlic spray can deter some pests. To make a garlic spray, just chop a whole head of garlic and steep in vegetable oil overnight. Strain and mix with an equal amount of water and a few drops of dish detergent.

COMMON PESTS AND HOW TO CONTROL THEM

APHIDS
Also known as greenfly. Small (1/8 inch/3 mm or less) pale green, pink, or nearly black insects, which may or may not have wings, cluster near growing tips and buds. They cause leaves and shoots to curl and sometimes to turn yellow or become sticky. Hose off with a blast of water, or use garlic spray or insecticidal soap. Repeat every few days as needed.

FLEA BEETLES
Various types of beetles affect herbs. The tiny black or metallic blue flea beetles are easily identified by the way they jump when a plant is touched. The adults eat tiny rounded holes in leaves, while the larvae feed on roots. The only really effective way to prevent damage is to cover plants with floating row cover (a lightweight, nonwoven cloth available from garden centers; cover edges with soil to prevent insects from crawling underneath). Keep the garden clear of plant debris and do a thorough fall cleanup to reduce future problems.

JAPANESE BEETLES
Adult Japanese beetles are 1/2 inch (1 cm) and metallic blue-green with copper-colored backs. They eat holes in leaves, or sometimes eat the whole leaf except the veins; the larvae, known as white grubs, feed on the roots and kill the plant. Handpick any large beetles into a jar of soapy water (beetles will drown overnight), or set out baited traps (traps specifically intended for Japanese beetles can be purchased from garden centers).

LEAF MINERS
A group of pests (the larvae of various flies, moths, and beetles) feed between upper and lower leaf surfaces, causing white tunnels or blotches on leaves. Remove affected leaves as soon as any damage is visible. Better yet, take preventive measures. Cover plants with floating row cover. A thorough fall cleanup should also help reduce problems in future years.

MEALYBUGS
Small (1/4 inch/5 mm or less) wingless insects covered with white waxy powder and often with tiny trailing white filaments. They secrete honeydew, making the plant sticky. Wipe it off with a cotton swab dipped in alcohol, hose off with a strong jet of water, or spray the plant with insecticidal soap.

PARSLEY WORMS
Black-striped caterpillars that feed on the leaves of parsley, dill, and other members of the carrot family. However, since they are the larvae of black swallowtail butterflies, you will probably not wish to harm them. Remove by hand. If Queen Anne's lace or other wild members of the carrot family grow nearby, you can move the caterpillars to those plants.

SCALES
Look like tiny bumps of wax; suck juices from plant leaves and stems. Hose off plants to remove sticky honeydew. Use a lightweight horticultural oil spray (follow directions). Remove severely infested branches or entire plants.

SLUGS AND SNAILS
Chew holes or large portions of leaves at night, leaving a slender shiny trail. Pick off by hand; sprinkle a ring of diatomaceous earth on soil around target plants (wear a dust mask to prevent inhalation); trap in shallow dishes of beer set into the soil, or in empty grapefruit halves set edge-down overnight.

SPIDER MITES
These are animals so tiny that they appear as small specks under a hand lens. They produce a mottling on leaves and cause them to fall prematurely; the whole plant may be covered with fine webs. Hose off plants with a jet of cold water every few days, or, alternatively, spray with insecticidal soap.

SPITTLEBUGS
Also known as froghoppers. These tiny (1/3 inch/8 mm) insects are easy to recognize as they are surrounded by masses of frothy bubbles. They suck plant juices and may cause wilting. Remove the bubble masses and the bugs inside, either by hand or by hosing off with a jet of water every couple of days. To minimize problems, keep the garden clear of weed debris.

WHITEFLIES
The small (1/12 inch/2 mm) white-winged adults lay eggs on the undersides of leaves. Adults and larvae suck plant juices, weakening plants. Hose off with a jet of water every few days or spray with insecticidal soap. You can also use yellow sticky traps (stiff yellow cards coated with a sticky substance that are available at some garden centers).

COMMON DISEASES AND HOW TO PREVENT THEM

DAMPING OFF

Stems of seedlings rot at soil level. To prevent, water seedling trays from the bottom and maintain good air circulation and soil drainage. Cover seeds sown indoors or directly in the garden with a thin layer of finely milled sphagnum moss (available at garden centers).

DOWNY MILDEW

White fluffy growth on underside of leaves; yellow spots on upper side. Remove infected leaves; this is most effective if the disease is caught early. To prevent, avoid overhead watering and ensure good air circulation and soil drainage.

LEAFSPOT DISEASES

Round or irregular blotches of fungus on leaves. Avoid wetting leaves; water soil at base of plants, not foliage. After working near diseased plants, wash hands and disinfect tools by wiping with rubbing alcohol.

POWDERY MILDEW

White powderlike mold on upper side of leaves, especially common on bee balm. If caught early, remove infected leaves or branches; cut back bee balm to the ground to stimulate fresh growth. To prevent, keep plants well watered, and thin clumps to improve air circulation.

ROOT, STEM, OR CROWN ROT

Fungus causes stems to discolor, wilt, and die. Remove diseased plants promptly. To prevent, improve soil drainage and keep mulch a few inches away from plant crowns.

RUSTS

Small orange or brown spots on leaves. The best control is to remove diseased plants promptly.

WILTS

There are many types of wilt diseases, each specific to a single plant or a group of plants in the same family. Wilts may be bacterial or fungal in origin. Sudden, severe wilting of the plants (when the soil is dry) is the primary symptom of all; sometimes plants also develop streaks or turn yellow. There are no effective organic or chemical controls for wilts. Remove diseased plants promptly. After working near diseased plants, wash hands and disinfect tools by wiping with rubbing alcohol. Avoid growing that type of plant in the same spot for at least three years.

HERBS AS COMPANIONS

If you are growing herbs among ornamental plants or vegetables, you might like to try positioning them so that other plants benefit from their presence. Research has not yet demonstrated that companion planting is a universally applicable method of pest and disease control, but many gardeners have a strong belief in its efficacy. The best advice is to watch your herbs carefully and take note of what appears to work in your garden.

Ideas for companion planting that you might try include growing chives or other onion relatives with other plants, as their oil may help against a range of risks from molds to caterpillars; grown with carrots, garlic is said to ward off carrot fly. The aroma of parsley is also believed to deter carrot fly. The scent of coriander is believed to repel aphids. Lavender has been grown traditionally at the base of roses to help ward off aphids, possibly because one of its components (linalool oil) is a good insect deterrent. Members of the daisy family such as tansy, elecampane, and feverfew, which were traditional insect repellents in the house, may have the same use in the garden.

Chamomile and yarrow are believed to protect plants around them perhaps because their flowers lure beneficial insects to the garden. The artemisias, especially wormwood, may help deter insects from a neighboring plant because of the thujone and other oils they contain. Note, however, that thujone can also inhibit the growth of nearby plants, so be on your guard to check whether your artemisias may be having a harmful effect.

Propagation

How you propagate an herb will be determined by the type of plant it is. It may be an annual, which completes its life cycle in one growing season; a biennial, which flowers and dies in the second growing season after germination; a perennial, which lives for at least three seasons; or a shrub, a woody-stemmed plant usually branching from near the base. Annuals and biennials are often grown from seed. Perennials and shrubs can be grown from seed, though this is usually a multiyear process. It is often easier to buy plants, or to propagate by one of the other methods described below. Usually one type of propagation is likely to be more advantageous than others. For example, true tarragon is sterile and cannot be grown from seed, so it needs to be propagated by division. For the easiest methods of propagation for individual herbs, see the chart on pages 20–21.

Depending on the size of your herb garden, the type of plant, and how easy it is to grow, it may be sensible to buy plants. If, for instance, you are gardening in a window box or in pots, or if you do not require large numbers of plants, it may well be easiest to purchase pre-grown herbs. You may also prefer to purchase plants if you require an herb that is hard to propagate—for instance, parsley can be difficult to germinate—or if you do not have the right conditions in which to grow tender plants from seed. Buy annuals and perennials in the spring and early summer. Hardy containerized shrubs and perennials may be bought and planted at any time of the growing season. They will tend to do better—and need less constant watering—if you avoid planting them at the height of summer; spring and fall are best.

If you are unable to find unusual herbs at your local garden center, you can order plants or seeds in late winter or early spring from specialty garden catalogues, either through the mail or over the Internet.

GROWING FROM SEED

Growing from seed is preferable if you require larger numbers of plants. Although it is more work than buying pre-grown plants, it is not difficult and is much cheaper. This is particularly true for annuals, biennials, and those perennials that sprout easily, such as chives, fennel, or feverfew. Growing from seed also enables you to grow more unusual plants that might not be available at your local garden center. See the chart on pages 20–21 for herbs that can be grown easily from seed.

To determine the time of sowing, follow the instructions on the seed packet. Tender annuals must be started indoors, or sown outdoors after all danger of frost has passed. Other herbs can be started either outdoors or indoors. The advantage of starting seeds indoors is that germination and development can take place earlier in the year and therefore the plants can enjoy a longer growing season.

Some herbs do not take well to being transplanted and should be sown directly into the soil where required. This particularly applies to herbs in the carrot family, such as angelica, anise, chervil, coriander, and dill, which have deep-growing roots. To grow seeds outdoors, rake the soil to produce a level, fine-textured seed bed. Scatter the seeds or sow them in drills according to the instructions on the packet, cover, and water using a nozzle with a fine rose (water breaker) or watering wand so you don't wash away the seeds.

Some seeds will only germinate if specific requirements are met. For example, chervil needs light to germinate and so requires minimal covering. Many perennial herbs, such as angelica, have extra-tough seed coats that have to be broken before germination is possible. This may occur naturally by the action of frost, but it may be necessary to stratify them: Sow seeds in moistened vermiculite or sterile seed-starting mix, place inside a plastic bag, close with a twist tie, and refrigerate for four to twelve weeks. Some seeds benefit from being soaked in water overnight before sowing. For instance, soaking parsley seed in warm water overnight before sowing will improve the germination rate.

The traditional way of starting seeds indoors is to use a soilless growing medium (this is a commercial potting mix especially designed for starting seeds). Pour this into a shallow pot or seed tray to a depth of 2 inches (5 cm). Firm it gently. Soak the tray in a pan of water, so that moisture is absorbed from below, and allow it to drain before sowing.

After sowing thinly and evenly, use a sieve to cover the seed with potting medium twice to three times the depth of the thickness of the seed used. Cover the tray with a sheet of glass or plastic wrap to maintain humidity, and keep it in the dark at a temperature of 70–75°F (21–24°C) until leaves begin to appear. (Heat promotes rapid germination; seeds will sprout more slowly at cooler temperatures.)

Many herb gardeners use convenient compartmentalized trays with individual seeds sown in each block. These eliminate the need

to transplant crowded seedlings into larger pots and so minimize the risk of disturbing tender roots, which can severely stunt the growth of young plants.

Unless you are growing seedlings in compartmentalized trays, once the seedlings have developed a couple of pairs of leaves transplant them to 3 inch (7 cm) pots. Keep them in good light (on a sunny windowsill, or a few inches below fluorescent lights that are set to stay on for sixteen hours a day) to prevent them from becoming spindly. If they are on a windowsill, rotate them every few days to prevent lopsided growth. Water whenever the surface of the potting medium feels dry.

When the seedlings have outgrown their pots or compartments, transplant them into larger pots filled with potting soil. Harden off the plants by moving them outdoors for a couple of hours a day at first, increasing their exposure in stages. After about two weeks of hardening off, provided the risk of frost has passed, transplant them into their final position in the garden.

Seedlings of calendula (center) and flax (right) have grown from seed directly sown into individual compartments in this seed tray.

These seedlings, including chervil (front left) and fennel (right), were sown in a seed tray and then transplanted into individual pots.

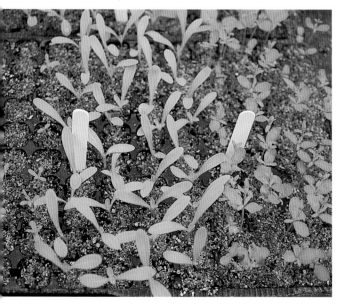

1 To divide plants, first loosen and ease the plant up.

2 Insert two forks into the clump back to back and push the handles apart.

3 Use the forks to continue to break off small clumps, and set the smaller divisions aside.

DIVISION

Perennial herbs can be propagated by division—that is, by dividing clumps in early autumn or in the spring into pieces, each with a root system and one or more shoots. You can do this to make more plants for other parts of the garden, to give plants to friends, or to make smaller clumps. Left to their own devices some perennial herbs increase in size until they take over an area. Dividing improves plant vigor. Overgrown clumps of perennials often die out in the center and have reduced flowering, which is a sign of the need to divide and replant.

To divide, water if the soil around the plant is dry, then loosen the soil and ease the clump up with a garden fork. Some clumps can then be teased apart by hand; for tougher rootstocks use two garden forks (see below).

Mints and bee balm have long rhizomes: Underground stems that spread out, putting down roots, and from which aerial stems shoot up. To propagate these herbs, ease up lengths of rhizomes with a fork and plant in pots or in the garden with the rhizomes half buried.

LAYERING

Some perennial herbs, such as pennyroyal, send out long scrambling stems overground that may sprout roots where they touch the soil. With these, you can encourage rooting by layering: Weighting or pegging down these stems with a stone or a loop of wire pushed into the soil. Most small shrubby herbs, such as thyme and winter savory, can be encouraged to root in a similar fashion, despite their woody stems. With plants such as sage and lavender, which have longer stems, you can mound up soil over a leggy stem to stimulate new root growth. Once roots have formed, cut the connecting stem to create a new plant.

4 Replant the new smaller clumps separately. Firm soil around roots and water well after planting.

CUTTINGS

Taking a cutting is simply a matter of cutting a length of stem and giving it the conditions needed to encourage root growth. With soft-stemmed plants such as tarragon or hops, take stem cuttings from new growth in early summer, cutting a young shoot just below a leaf about 2–4 inches (5–10 cm) from the tip.

With woody shrubs such as rosemary or bay, take semi-ripe cuttings in late summer once new stems have hardened slightly, cutting a shoot just below a leaf about 4–6 inches (10–15 cm) from the tip.

When you are dealing with roses, you need to wait until midfall, when you can take fully ripened hardwood cuttings. Make the cut at the junction between the current season's growth and the growth of previous seasons, and trim to 6 inch (15 cm) lengths.

Dip the cuttings in rooting hormone powder (available at garden centers), and put them into pots of a commercial soilless mix, ideally one that has been designed for cuttings. Place them in a cool greenhouse or cold frame, or cover with a transparent plastic bag to stop them from drying out, and keep at about 65–70°F (18–21°C). When the cuttings have rooted—indicated by growth at the tips— transplant into 4 inch (10 cm) pots and harden off (see page 33) before transplanting into the garden.

A few herbs, such as the mints, root easily in water. Cut a stem 6–8 inches long (15–20 cm) at any time during the growing season, drop it into a glass of water (remove any leaves below the water level), and stand it on a sunny windowsill at 65–70°F (18–21°C).

Root cuttings are an easy way to propagate comfrey and horseradish. Take sections of root about 2–4 inches (5–10 cm) long in the autumn, and simply plant them directly where you want them in the garden. They should root by the following spring.

Some herbs, such as mint (left) or basil, will begin to root from stems kept in water.

Harvesting herbs

You harvest herbs every time you pick a few leaves—to throw into a salad, for instance. But for out-of-season culinary and home use and medicinal availability, systematic gathering and preserving becomes necessary. For methods of making preparations from fresh or preserved herbs, see *Herbs at Home,* pages 150–165.

In mild climates, evergreen herbs such as rosemary and thyme can be gathered fresh all year. In colder climates, unless they are grown indoors, they must be harvested before the winter. The leaves of most perennial herbs can be gathered at any time during the growing season, and you can cut as much as three-quarters of the current season's growth in a given harvest. However, for many herbs there are optimal times for gathering. For leaves such as basil, thyme, sage, mint, and lemon balm, the peak time for flavor, fragrance, and tenderness is before they flower (see individual entries in *Useful Herbs,* pages 38–113, for flowering times). Salad leaves are best picked young, while they are still succulent.

Collect herbal flowers for the vase or potpourri as soon as the blooms begin to open. For medicinal use, gather whole plants just

> ## CAUTION
>
> When gathering wild plants, do not on any account pick those that are endangered or legally protected (see page 6). Also, be absolutely certain that you have correctly identified what you are collecting. Mistakes can be fatal: For instance, inexperienced gatherers have been known to confuse the leaves of the poisonous foxglove, before flowering, with the young leaves of comfrey.

before they begin flowering. Gather roots such as licorice in the autumn as the top growth dies. Gather seeds on a dry day when they are no longer green and are almost ripe. Cut the stalks before the seeds begin to fall from the heads. Tie stalks into small bunches, hang upside down, and tie a paper bag over the seed heads. Note: if you want the herb to self-seed, leave some seed heads on the plant.

When you gather herbs, carry a tray or basket big enough to lay herbs flat to avoid crumpling or bruising them. Harvest on a dry day, ideally—particularly in hot-summer climates—in the cool morning hours after the dew has evaporated but before the sun has begun to affect the plant and evaporate its volatile oils.

Harvested herbs need to be treated with the utmost care. To ensure that the plants retain their active properties, you should avoid damaging them.

Once seed heads of plants such as angelica have dried, remove them from their paper bags and separate seeds from stems by rubbing gently with your fingers.

Preserving herbs

FREEZING

When you want to preserve herbs with tender leaves such as fennel, dill, basil, chives, and chervil for culinary purposes, freezing is the easiest method to use, and the one that best preserves their flavor. Chop herbs onto a small tray, freeze, and then shake the frozen leaves into a resealable plastic bag. You can easily shake out the amount you need: It is already chopped and ready to use. You can also chop sprigs into the compartments of an ice tray and fill them up with water, and freeze.

DRYING

Drying works well for most herbs, except those tender-leaved ones mentioned under *Freezing* (above). To preserve quality, herbs need to dry as quickly as possible in a warm, dry, dark space with good ventilation. For long-stemmed and bushy herbs such as sage, rosemary, thyme, the artemisias, the mints, and summer savory, make small bunches tied with string. Hang the bunches upside down. With soft-stemmed herbs such as chamomile, lay them out on a wire cooling rack, a drying tray, muslin stretched across a wooden frame, or anything similar that allows air to circulate around the plants. Dry the bunches or trays in a shaded place away from direct sunlight, such as in an attic or dry closet, until they are thoroughly dried. Leaves are ready when they have become brittle and break easily; flowers should rustle like tissue paper. Most herbs take four or five days to dry; those with thicker leaves may take a week or even two.

Hang seed heads in paper bags in an airy place until they are thoroughly dry and the seeds are falling from their heads or pods. This will probably take at least three weeks.

During very humid weather, when herbs may mold or spoil before they dry, a quicker method is needed. You can dry the herbs in a

STORING DRIED HERBS
Place herbs into airtight containers as soon as they have dried. Keep them out of direct sunlight in a cool place—warmth will shorten their useful life. Store flowers flat, if possible. Strip leaves whole from the stem before storing, and crumble just before use. Dried roots are extremely difficult to crumble; you should chop them, as directed below, before drying.

cool oven or food dehydrator at a temperature not higher than 90°F (33°C) for one to three days, turning once or twice daily. Or, quickest of all, you can use a microwave oven. Seeds and small-leaved herbs will take only about a minute on a low setting; even larger, juicier herbs will not take longer than about three minutes.

Roots need a slightly different procedure. Wash or wipe them clean, cut them lengthways, and slice into small pieces. Lay the pieces on drying trays and dry in an oven or food dehydrator set to 130°F (55°C). Stir pieces every couple of hours until they have lost their elasticity and snap rather than bend between the fingers. You can also tie roots in bunches and hang to dry, but they take a long time.

OTHER METHODS OF PRESERVING

Herbs can also be preserved in oil or vinegar (see page 120). You can make syrups with some herb flowers, such as those of elderberries, or with the stems of angelica, or with aromatic roots such as elecampane (see page 140). Syrups can be kept in the refrigerator for a few weeks, or for longer in sterilized jars.

LABELING

However you preserve herbs, it is essential to label the herbs rather than hope you will remember what they are. Most crumbled dried herbs look alike. Confusing two medicinal herbs, or a medicinal herb with a culinary herb, could have undesirable—even fatal—consequences.

Useful Herbs

Yarrow *Achillea millefolium*   English mace *Achillea ageratum*   Agrimony *Agrimonia eupatoria*

YARROW *Achillea millefolium*
G M H
other names milfoil, nose-bleed, soldier's woundwort
plant family Compositae (daisy family)
height up to 3 feet (90 cm)
habit hardy perennial with many sturdy stems and grayish green fernlike leaves; flat rosettes of tiny white or red flowers bloom from early summer to autumn
habitat plant of the waysides and pastures; prefers full sun and moderately fertile soil
zones 3–9
This roadside plant is often grown in meadow gardens; colorful cultivars of yarrow are mainstays of the summer perennial garden. Its flowers are good for cutting and drying. Infusions are used in shampoos or as rinses for oily skin and greasy hair, and yarrow's essential oil can be added to a soothing bath.

The genus is named after Achilles, the bravest of the ancient Greeks in the Trojan War. He used yarrow to staunch the wounds of his soldiers, but the efficiency of this historic use has not been proven. Traditionally, yarrow tea was also popular for combating colds and flu,

and for reducing heavy menstruation, but these uses are not proven either.

Yarrow helps promote good digestion; it contains bitter compounds (sesquiterpene lactones) that stimulate the release of bile. It is approved by Germany's Commission E (see page 167) for indigestion and loss of appetite.
Caution *At proper doses side effects of yarrow are minimal, but do not take it if you are allergic to yarrow or to any other member of the daisy family. The American Pharmaceutical Association recommends that it should be avoided during pregnancy because of the presence of small amounts of a toxic compound (thujone).*
other species
English mace (*Achillea ageratum*), a hardy European perennial, is an underused culinary herb. Its saw-toothed leaves are a decorative addition to potato salads. Its flavor blends well with other herbs in chicken dishes.

AGRIMONY *Agrimonia eupatoria*
G M
other names church steeples, sticklewort, cocklebur
plant family Rosaceae (rose family)
height up to 3 feet (90 cm)
habit hardy perennial with distinctive multipart leaves made up of paired toothed leaflets that alternate small ones between large ones along

Key to herb uses

G In the garden	M In medicine
C In cooking	H In the home

the leaf; numerous small yellow flowers on a long spike in summer

habitat prefers sunny conditions; tolerates wet to dry, well-drained alkaline soil

zones 6–9

Agrimony's pretty, erect spikes of small yellow flowers are decorative in the flower border or in the herb garden. A yellow dye can be obtained from the plant. Historically, agrimony was one of the most highly regarded wound-healing herbs. The species name *eupatoria* is linked to Mithridates Eupator, the King of Pontus, who in the first century BC was renowned for the depth of his herbal knowledge.

Agrimony has an astringent action, the result of the large amounts of tannins it contains. Commission E approves its use for inflammations of the skin, mouth, and pharynx, and also for occasional use against mild diarrhea. An infusion of the dried flowering plant is taken as a tea or used as a gargle. It may also be applied as a poultice.

LADY'S MANTLE *Alchemilla mollis*
formerly *A. vulgaris*

G M H

other names lion's foot, bear's foot, nine hooks, Our Lady's mantle

plant family Rosaceae (rose family)

height up to 1 foot (30 cm)

habit hardy perennial with large cape- or mantle-shaped leaves with indented edges; clusters of small yellow-green flowers from late spring to early autumn

habitat full sun to partial shade and rich, moist soil

zones 4–7

The genus name *Alchemilla,* from the word alchemy, is a reminder of the medieval belief in this plant's special powers. Herbalists and alchemists would gather the early morning dew lying in its mantle-shaped leaves and use this to mix potions that required special purity. The attractive way its beautiful leaves capture dew still fascinates gardeners, who plant lady's

mantle as an edging plant. Both flowers and leaves enhance gardens and look pretty in flower arrangements. In moist, fertile soil it is a prolific self-seeder.

The first written record of the common name was in German (*Frauenmantle*) by the botanist Tragus in his *History of Plants* (1532). Traditionally the herb was used to treat irregular or excessively heavy menstrual periods and vaginal itching. (Since it contains highly astringent tannins that can tighten tissues, there was even a tradition of using an infusion to restore the appearance of virginity.) None of these uses has been shown to be effective. An infusion is good as a skin toner.

Commission E has approved the herb's short-term use to treat light, nonspecific diarrhea. It has also been used for digestive problems, skin rashes, and inflammation of the mouth and pharynx, but these uses have not been proven.

Caution *Lady's mantle has a good record as a safe herb. However, it is best to avoid prolonged ingestion of high amounts of tannins from any source, because this does increase the risk of cancer. Do not take this herb for diarrhea for more than three days without consulting a medical professional. It is advisable to avoid taking lady's mantle during pregnancy.*

Lady's mantle *Alchemilla mollis*

GARLIC *Allium sativum*

G C M

plant family Liliaceae (lily family)
height around 1 foot (30 cm)
habit hardy perennial with bulbs containing 5
to 15 bulblets (cloves); long narrow, basal
leaves; small, ball-shaped cluster of greenish
white to pink flowers in summer
habitat prefers full sun and light, fertile, well-
drained soil
zones 4–9

Garlic is one of the oldest and best-known
herbs. Its use was recorded over five thousand
years ago in Mesopotamia, and well over two
thousand scientific papers have been written
about its properties. This strongly flavored
seasoning is used in many types of cooking.
Garlic is used with meat and vegetables, and in
sauces, soups, salads, and many other dishes. It

Chives *Allium schoenoprasum*

Garlic *Allium sativum*

is also used to flavor butter, oils, and vinegars.
It should be harvested when the leaves and
bulbs are dry, and stored in a cool place.

The sulfur compounds in the volatile oils are
responsible for garlic's distinctive strong aroma,
but they are also the basis of its healthy
properties. The specific compound responsible
for most of garlic's smell and healthy qualities is
allicin, which is formed by enzyme action only
when the raw bulb is crushed or chewed. Allicin
is destroyed by cooking, so garlic is most
beneficial if eaten raw. Garlic has been shown to
reduce low-density lipoproteins (LDL, the so-
called "bad" cholesterol) in the blood. It has
also been found to reduce blood pressure
slightly. There is some evidence that garlic may
reduce the aggregation of platelets, which may
help reduce the risk of blood clots.

Garlic has also been used for digestive
problems and for chest infections and colds. It
has been shown to have antibacterial,
antifungal, and antiviral properties, and for this
reason has sometimes been used on wounds,
athlete's foot, and warts.

It is thought that deodorized forms of garlic,
available as commercial products, do not have

as many health benefits as raw garlic. The recommended prophylactic dose is one fresh clove, eaten raw, one or two times daily.

Caution *In a minority of people garlic may irritate the digestive tract.*

other species

Garlic has the strongest pungency of all the alliums (onion relatives including leeks, scallions, and chives). Most of the onions have similar properties, but the less pungent they are the less therapeutic value they tend to have. For example, chives (*A. schoenoprasum*) are mild-tasting and not nearly as effective as onions; they are mainly used in salads and seasonings such as herb butters.

Onions (*A. cepa*), eaten raw or as juice, are approved by Commission E for treating poor appetite, bronchial infections and colds, and inflammation of the mouth and pharynx. They are indispensable components of both Eastern and Western cuisines, and have a role in traditional treatments for bronchial infections and colds. There are also wild *Allium* species growing throughout much of the world.

ALOE *Aloe vera* syn. *Aloe barbadensis*

G M H

other names Barbados aloe, first-aid plant, burn plant

plant family Liliaceae (lily family)

height 2 feet (60 cm)

habit tender perennial, a clump-forming succulent with thick, white-mottled green leaves that have small spiny teeth along the edges; tall spikes of many small, tubular yellow flowers bloom in summer

habitat prefers sun and well-drained, dry to average soil

zones 10–11

Aloe is a very common houseplant and, in warm climates, a strikingly architectural garden plant. It has two main products: A useful soothing gel (consisting of polysaccharides) which is packed in its succulent leaves; and bitter aloe, the liquid or dried sap from the outer leaf and leaf base, which should only be used under medical supervision.

It is easy to obtain the gel: Just break off a leaf and cut it open lengthwise. It has a cooling, anti-inflammatory action and is often used to soothe burns, cuts, bites, stings, and rashes. It is thought to seal and protect wounds and help speed up cell regeneration. It also acts as a skin moisturizer, and for this reason it is sometimes used in commercial creams and lotions.

Caution *The anthraquinones contained in bitter aloe make it a strong laxative as they stimulate propulsive contractions. Bitter aloe should never be used during pregnancy and should be considered for use only under strict medical supervision. It is wise to avoid taking commercial aloe gel internally; though the pure gel should have no harmful effects, it is possible that the commercial product may be contaminated by bitter aloe.*

Aloe *Aloe vera*

MARSHMALLOW *Althaea officinalis*
G C M H
other names mallard, althea, sweet weed, mortification root
plant family Malvaceae (mallow family)
height up to 7 feet (2 m)
habit hardy perennial with velvety lobed leaves and densely downy stems; pale pink flowers up to 2 inches (5 cm) across in mid- to late summer
habitat marshland plant; prefers full sun and damp to wet, light soil
zones 3–9

Because of its statuesque height and beautiful flowers, marshmallow has long been an attractive feature in an herb garden. The genus name *Althaea* is from the Greek *altho,* meaning "to cure." According to the Roman natural historian Pliny, "Whoever shall daily swallow a spoonful of mallow shall be free from disease."

Originally, a paste of the root's mucilage was cooked to produce marshmallow candy. Today, marshmallows are made from flour, gums, and other ingredients—but not mallow.

Cosmetically, an infusion of marshmallow leaves makes a soothing skin toner. It can also be used as a rinse for dry hair.

Marshmallow's traditional use for soothing sore throats and dry coughs has been substantiated by modern studies. It is approved by Commission E for treating coughs and bronchitis. An infusion of dried leaves or dried root can be used as a gargle, or taken as a tea. A commercial syrup of roots may help a dry cough.
other species
Musk mallow (*Malva moschata*) and hollyhock (*Alcea rosea*) are more commonly grown in gardens because they have showier flowers. They and other mallows have herbal properties similar to those of marshmallow.

DILL *Anethum graveolens*
G C M H
other names dillweed, dillseed
plant family Umbelliferae (carrot family)
height up to 3 feet (90 cm)
habit hardy annual, usually with one upright stem and finely cut aromatic leaves; flat-topped clusters of tiny yellow flowers in summer, followed by aromatic seeds
habitat full sun and well-drained, evenly moist, moderately fertile soil
all zones (annual)

Marshmallow *Althaea officinalis*

Dill *Anethum graveolens*

The blue-green, filigree fronds and large but dainty flower heads of dill look attractive in flower arrangements. Dried flowers and seed heads add a sculptural presence to dried flower arrangements.

Dill is so closely related to fennel, also yellow-flowered but larger, that the two tend to hybridize. If you intend to save their seeds for cooking, or to plant in future years, avoid planting them close together when planning your herb garden. Choose a sheltered spot, as the long stalks can be damaged by wind.

Dill seeds are traditionally used in pickling vegetables such as cucumbers, gherkins, and cauliflowers, particularly in Germany and the United States, home of the dill pickle. They are also commonly used to flavor herb vinegars. When ground, they make a useful salt substitute to enhance flavor for salt-free diets. The seeds have a stronger flavor than the leaves, partly due to their greater carvone content. Feathery dill leaves are used in salads and sauces and on vegetables. They combine especially well with eggs, fish, and—rather surprisingly—with strawberries.

Dill has been approved by Commission E for the treatment of indigestion. An infusion made from the dried seeds or leaves can be used for this purpose; such an infusion may also be helpful against flatulence and even hiccups.

The seeds help to relax the muscles of the gastrointestinal tract. The aromatic qualities of the oils in the plant's seeds have led to their use in Indian medicine to counteract bad breath.

ANGELICA *Angelica archangelica*
G C M H
other names garden angelica, archangel, root of the Holy Ghost
plant family Umbelliferae (carrot family)
height up to 7 feet (2 m)
habit hardy biennial with upright hollow stems and coarsely segmented leaves; globe-shaped clusters of tiny yellowish green flowers bloom in early summer

Angelica *Angelica archangelica*

habitat partial shade with rich, damp, well-drained soil
zones 4–9
Angelica is a stately plant in a woodland garden. It has a beguiling aroma, and its essential oil is used in aromatherapy and perfumes. Its foliage is scented when dried, its seeds can be used as a fixative for potpourris, and the tiny flowers also have a sweet fragrance. It was beloved by medieval herbalists, and John Parkinson in his book *Paradisi in Sole Paradisus Terrestris* (1629) placed it above all medicinal plants. It was called "*herba angelica*"—the herb of the angels.

Most people knowingly encounter angelica only as green pieces of candied stem on cake decorations. However, it is also used to flavor Benedictine liqueur and gin.

Angelica root has been approved by Commission E for the treatment of digestive problems and loss of appetite; it can be taken in the form of infusions of the dried roots.

However, the American Pharmaceutical Association state that ingesting angelica root carries a health risk.

Caution *Unfortunately, two of the compounds in angelica's root oil (xanthotoxin and bergaptene) are furocoumarins. These are phototoxic—that is, they sensitize the skin to light, so you should avoid ultraviolet sun beds or extended sunbathing if using angelica root. Dried roots have less of this effect and so are safer than fresh ones. In animal studies it was found that the furocoumarins could cause cancer. Avoid using angelica preparations during pregnancy and if you are diabetic. Avoid gathering angelica in the wild. It can easily be mistaken for similar-looking but poisonous plants, including spotted water hemlock (Cicuta maculata).*

other species

Great angelica, also known as masterwort (*Angelica atropurpurea*), grows wild in much of eastern North America. It looks similar but has purple stems and grows in wet places. It has been used in similar ways to the garden angelica, particularly as a leaf tea for indigestion and colds. It carries the same cautions.

In Europe wild angelica (*A. sylvestris*), a striking plant with purple-flushed stems, also grows in freshwater marshes and wet woodlands. A yellow dye can be extracted from it.

CHERVIL *Anthriscus cerefolium*
G C H

other names garden chervil
plant family Umbelliferae (carrot family)
height up to 2 feet (60 cm)
habit hardy biennial with finely cut aromatic leaves; flat-topped clusters of tiny white flowers bloom in early summer
habitat partial shade and moist, rich soil
zones 3–8

Chervil, closely related to a plant known in Europe as cow parsley (*Anthriscus sylvestris*), is often grown in kitchen gardens. Since it quickly goes to seed, it is usually grown as an annual. Its flavor falls between that of parsley and anise.

The leaves and sprigs are often used in French recipes and in salads, vinegars, and for garnishes. When used in hot dishes such as soups, chervil is best added near the end of cooking. Chervil forms part of the traditional *fines herbes* mixture. In celebration of its aroma and taste, its name derives from a Greek word meaning "to rejoice."

An infusion of chervil makes a good toner for oily skin; the herb's astringent qualities help to close the pores.

Caution *Avoid use of chervil's essential oil, as two of its components (estragole and anethole) can be an irritant. Estragole is also suspected to be carcinogenic.*

CELERY *Apium graveolens*
G C M

plant family Umbelliferae (carrot family)
height up to 3 feet (90 cm)
habit hardy biennial grown as an annual with grooved stems and segmented leaves; clusters of small white flowers bloom in the summer of the second year
habitat prefers full sun and rich, fertile, well-drained soil
all zones (grown as annual)

Celery was cultivated in ancient Egypt and China. The cultivated form, *Apium graveolens* var. *dulce*, requires moist, well-drained, fertile soil, which is piled up around stems to blanch them. If grown only for its seeds, celery tolerates poor soil. Celery growing wild or in poor soil has a darker stem and is more bitter.

Celery is a culinary favorite, stuffed as an hors d'oeuvre, eaten raw in salads, and cooked in soups and stews. The seeds are a popular seasoning, used in salads and salad dressings or to give the flavor of celery to some hot dishes.

The seeds are the part of the celery plant that has been used medicinally. Though no medical uses have been proven, infusions of the seeds and leaves have been used to treat indigestion and loss of appetite, and for coughs. Infusions or commercial capsules have also been

Chervil *Anthriscus cerefolium*

Celery *Apium graveolens*

Horseradish *Armoracia rusticana*

taken to combat gout and rheumatoid arthritis, in the unproven belief that they are mildly diuretic and thus flush harmful compounds out of the body. The U.S. Food and Drug Administration has approved the plant and its seeds as safe for food use.

Caution *Do not eat celery seeds intended for cultivation, as they may have been treated with fungicide. During pregnancy avoid using large quantities of seed or the essential oil. Do not use celery medicinally if you are suffering from any kidney infections. Celery, especially the seeds, can cause serious allergic reactions. One compound contained in celery, the furocoumarin bergaptene, can cause sun sensitivity. This compound is especially concentrated in celeriac, also called celery root, which is a variety of celery (A. graveolens var. rapaceum) grown for its swollen root. The combination of eating a lot of celery root and lying under ultraviolet sunlamps can cause a sunburn-like skin reaction.*

HORSERADISH *Armoracia rusticana*
(formerly *Cochlearia armoracia*)
G C M
other names red cole, redcol
plant family Cruciferae (mustard family)
height up to 5 feet (1.5 m)

habit hardy perennial with long thick roots and long coarse leaves; bears small white flowers in early summer
habitat prefers full sun and rich, moist, well-drained soil
zones 3–9

Horseradish is easy to grow in the vegetable or herb garden, but its location must be chosen with care. It is extremely difficult to remove from an area; even the smallest pieces of roots left behind will grow back. The root of horseradish, either grated fresh or the purchased condiment (which is preserved in vinegar), has many culinary uses. It traditionally accompanies roast beef and is also used in dips, cheese spreads, and coleslaw.

The mustard oil that gives horseradish sauce its kick has antibiotic properties and has been used to treat inflammations of the respiratory tract. Commission E has approved the use of horseradish to treat coughs and bronchitis. For this purpose, the grated fresh or dried root can be eaten, drunk as an infusion, or pressed to extract the juice, which is usually drunk diluted—traditionally with wine.

Caution *Overconsumption of horseradish can cause discomfort to the digestive tract. Avoid taking it if you have kidney or thyroid problems.*

TARRAGON *Artemisia dracunculus*
G C M H
other names French tarragon, little dragon
plant family Compositae (daisy family)
height up to 3 feet (90 cm)
habit hardy perennial with sturdy, branched stems and slender linear, aromatic leaves; rarely produces tiny tassels of yellowish green flowers in summer
habitat full sun and rich, well-drained soil
zones 3–9

Tarragon is a popular plant for herb and kitchen gardens. It has tiny flowers and rarely produces viable seeds. To grow this herb, you need to purchase plants or start cuttings from a friend's plant. Avoid seeds, as the only seeds sold as tarragon will be its flavorless relative Russian tarragon.

Tarragon is used in cooking throughout the world, especially to flavor vinegars, and in chicken and egg dishes; it is also good in dips and spreads. It is often included in the *fines herbes* mixture. It owes its popularity as a culinary herb to its distinctive, spicy anise taste, caused largely by its essential oil component, estragole. The fresh herb has the best anise flavor; when dried the flavor is less pronounced. Tarragon has been used as an appetite stimulant, perhaps because it adds such wonderful flavor to food. It has also been used to help relieve flatulence.

Tarragon has also been used in perfumes for its fragrance. It keeps its scent when used in dried herb arrangements.

Caution *Tarragon (except for the small quantities used as seasoning) should not be taken during pregnancy. The estragole present in its essential oil has been identified as potentially carcinogenic. Do not consume tarragon in large quantities.*

other species
Artemisias are among the favorite garden plants of those who love soft, silvery, gray-green foliage. These silvery tones are produced by a covering of fine hairs on each leaf. Artemisias make a visually calm background to other garden plants. The genus was named after

Tarragon *Artemisia dracunculus*

Southernwood *Artemisia abrotanum*

Artemis, the Greek goddess of women's fertility. Most artemisias have strong scents, though sometimes these are not obvious until you rub a leaf. Fresh or dried, they make attractive additions to flower arrangements. The dried leaves are often used in insect-repelling sachets. Pharmacologically the various species are also very active and similar to each other, containing bitter sesquiterpene lactones such as absinthin and strong volatile oils such as the ketone thujone. With the exception of tarragon, artemisias should not be taken internally as they can be highly toxic (see *Wormwood*, page 104).

The strong aroma of southernwood (*Artemisia abrotanum*) is softened by an overtone of lemon. The feathery texture of its lacy leaves, along with its fragrance, makes it a favorite in the garden. It can reach 5 feet (1.5 m) tall. Because of its pungent scent, it can be rubbed directly on to the skin to keep insects at bay. Dried sprigs (or sachets containing dried leaves) can be placed between clothing to deter moth attack—a use suggested by its alternative name of garderobe. An infusion makes a good tonic for dry or dull hair.

Sweet wormwood (*A. annua*), unlike most artemisias, is an annual. It rapidly grows to 6 or more feet (1.8 m) tall and is topped by sprays of tiny yellow-green flowers. Both its feathery leaves and flowers are aromatic, with a sweeter scent than other artemisias. It has been used in China for nearly 2,000 years to treat fevers and chills, including malaria. Recent research shows that one of its components (artemisinin, a sesquiterpene lactone) may prove to be a powerful antimalarial drug. It has been licensed for use in commercial form in several countries.

Roman wormwood (*A. pontica*) grows only about 15 inches (38 cm) tall, a good size for most gardens. It spreads rapidly, so clumps must be edged with a sharp spade every year to keep them from running into other plants. Its fine, lacy leaves are pewter gray. It has a less bitter smell and flavor than the common wormwood (see page 104), which led to its use as a preferred flavoring for vermouth.

Sweet wormwood *Artemisia annua*

Roman wormwood *Artemisia pontica*

CALENDULA *Calendula officinalis*
G C M H
other names pot marigold, marygold
plant family Compositae (daisy family)
height 20 inches (50 cm)
habit hardy annual with oblong gray-green leaves; large flowers in shades of yellow and orange bloom throughout the summer and fall, even in winter in mild climates
habitat full sun to light shade and average, well-drained soil; prefers cool conditions
all zones (annual)

Once established in the flower garden, calendula looks after itself and some plants will be in flower for most of the year until the first frosts hit. It frequently reseeds, saving you the trouble of replanting the following year. The flowers are good for cutting, and they dry well.

The English herbalist Henry Lyte described the plant well in his *Niewe Herball* (1578): "It hath pleasant, bright and shining yellow flowers, the which do close at the setting downe of the sunne, and do spread and open againe at the sunne rising."

As a garnish the flower petals bring a colorful, sunny note to salads. They have been termed "poor man's saffron," as they will give a yellow color to foods if they are added during the cooking process. The flowers have long been used on the Indian subcontinent as a holy adornment to statues of gods.

Calendula's alternative names of pot marigold and marygold, echoing the name of the Virgin Mary, are thought to derive from the herb's reputation for healing sore nipples and promoting menstruation. An infusion of the flowers is a good toner for oily skin or greasy hair.

In folk medicine calendula has been used for many purposes, including as an antifungal douche, a gargle for sore throats, and a remedy for stomach disorders and hemorrhoids. However, it is now most commonly used to treat inflammations of the skin. Its flowers are approved by Commission E for treating cuts, scrapes, burns, and inflammations, and for bringing relief to sore skin. Commission E also approves their use for inflammations of the mouth and throat. Research has shown that the flowers have antifungal, antibacterial, antiviral, and anti-inflammatory properties. An infusion of the flowers can be used as a wash or a compress. A commercial calendula cream is readily available and very convenient.

Calendula *Calendula officinalis*

CENTAURY *Centaurium erythraea*
syn. *Erythraea centaurium*
G M
other names bitterherb, feverwort
plant family Gentianaceae (gentian family)
height up to 10 inches (25 cm)
habit hardy biennial with a rosette of leaves at the base; pink flowers in loose clusters through summer and fall
habitat found on dry grasslands and dunes; prefers full sun and well-drained, sandy soil
zones 4–8

Centaury *Centaurium erythraea*

PERENNIAL CHAMOMILE
Chamaemelum nobile
G M H
other names Roman chamomile, English chamomile
plant family Compositae (daisy family)
height up to 1 foot (30 cm)
habit hardy perennial with creeping stems and low, finely cut scented leaves; bears small white daisy flowers in summer
habitat full sun to light shade; most soils
zones 4–8

Perennial chamomile grows low and multiplies by means of runners. The name chamomile is from the Greek for "earth-apple," because of its applelike scent when crushed. These qualities led to its popular use as a scented lawn. In the medieval garden chamomile was even planted to cover earth seats. Its scent also led to its use as a strewing herb, an herb scattered on floors to release pleasant scents when walked upon.

Perennial chamomile *Chamaemelum nobile*

With its clusters of small starlike flowers measuring about ½ inch (1.5 cm) in diameter, centaury makes a pretty garden plant. Its unusual name is derived from Chiron the centaur, the mythological Greek figure, half-human, half-horse, who, according to legend, taught humans the use of medicinal herbs.

One of the most valuable of the bitter herbs, centaury has a relatively mild bitter action that stimulates the appetite and helps to trigger salivation and the secretion of gastric juices. It is recommended by Commission E for overcoming poor appetites and for the treatment of indigestion. The flowers, leaves, and stems are used to make a bitter infusion that can be slowly sipped before meals.

Centaury's value in arousing appetite led to its inclusion with other herbs in vermouth and bitter liqueurs used as aperitif drinks.

Caution *You should avoid using centaury during pregnancy or if you suffer from stomach or intestinal ulcers.*

Perennial chamomile contains aromatic oils and sesquiterpene lactones that help protect it from insect attack. It also has a reputation for protecting sickly neighboring plants, which has led to its being termed a "physician plant." It supposedly repels insects on adjacent plants.

Chamomile makes a good dried flower and is a popular ingredient in potpourri. Chamomile oil is used in aromatherapy. An infusion of the fresh or dried flowers can be used as a toner for oily skin and as a rinse to brighten blond hair.

An infusion of dried flower heads has been used to treat indigestion arising from stress. The sweet smell of perennial chamomile contrasts with its slightly bitter taste, and this may stimulate digestion. It has also been used to calm hyperactivity and to prevent insomnia. However, none of these uses has been approved by Commission E, and it seems that annual chamomile (see page 68) may be more effective.

Historically the annual (German) and perennial (Roman) chamomile were not distinguished from each other. Chamomile was one of the nine sacred Saxon herbs, and it has been among the most popular herbal treatments of the last two hundred years. Both the annual and the perennial chamomiles are most often taken as a tea; according to one estimate, a million cups of chamomile tea are drunk each day worldwide.

Caution *The use of perennial chamomile's essential oil should be avoided during pregnancy as it is a uterine stimulant. Generally, internal use of the essential oil is not advisable.*

CHICORY *Cichorium intybus*
G C M
other names wild succory, blue endive, coffee-weed
plant family Compositae (daisy family)
height up to 5 feet (1.5 m)
habit hardy perennial with deep roots and long, toothed leaves on erect tough stems; bright blue flowers all summer into fall

Chicory *Cichorium intybus*

habitat prefers open conditions; full sun and rich, well-drained soil
zones 3–9

Chicory is an attractive plant whose pale blue flowers can be seen on roadsides. Now generally considered a weed, in former times chicory was often included in herb and kitchen gardens. Its young nutritious leaves have been eaten in salads since classical times. In France and Belgium the plant is forced for winter or early spring greens, as is its cousin the endive. Chicory roots are dried and roasted to make a coffee substitute (or to mix with coffee for the distinctive chicory flavor); chicory roots contain up to 60 percent of the carbohydrate inulin.

Chicory is similar to dandelion, not just in its leaf shape but in other characteristics as well. Its stems are filled with a white sticky sap or latex that contains sesquiterpene lactones. These bitter compounds help deter some insects from feeding on the plant. For humans, they give the plant a pleasing bitterness that stimulates the appetite and the flow of bile to aid digestion. Commission E approves both these uses.

In addition to eating the leaves and drinking a decoction of the roasted root, users may take an infusion of the dried leaves and roots of the whole fresh chicory plant.

Caution *There have been rare instances of allergic reaction to chicory; avoid eating it if you have any sensitivity to other plants of the daisy family, including ragweed.*

CORIANDER *Coriandrum sativum*

G C M H

other names coriander seed, Chinese parsley, cilantro
plant family Umbelliferae (carrot family)
height up to 20 inches (50 cm)
habit hardy annual with erect stems and moderately to finely cut aromatic leaves; flat clusters of tiny white to mauve flowers in summer, followed by round seeds
habitat full sun to light shade; moderately rich, well-drained soil
all zones (annual)

This pungently aromatic herb with a spicy flavor has long enjoyed popularity. Its seeds were found in an Egyptian tomb from the twenty-first dynasty, confirming that it has been used for over three thousand years. It was originally a Mediterranean plant, but the seeds are used on the Indian subcontinent on a huge scale in curries, including the garam masala seasoning mixture. The ground seeds are also used to flavor baked goods, candy, and alcoholic beverages such as gin, and even to mask unappetizing smells or flavors in pharmaceuticals. The strongly flavored leaves, more commonly known as cilantro, have long been used in the cuisines of Southeast Asia, India, and Mexico. In recent years, they have also become widely used in Britain and North America. The fresh leaves are used in salads, soups, sauces, dips, and spreads, and as a

garnish. Crushed coriander seeds are wonderfully fragrant and make a good fixative for potpourri. The oil extracted from the seeds is used in aromatherapy.

Coriander also has curiously English connections. It was the first aromatic herb to be taken to Britain, ahead of the Roman invasion, and its seeds were excavated from a late Bronze Age hut in Kent. In medieval and later times coriander was grown alongside saffron at Saffron Walden in Essex. In the seventeenth century one of coriander's major uses was in "comfits," or sugared candies, which were sucked to settle digestion. The seeds, rather than the leaves, were used for this because they have a sweeter taste. The leaves were also used medicinally at that time, but the diarist John Evelyn noted in 1699 that the leaves were "profitable indeed to the stomach, but offensive to the head."

Commission E has approved the use of coriander for indigestion and loss of appetite. It may be taken as either an infusion or a tincture of the crushed seeds.

Coriander *Coriandrum sativum*

ECHINACEA *Echinacea purpurea* and
E. angustifolia
G M
other names purple coneflower
plant family Compositae (daisy family)
height up to 4 feet (1.2 m)
habit hardy perennial with large, coarse-textured, pointed leaves; large daisylike flowers with rosy purple petals and orange-tipped black central cone in summer
habitat prefers full sun but tolerates light shade and grows in most soils
zones 3–9

Echinacea's flowers are large, attractive, and colorful, and well worth growing in the garden. Provided they get enough sunlight, the spectacular pink blooms with dark raised centers attract butterflies and brighten an herbaceous border or woodland garden.

Narrow-leaved coneflower (*Echinacea angustifolia*) was used extensively by Native American tribes to treat snakebites, infected wounds, and other conditions. The use of echinacea spread worldwide when, in the 1930s, a Dr. Madaus returned to Germany from an American visit bearing seeds. He brought seeds of *E. purpurea,* believing them to be of *E. angustifolia,* and found that this plant was equally useful. His company (the Madaus pharmaceutical company) made standardized echinacea products widely available.

Today echinacea is one of the most popular and most researched herbal treatments. It has been demonstrated to stimulate the body's immune system and improve resistance to bacterial and viral infections. Current research suggests that echinacea may help to decrease the severity and duration of cold and flu symptoms, but it is not effective at preventing symptoms. Many components contribute to echinacea's action, so the herb works as the sum of its parts rather than with a single component. The complex sugar (polysaccharide) arabinogalactan has been demonstrated to stimulate the immune system, while other components (alkylamides) stimulate white blood cell activity. Another component (caffeic acid) inhibits *Staphylococcus aureus* bacteria; derivatives of this

Echinacea *Echinacea purpurea*

Echinacea *Echinacea angustifolia*

compound, along with the flavonoid components, have been found to have antibacterial, antiviral, and anti-inflammatory properties.

There are differences between *E. angustifolia* and *E. purpurea,* but how significant they are is not yet clear. *E. purpurea* is better researched. This species is approved by Commission E for use in treating colds, fevers, coughs and bronchitis, urinary tract infections, inflammation of the mouth and throat, a general tendency to infection, and (externally) for wounds and burns.

Caution *Those suffering from autoimmune and systemic diseases including tuberculosis, multiple sclerosis, AIDS, and HIV infections should not take echinacea internally. Similarly, avoid using it during pregnancy or if you have any sensitivity to other plants of the daisy family.*

other species
There are a number of echinacea species native to North America, but the only other one so far demonstrated to have marked medicinal value is pale coneflower (*E. pallida*). Its use is approved by Commission E for treating fevers and colds.

EUCALYPTUS *Eucalyptus globulus*
G M

other names blue gum, Tasmanian blue gum, gum tree
plant family Myrtaceae (myrtle)
height up to 150 ft (45 m)
habit tender tree with smooth, creamy white to gray bark that peels off in ribbonlike shreds and long, silvery blue evergreen leaves; single white petal-less flowers from spring to summer, followed by hard woody seedpods
habitat full sun and fertile, well-drained soil
zones 9–11

Given the right conditions, this fast-growing tree can be grown as a windbreak or as a specimen. Eucalyptus are the archetypal Australian trees on which koala bears live and feed. There are over five hundred species. The juvenile leaves are ovate; those on adult trees are sickle-shaped and glossy. They are aromatic, and

Eucalyptus *Eucalyptus globulus*

can be dried and added to potpourris. When boiled, the leaves produce a red dye.

Species used for medicinal purposes, such as *Eucalyptus globulus,* contain mainly eucalyptol (cineole) in their volatile oil. This has been demonstrated to have antibacterial and antifungal properties. The oil can be used in diluted form as an expectorant to help clear the lungs. Used in a steam inhalation, the oil can ease blocked-up noses. It is also used in commercial eucalyptus lozenges to stimulate saliva production, which eases coughing. Commission E approves the use of diluted eucalyptus oil to treat coughs and bronchitis, and, externally, for rheumatic complaints.

Caution *Use only the recommended dosage, as large doses of the essential oil can be life-threatening. Avoid using eucalpytus during pregnancy. Do not give eucalyptus to babies or toddlers. Do not apply eucalyptus preparations to or near the faces of babies or young children, as it is possible that they might cause dangerous breathing difficulties.*

Boneset *Eupatorium perfoliatum*

Joe Pye weed *Eupatorium purpureum*

BONESET *Eupatorium perfoliatum*
G M

other names thoroughwort, ague-weed,
feverwort, Indian sage
plant family Compositae (daisy family)
height up to 5 feet (1.5 m)
habit hardy perennial with long, pointed,
stalkless leaves; clusters of small, shaggy white
flowers bloom from summer through to fall
habitat full sun to partial shade and moist to
damp, rich soil
zones 3–9

Boneset has shaggy flowers like other species of
Eupatorium, though the herb's clusters are
smaller and somewhat more open. This
handsome plant can be found in wet meadows
and low-lying woods all over North America. It
makes a highly attractive feature in wild gardens
and naturalistic plantings, especially at the
edges of woods.

According to some sources, the plant
received the name boneset because it was used
to treat a highly debilitating type of influenza
known as "break-bone fever." It was a Native

American treatment for fevers, which gave it its
alternative name of feverwort. It caused patients
to sweat, which seemed to cool the fever.
Boneset was also used by people living in and
around swamps to treat rheumatic conditions.
These effects have not been proven.

other species

Joe Pye weed (*E. purpureum*) has handsome
clusters of shaggy pink to rosy purple flowers
and a sweet scent with a hint of apple in its
flowers and its crushed leaves. It thrives in the
same conditions as boneset. Joe Pye weed was
also used by Native Americans to treat fevers,
and it takes its common name from the Native
American Joe Pye (or Jopi), who used it to help
settlers in New England when they were dying of
typhus. Joe Pye weed has also been used as a
diuretic to treat problems of the urinary tract. Its
other common name, gravel root, refers to kidney
gravel, and it has been used to "wash out" kidney
stones. These effects are unproven, and internal
use of Joe Pye weed is no longer advised because
the plant contains the same pyrrolizidine alkaloids
as comfrey (see page 95).

MEADOWSWEET *Filipendula ulmaria*
G M H
other names queen-of-the-meadow, bridewort
plant family Rosaceae (rose family)
height up to 5 feet (1.5 m)
habit hardy perennial with dark green, toothed leaves; red stems bear large heads of creamy white, fragrant flowers from midsummer to early autumn
habitat full sun to partial shade and constantly wet to moist, fertile soil
zones 3–9

The blooms of this wildflower smell of vanilla, while the leaves, in contrast, have a musky scent. Meadowsweet is said to have been Elizabeth I's favorite strewing herb. It was also one of the three most sacred and magic herbs of the Druids, along with water mint and valerian. It adds a pleasant fragrance to fresh or dried flower arrangements.

Though meadowsweet thrives in wet meadows, that does not seem to be the source of its name. It was once used as a flavoring of the fermented honey-based drink called mead. Thanks to meadowsweet, this alcoholic Saxon drink seems to have had a built-in hangover cure, for meadowsweet contains salicin, from which salicylic acid and aspirin are derived. Meadowsweet has been used like aspirin to bring relief from pain.

In 1853, German chemists working with an extract of meadowsweet synthesized acetylsalicylic acid. To name this potent new drug (patented in 1899), they took the "a" from acetyl—the chemical they added to the extract—and "spirin" from meadowsweet's former Latin genus name, *Spiraea*.

A dried meadowsweet flower head infused in a hot cup of water provides a soothing drink for a cold. Commission E approves the use of meadowsweet for coughs, bronchitis, and fevers as well as colds.

Caution *Continuous use of salicylates can cause gastric bleeding. In meadowsweet and similar plants, the salicylates may be partially buffered by the plant's tannins and mucilage, but this has not been proven. Avoid meadowsweet if you are sensitive to aspirin. Children under sixteen should avoid all aspirin-related substances because of the risk of the rare Reye's syndrome, which can cause potentially lethal liver damage.*

Meadowsweet *Filipendula ulmaria*

Bronze fennel *Foeniculum vulgare* 'Purpurascens'

FENNEL *Foeniculum vulgare*
G C M H

other name fenkel, finocchio
plant family Umbelliferae (carrot family)
height up to 7 feet (2 m)
habit hardy perennial with threadlike leaves; flat yellow clusters of small flowers in summer
habitat prefers warm, dry, sunny positions and well-drained soil
zones 5–9; Florence fennel all zones (half-hardy annual)

Fennel is one of the tallest and most graceful plants in the herb garden. It resembles a larger version of dill. The purplish foliage of bronze fennel (*Foeniculum vulgare* 'Purpurascens') is particularly ornamental. Fennel has a distinctive aniseed scent and taste; the main volatile oil of both anise and fennel is anethole.

Fennel has long been praised for its use in cooking and medicine. The Roman natural historian Pliny credited it with twenty-two remedies. As the herbalist Parkinson noted in *Theatricum Botanicum* (1640): "The leaves, seede and rootes are both for meate and medicine."

One form, known as "sweet" or Florence fennel (*F. v.* var. *dulce*), is grown as an annual in vegetable and herb gardens. It has a bulbous base to its stalk that is eaten raw in salads or cooked as a vegetable, with fish, and in soups, casseroles, and stews. The leaves are also used as a seasoning or garnish. Florence fennel has a sweeter flavor because it contains more anise-flavored anethole and less of the bitter volatile oil fenchone than the perennial wild fennel of the Mediterranean, which is also known as bitter fennel. The foliage of both plants is attractive in flower arrangements. The essential oil extracted from the seeds of Florence fennel is often used in aromatherapy.

Fennel is a mild expectorant; an infusion made from the crushed seeds or essential oil is approved by Commission E for treating coughs and bronchitis. In tests on frogs, two of its components (anethole and fenchone) have been found to break down mucous secretions. Fennel is also approved by Commission E for treating indigestion. A dish of dried fennel seeds is often provided after a meal at an Indian restaurant to promote digestion and alleviate gas. The seeds may also be crushed or ground and then made into a tea. Fennel tea has traditionally been used

Florence fennel *Foeniculum vulgare* var. *dulce*

to soothe babies' colic. In the nineteenth century, doctors recommended fennel to aid in the production of breast milk.

Caution *Fennel has a long history of safe use, but a few individuals can be allergic to the anethole it contains. For aromatherapy, it is best to use the essential oil of Florence fennel rather than bitter fennel. The oil should not be used by pregnant women or children. In a few sensitive individuals, fennel may cause light-triggered skin reactions because of trace amounts of the compound bergaptene and other furocoumarins.*

LICORICE *Glycyrrhiza glabra*
M

other name liquorice, sweetwood
plant family Leguminosae (pea family)
height up to 5 feet (1.5 m)
habit hardy perennial with woody stems and fine leaflets arranged like rungs of a ladder; loose spikes of pale blue to violet flowers in summer
habitat full sun to partial shade and deep, well-drained fertile soil
zones 7–9

The early Greek physician Dioscorides called this plant *glycyrrhiza,* from *glukos* meaning "sweet" and *riza* meaning "root." Over the centuries, the name became corrupted: In English it became lycorys and eventually licorice; in German it became *lacrisse.* The compound responsible for the sweet taste of licorice is glycyrrhizin. Each molecule of glycyrrhizin is fifty times as sweet as one molecule of sucrose in table sugar. Because of its sweetness, it was inevitable that licorice would be used for candy. The traditional means of extraction was to crush the thick roots in a mill, boil them in water, and then concentrate the liquid by evaporation. Today, European licorice confectionery is still usually made from licorice, while American candy products often substitute the similar-tasting anise (see page 80).

One of licorice's historic "medicinal" uses was as a sweetener mixed with bitter herbs to make them more palatable. For thousands of years, though, licorice has also been used for its soothing effects. Some of its compounds (liquirtin and other flavonoids) have been found to accelerate the healing of gastric ulcers.

In experiments, licorice has been shown to have anti-inflammatory effects and possibly also antiarthritic, antibacterial, and antiviral effects. It is approved by Commission E for treating coughs and bronchitis. Licorice can be taken as a decoction or infusion of the roots.

Caution *Do not take licorice for longer than a month without professional advice. Avoid using it at any stage of pregnancy or while breast-feeding. Also avoid using it if you are suffering from high blood pressure, diabetes, liver, or kidney disorders. Prolonged high levels of licorice can cause severe fluid retention, high blood pressure, and weakness; eventually these could escalate to the point of requiring hospitalization. Individual responses vary, but these effects are unusual when less than 100 mg are taken per day. Drink no more than three cups of licorice decoction or infusion within 24 hours. Always seek medical advice before using at larger doses.*

Licorice *Glycyrrhiza glabra*

59

Witch hazel *(Hamamelis virginiana)* in spring

Witch hazel *(Hamamelis virginiana)* in fall

WITCH HAZEL *Hamamelis virginiana*
G M H

other names winterbloom, snapping hazel, striped alder
plant family Hamameldaceae (witch hazel family)
height up to 17 feet (5 m)
habit hardy tree with deciduous, oval leaves; yellow aromatic flowers with threadlike petals in shaggy clusters in the fall
habitat damp woodlands; prefers partial shade and moist, fertile soil
zones 3–8

The attractive late-season color of witch hazel's spidery flowers has made it and its hybrids garden favorites. Sometimes the leaves also turn brilliant colors in autumn. Chinese witch hazel (*Hamamelis mollis*) is the most handsome, but it blooms in late winter to early spring, and is less hardy than common witch hazel.

The combination of tannins in witch hazel exerts a strong astringent effect. This contracts and tightens the skin surface, which slows bleeding and creates a protective film to accelerate healing. The tannins also have an antiseptic role because of their astringent action on surface bacteria. Consequently a decoction of witch hazel leaves is useful as a mouthwash.

Distilled witch hazel (steam-distilled from the leaves and bark of *H. virginiana*) is used around the world for treating minor skin ailments, but it is unclear why it works. Commercial witch hazel contains only minimal amounts of tannins, as tannins are very large molecules and so are not readily distilled. It is likely that, as the American Pharmaceutical Association suggests, the effect is attributable to the alcohol that is added to the distillate. Alcohol has a somewhat similar astringent action to tannins.

Rather than using a distillation, a more effective preparation of witch hazel is to make a decoction or infusion of the bark and leaves. The decoction or infusion can be made into an ointment for convenience, or a tincture of witch hazel can be used.

Commission E approves the leaf and bark for treating varicose veins (including hemorrhoids) and skin inflammations, and for healing wounds and burns. The leaf only is approved for treating inflammations of the mouth and pharynx.

Caution *Although witch hazel has been used at times in an infusion or distillation to treat diarrhea, some authorities advise against internal use, particularly over long periods of time. It can trigger digestive problems and, potentially, may cause liver damage.*

HOPS *Humulus lupulus*
G M H

other name common hops
plant family Cannabidaceae (hemp family)
height up to 20 feet (6 m) or more
habit hardy perennial vine with twining stems and lobed leaves; conelike flowers dangle from female plants in summer
habitat full sun and moist but well-drained, fertile soil
zones 3–8

Hops are cultivated on a large scale worldwide. This perennial vine, which grows very rapidly but dies back to the ground each winter, is easy to grow: All it requires is sun, rich soil, and a tall support. It is often grown to twine up strings or wires running diagonally between sturdy posts. Gold-leaved 'Aureus' is more ornamental than the common form.

The name hop derives from the Anglo-Saxon word *hoppan*, meaning "to climb," which hops do, with rough twining stems. There are separate male and female plants. The ripe, conelike female flowers are used in herb pillows and in brewing; they contain small surface glands that produce an aromatic yellow powder called lupulin. This powder is the source of the bitter resins and volatile oils used to give beer its bitter flavor. A few especially aromatic hop varieties also give beer a heady aroma.

Hops have had a wide variety of other uses. Pliny, writing in the first century AD, relates

Hops *Humulus lupulus*

that the Romans used to eat spring shoots of hops as we eat asparagus. In the eighteenth century George III of England popularized the use of hops in herb pillows. The vines are also attractive in dried flower arrangements and wreaths. Today, hops are used primarily in the production of beer.

The bitter acids in hops (humulone and lupulone) have been found to have antibacterial and antifungal properties, and are likely to be the reason why hops preserve beer. Different types of hops are used in different types of beer. Lager-style beers (popular in the United States) normally have a lower hop content than darker and more bitter beers.

Hops have been shown to have sedative properties, and are approved by Commission E for treating nervousness and insomnia. They are prepared as an infusion of the dried female flowers, as a tincture, or as a bath additive. In sleep-inducing infusions, hops are often combined with other herbs such as valerian and linden flowers.

GOLDENSEAL *Hydrastis canadensis*
G M
other names yellow root, eye-root, yellow puccoon, Indian paint, wild curcuma
plant family Ranunculaceae (buttercup family)
height up to 1 foot (30 cm)
habit hardy perennial with a few, deeply lobed, toothed leaves; solitary greenish white flowers in late spring followed by inedible red fruits that resemble raspberries
habitat moist, shaded conditions in most soils, with some partial to full shade in moist soils, rich in organic matter
zones 3–8

Goldenseal is a strange-looking plant that grows in the damp mountain woodlands of eastern North America. Its red fruit sits at the center of the leaf like a jewel on a cushion. In the right

Goldenseal *Hydrastis canadensis*

growing conditions, the roots spread underground to form large patches. Goldenseal is somewhat challenging to grow. Though easiest to start from seeds, these can take over a year to sprout. It rarely survives being transplanted from the wild, so purchase nursery-propagated plants.

Its use by Native Americans was recorded as early as 1793. The Cherokees used goldenseal to cure snakebites and as a wash for eye inflammations, and the Iroquois used it to treat diarrhea, fevers, and pneumonia. Above all, it was used as the source of a golden yellow dye. Goldenseal attracted more general popularity in the mid-nineteenth century, but over-collecting caused it to decline rapidly. In the first half of the twentieth century the U.S. Department of Agriculture began experimenting with cultivation. Today the massive demand for goldenseal is met largely by field-grown roots.

Goldenseal is now one of the top-selling herbs in the United States for a wide range of uses. Goldenseal mouthwashes and commercial sterile eyewashes are available over the counter, and the herb is frequently used to treat disorders affecting the mucous membranes of the body, especially of the eyes, the mouth, the ears, nose, and throat, the digestive system, and the vagina. Though its benefits have not been proven, it has come to be used for anything from hemorrhoids to cold sores.

However, for such a commonly used medicinal herb only a comparatively small amount of research has been done. There is clinical evidence that one of the alkaloids it contains (berberine) has antibacterial properties and may assist digestion. Another alkaloid, hydrastine, can constrict blood vessels and so may assist the control of bleeding. Both these alkaloids have astringent and mild antiseptic qualities, supporting their use as a mouthwash.
Caution *Goldenseal should not be used continuously for long periods. Overdoses can cause convulsions, difficulty in breathing, and vomiting. You should not use goldenseal during pregnancy, as berberine has been shown to stimulate the uterus.*

ST.-JOHN'S-WORT *Hypericum perforatum*
G M

other names Klamath weed, perforate
St.-John's-wort, common St.-John's-wort
plant family Hypericaceae (St.-John's-wort
family)
height up to 3 feet (90 cm)
habit hardy perennial with small oblong leaves
dotted with tiny transparent spots; small yellow
starlike flowers in summer with dense golden
tufts (anthers) in their centers
habitat full sun and average to poor or
alkaline soil
zones 3–8

The Knights Hospitallers of St. John are said to
have used St.-John's-wort to treat wounds
sustained by the Crusaders in battle. The
original link with St. John may even predate the
Crusades, since the plant produces its small
yellow blooms in the middle of the summer,
near St. John's Day (24 June).

In recent years the Crusaders' use of the
plant has been vindicated. Some compounds in
St.-John's-wort, including flavonoids, have been
found to have an antibacterial and anti-
inflammatory action. The herb is approved by
Commission E for treating skin inflammation,
wounds, burns, and bruises. Rub a cream made
from the flowering tops (see page 119) on to
the affected part.

This sunny yellow flower has a long
tradition of repelling the "evil spirits" of mild or
temporary depression, and is in widespread use
in this way in the United States and Europe. In
Germany it outsells pharmaceutical
antidepressants. However, the effectiveness of
St.-John's-wort for treating depression has not
been fully established in clinical trials. Self-
treatment of depression is not recommended.
Consult your medical practitioner if you feel
depressed for more than a few weeks.

Caution *There is a potential sun risk from this
popular herb. In tests, animals fed very large doses
of St.-John's-wort developed photosensitization
(skin reactions resulting from exposure to the sun).*

St-John's-wort *Hypericum perforatum*

*Although this effect is more likely to be suffered
when taking hypericin extracted from the plant
(rather than the whole herb), light-skinned people
or those who are particularly sensitive to the sun
should avoid direct sunlight or ultraviolet lamps
while taking St.-John's-wort.*

*St.-John's-wort should not be taken in
conjunction with any prescription antidepressants
that work either as MAO (monoamine oxidase) or
SSR (selective serotonin reuptake) inhibitors except
on medical advice, as the cumulative dosage may
carry risks. Some concerns have also arisen about
possible reactions with other drugs. Raised blood
pressure is also a hazard. Because of these potential
side effects, you should always consult a medical
professional before taking St.-John's-wort.*

Hyssop *Hyssopus officinalis*

HYSSOP *Hyssopus officinalis*
G M
other name azob
plant family Labiatae (mint family)
height 2 feet (60 cm)
habit hardy perennial with small, linear leaves along the square stem, and small spikes of violet-blue, pink, or white flowers from mid-summer until early autumn.
habitat prefers full sun and well-drained, average to dry or sandy soil
zones 4–9

Hyssop loves dry conditions and is perfect for rock gardens or for low hedges. Its flower heads, which are attractive to bees, have a camphorous smell and a slightly bitter minty taste. They are the prime flavoring agent of Chartreuse liqueur. The bitter leaves are sometimes used in small quantities as an alternative to sage in meat or fish dishes. This bitterness comes from the diterpene marrubiin, a compound which may also give the herb some expectorant properties. Hyssop leaves and flowers have traditionally

been included in infusions for soothing coughs and colds. Hyssop is also used in a number of commercial herbal cough and cold preparations. However, its effects have not yet been supported by clinical trials.

Caution *Hyssop oil is under legal restrictions in some countries. Epileptic seizures have occurred with its ingestion, so internal use of the essential oil should be avoided.*

ELECAMPANE *Inula helenium*
G M
other names horse heal, scabwort, elf dock
plant family Compositae (daisy family)
height up to 10 feet (3 m)
habit hardy perennial with large basal leaves and small upper leaves with downy undersides; it bears big, showy, daisylike yellow flowers that bloom in summer
habitat full sun and moist, well-drained soil of average fertility
zones 3–9

Elecampane is a striking herb; its spectacular huge yellow flowers with spiky petals will brighten the herb garden through high summer. Individual flowers may reach 3 inches (8 cm) across. It is happiest in a sheltered spot such as a walled garden; otherwise, it will need staking against the wind.

According to Pliny, the Roman Emperor Augustus declared: "Let no day pass without eating some of the roots of enula [elecampane], considered to help digestion as well as mirth." By the medieval period elecampane's root was used medicinally and made into a confection. The candy remained popular until the early twentieth century. The candies would be sucked for chest complaints and asthma.

Some components found in elecampane (sesquiterpene lactones, including helenin and isohelenin) have been found to have antifungal, antibacterial, and anti-inflammatory properties. Its essential oil has traditionally been used as an expectorant. The dried roots, harvested in the fall, were traditionally taken as a tea to treat

Elecampane *Inula helenium*

This plant is the laurel that was given as crowns for the victors of poetry and sports tournaments in ancient Greece and Rome, and the name of the degree award of Bachelor of Art or Science today derives from the Latin *bacca laureus* (the "berried laurel"). The death of the tree was felt to be a bad omen.

Bay makes a good specimen tree. In harsher climates it is often grown in a container so that it can be brought indoors over the winter.

In cooking, fresh or dried bay leaves are used whole to impart flavor to soups, casseroles and stews, tomato sauces, and rice dishes. Bay leaves are an essential component of *bouquets garnis*. A popular ingredient of potpourris and herbal wreaths, bay is also a good scented herb for the home, as it discourages insects. Its oil is used in aromatherapy.

Bay is thought to promote the digestion of meat and other food, and an infusion of bay leaves has been used to treat digestive disorders. It has also been used in ointments for aches and pains. However, none of these uses has been supported by clinical evidence.

Caution *Do not ingest the essential oil of bay leaves; use it only in diluted form, and never during pregnancy.*

Bay *Laurus nobilis*

bronchitis and bronchial catarrh. (The tea tastes mildly bitter, so it was sometimes sweetened with honey.) However, none of these traditional medicinal uses have been proven, so use of this herb is not recommended by Commission E.

Caution *Elecampane contains compounds (lactones) that can trigger an allergic rash. Large amounts of the herb taken internally can lead to vomiting and even paralysis. Do not take elecampane in pregnancy or while breast-feeding.*

BAY *Laurus nobilis*
G C M H
other names sweet bay, bay laurel, Grecian laurel, true bay
plant family Lauraceae (laurel family)
height up to 70 feet (20 m)
habit half-hardy shrub with leathery, evergreen leaves; bears clusters of small, yellow flowers in spring, followed by purple berries
habitat full sun to afternoon shade and moderately rich, moist, well-drained soil
zones 8–10

LAVENDER *Lavandula angustifolia*
formerly *L. officinalis*
G C M H
other names common lavender, nard
plant family Labiatae (mint family)
height up to 3½ feet (1 m)
habit hardy perennial with narrow, aromatic, gray leaves along square stems; small clusters of tiny purple flowers in early summer
habitat prefers full sun and average to dry, well-drained soil
zones 5–8

Lavender's pretty cushioned form and seductive scent make it a garden favorite. The downy gray leaves contrast nicely with many other herbs and ornamental plants; in milder climates, leaves remain attractive all year. (In cold winters, leaves may discolor or die back.) It is a key ingredient of the culinary herb blend *herbes de Provence.*

Lavender has long been used to scent linen closets and to deter moths and other insects. The scent is primarily due to its esters, which are most abundant at the peak flowering period. The flowers are harvested for drying just before they open. Esters remain active in the dried flowers used in decorations and potpourri.

Lavender's essential oil is used to perfume bath soaps and oils, among many other products. It is a favorite in skin toners and hair rinses. The Romans used lavender as a perfumed bath oil—the name lavender comes from the Latin *lavare*, meaning "to wash"—and a few drops of essential oil in the bath can be relaxing. It is one of the most frequently used aromatherapy oils. The essential oil can be diluted in a carrier oil and massaged on the temples and nape of the neck to reduce tension, anxiety, or headaches.

Infusions made from the flowers are approved by Commission E for treating loss of appetite, nervous indigestion, and insomnia, and also to improve circulation.

Caution *Avoid taking lavender internally during pregnancy.*

other species

Rarely grown in gardens but commercially grown in Spain for the perfume trade, spike lavender (*Lavandula latifolia*) produces a more pungent oil that is used in perfumes, soaps, and other products.

French or Spanish lavender (*L. stoechas*) has distinctive long tufts on the top of the flower head. These are long bracts of the tiny flowers. This species may have been the lavender most commonly used in Roman times. Both of these species are only hardy to zone 7.

Lavender *Lavandula angustifolia*

FLAX *Linum usitatissimum*
G M
other names linseed, flaxseed
plant family Linaceae (flax family)
height up to 4 feet (1.2 m)
habit hardy annual with narrow, gray-green
leaves; it bears pale blue flowers in summer,
followed by round capsules containing oval,
flattened seeds
habitat prefers full sun and well-drained soil
all zones (annual)

Pretty pale blue fields of flax can be seen
worldwide. The plant has been cultivated for
7,000 years for its oil, which is produced by
pressing the seeds. A taller form of the same
species is cultivated for its fibers, used to make
linen. The Roman natural historian Pliny was a
great admirer of flax; in the first century AD he
wrote, "What area of active life is there in
which linseed is not used, and what produce of
the earth can show greater marvels?"

When the seeds make contact with water,
their outer coat of mucilage swells to form a gel,
which acts as dietary fiber. If the seeds are
cracked or roughly ground, the linseed oil they
contain assists the passage of food through the
intestine. Commission E approves flax seeds
(linseed) in an infusion for easing constipation.
They may also be helpful for easing cases of
irritable colon. For these uses, the seeds must be
taken with at least ⅔ cup (150 ml) of water to
¼ ounce (7 g) of seeds. The seeds can also be
boiled and then used as a poultice for sore or
inflamed skin; this use is also approved by
Commission E.

Linseed oil is rich in the essential fatty acids
linolenic acid and linoleic acid, which may help
protect against strokes and heart attacks by
reducing cholesterol in the blood, particularly
LDL cholesterol (the so-called bad cholesterol).
To get the most benefit, seeds should be stored
in the refrigerator and ground within a day or
two of use; a spoonful or two can be sprinkled
on top of breakfast cereal or salads. Whole seeds
can be added to breads before baking.

Flax *Linum usitatissimum*

Caution *Do not use flax seeds in any form in
cases of bowel obstruction (a caution that applies
to any other laxative). Note that, as with any
dietary mucilage, taking linseed may reduce the
amount of other drugs absorbed by the body, so
always consult a physician before using linseed if
you are taking other medications. Do not consume
flax seeds in very large quantities as cyanogenic
glycosides may have a toxic effect. Do not in any
circumstances take any flax preparations that are
not intended for human consumption.*

White horehound *Marrubium vulgare*

WHITE HOREHOUND *Marrubium vulgare*
G M

other names common horehound, hoarhound, marvel, marribium
plant family Labiatae (mint family)
height up to 20 inches (50 cm)
habit hardy perennial with downy gray-green leaves and stems; small white flowers
habitat prefers full sun and well-drained to dry soil
zones 4–8

The wrinkled texture and silvery color of white horehound makes it an attractive addition to herb gardens. In summer, small white flowers appear in clusters around the stems. Horehound is especially useful in hot and dry climates; in less harsh conditions it may get floppy and need shearing to keep it tidy. Though rarely used today, it was used medicinally in former times. The Greek physician Dioscorides (first century AD) recommended a decoction of white horehound for coughs and asthma. The sixteenth-century English herbalist John Gerard said that it was a "most singular remedy against the cough and wheezing." It was grown in herb gardens in Britain and the United States to make homemade cough drops. In the United States white horehound candy was especially popular. Many were surprised when, in 1989, the U.S. Food and Drug Administration banned horehound from being sold as a cough remedy, citing a lack of evidence of effectiveness.

However, Commission E has approved the herb as a decoction for other uses: Indigestion and loss of appetite.

ANNUAL CHAMOMILE *Matricaria recutita*
G M H

other name German chamomile
plant family Compositae (daisy family)
height up to 2 feet (60 cm)
habit aromatic annual with finely cut scented leaves; white-petalled yellow-centered daisy flowers
habitat prefers full sun and sandy, well-drained soil
all zones (annual)

Annual chamomile grows much taller than its perennial relative, so it is unsuitable for use in chamomile lawns. With its sunny flowers, however, it adds bright color to the herb garden. It makes a pretty dried flower and is a useful ingredient in potpourri. It has long been used cosmetically. An infusion of the fresh or dried flowers makes a toner for oily skin and a rinse to bring out the highlights in blond hair.

Annual chamomile is a useful medicinal herb; the strength of its essential oils makes it more effective than perennial chamomile. It has been approved by Commission E for treating coughs (including bronchitis), fevers, and colds. Approved external uses include treating inflammations of the mouth and skin, as well as wounds and burns.

Annual chamomile *Matricaria recutita*

The components and effects of annual chamomile have been well investigated because of its widespread commercial use. The plant's action has been identified as the combined effect of many components: 28 terpenoids and 36 flavonoids.

A group of compounds present in chamomile, the azulenes, have been found to be antiallergenic. One of these—chamazulene—is particularly active. However, chamazulene forms only during the manufacture of extracts or on being heated, as the chamomile is made into an infusion or tea. Chamazulene and another compound, alpha-bisabolol in the volatile oil, contribute to the anti-inflammatory and antiseptic properties of this herb.

Chamomile tea traditionally has been used to treat sleeplessness. It is thought to have a calming effect on most gastrointestinal upsets, including flatulence, heartburn, indigestion, and diarrhea. These uses have not been proven.

Caution *Commission E found no adverse reactions to annual chamomile, and it has a good reputation for safety. However, anyone who is sensitive to any other plants of the daisy family should be aware that he or she is at some risk of an allergic reaction.*

TEA TREE *Melaleuca alternifolia*
M

other names ti-trol, melasol, narrow-leaved paperbark
plant family Myrtaceae (myrtle family)
height up to 25 feet (7.5 m)
habit tender evergreen small tree with needlelike leaves; white, shaggy "bottlebrush" flower spikes from late spring until the middle of summer
habitat full sun and average to dry or poor soil
zones 9–11

Tea trees were long used as Australian Aboriginal remedies, and have had a medicinal reputation since the earliest days of European involvement with the continent. There is a bewildering array of species of tea tree, all native to Australia and belonging to the *Leptospermum* and *Melaleuca* genera. It is *M. alternifolia,* an evergreen with layers of papery bark, pointed leaves, and a profusion of white flowers, that has now become renowned the world over as "tea tree."

The commercially available tea tree oil is often a blended product from a number of different species, such as the narrow-leaved paperbark (*M. linariifolia*). The primary active constituent is a terpene, terpinene-4-ol, which has a strong antiseptic action. The monoterpene p-cymene, which makes up only a small percentage of the essential oil, also exerts a powerful antibacterial effect. Tea tree oil also appears to be able to act against both viral and fungal agents, and it is remarkably well tolerated on the skin. These qualities have led to its widespread use as a treatment for infections and inflammation of the skin and of the respiratory tract and mouth. It has even been used against acne—tea tree oil is slower-acting than standard treatments such as benzoyl peroxide, but without the irritation that can arise as a side effect.

Tea tree oil is so well tolerated that it can be used at full strength to treat warts and verrucas. However, for most skin contact it is normal to have a 1 in 10 dilution: For example, to treat acne or athlete's foot 1 part of tea tree oil is diluted with 10 parts of water, while for cold sores it is used at the same dilution with a carrier oil such as almond oil. For treating vaginal infections such as *Candida albicans* and *Trichomonas vaginalis,* it is diluted with carrier oil in proportions of 1 to 15: A few drops can then be put on a tampon, which is left in place for 3 to 4 hours.

Caution *Although tea tree oil is normally easily tolerated, as with anything, there are some individuals who have an unusual sensitivity. In the event of mild irritation, the general advice is to experiment with weaker dilutions; if the adverse reaction is more pronounced, it is probably wiser to avoid tea tree oil altogether.*

LEMON BALM *Melissa officinalis*
G C M H
other names balm, sweet balm
plant family Labiatae (mint family)
height up to 5 feet (1.5 m)
habit hardy perennial with scalloped, lemon-scented leaves on square stems; small white flowers clustered in leaf axils (where leaves attach to stems) in summer
habitat prefers partial shade to full sun and moist, well-drained soil
zones 4–9

Lemon balm is an attractive plant that produces a wonderful scent when brushed against, and more so when it is crushed. The flowers are a magnet for bees, and its genus name comes from the Greek word for bee. Like its mint relatives it creeps, forming large clumps, and it also self-sows readily. Shearing plants a couple of times a season will keep them tidy and also prevent numerous volunteer seedlings. The

Lemon balm *Melissa officinalis*

fresh leaves make a pleasant addition to fruit salads, punches, and iced tea; they are also one of the many flavorings in Chartreuse liqueur. When dried, the leaves lose most of their flavor, so they are best as a summertime seasoning.

Over three hundred years ago the English naturalist and diarist John Evelyn wrote: "Balm is sovereign for the brain, strengthening the memory and powerfully chasing away melancholy." Even earlier, the eleventh-century Arab physician Avicenna wrote that "it makes the heart merry." Lemon balm is not an herb to raise deep depression (for which a medical practitioner should be consulted), but many people find that their spirits are lifted by lemon balm tea. Lemon balm is approved by Commission E for treating stress and insomnia.

The herb's scented foliage is attractive in fresh flower arrangements. Either the fresh or dried foliage can be used in rinses for oily hair. Lemon balm repels some insects due to various components of its volatile oil, including citronella. Try rubbing the fresh plant on your skin to keep insects away when working in the garden.

The plant has a low yield of oil, so most commercially available lemon balm preparations are made from a mixture of synthetic constituents. Consequently the proportions, composition, and effectiveness can vary considerably. For best results (and for the most aroma and flavor), make infusions from the fresh leaves. To dry for winter use, harvest the plant before it flowers.
Caution *Lemon balm can inhibit thyroid function, so be certain to consult a medical professional before taking lemon balm if you have a thyroid condition.*

PEPPERMINT *Mentha × piperita*
G M H
other names brandy mint
plant family Labiatae (mint family)
height up to 3 feet (90 cm)
habit hardy perennial with extensive creeping roots and dark green aromatic leaves that are

often tinged purple; square stems are topped by lilac-pink flowers from summer to fall
habitat full sun to partial shade, and moist, rich, loose soil
zones 5–9

Like all mints, peppermint spreads quickly and can be invasive. To keep it from taking over the garden, grow it in a sunken tub (with the bottom removed), in an isolated patch, or dig it up and divide it every two years. Peppermint occurred as a natural cross between spearmint and water mint (*Mentha aquatica*); it was identified as a distinct plant in 1696 by the English botanist John Ray. In naming the plant "peper mint," Ray accurately described the initially hot then minty cool effect it has on the mouth. He noted that it was superior to all other mints for the alleviation of stomach weakness and also for calming diarrhea.

Commercial production began in the mid-eighteenth century at Mitcham, England. The first recorded American reference was made by Samuel Stearn in 1801, who noted that "it restores the functions of the stomach, promotes digestion, cures the hiccups and flatulent colic." Essence of peppermint was a medicine-chest staple for pioneers traveling westward.

Peppermint is famous for its antispasmodic action on the smooth muscles of the digestive system. Recent medical trials with enteric-coated capsules of peppermint oil have found it to lessen symptoms of irritable bowel syndrome. An infusion of fresh or dried peppermint leaves is a trusted remedy, approved by Commission E for indigestion, colic, and nausea. Commission E also approves peppermint for treating inflammation of the mouth and pharynx, colds, and bronchitis.

When taken internally, peppermint induces sweating. An infusion of leaves made with equal amounts of elderflowers is a traditional remedy for colds or mild flu. Occasional inhalation of the steam from hot water poured over peppermint leaves may be helpful in opening up the nasal passages and combating congestion or bronchitis.

Menthol gives peppermint its cooling property, and methyl acetate its distinctive smell. Peppermint is one of the most popular (and most flavorful) herbs for herbal teas, either alone or mixed with other herbs. The distilled oil is a popular flavoring for everything from candy to toothpaste. Peppermint oil can also be soothing when used externally as a diluted oil in massage and for pain relief. It is used in aromatherapy. Peppermint also has cosmetic uses. An infusion of the leaves makes a good rinse for oily hair and, when cooled and diluted, a refreshing splash for the face.

Caution *Do not give peppermint in any form to small babies and infants. Internal consumption should also be avoided by anyone with gallstones. Peppermint can reduce breast milk flow. The concentrated amounts of menthol in peppermint oil can irritate the skin and mucous membranes, so always dilute it in a carrier oil or use infusions of the leaves.*

Peppermint *Mentha × piperita*

Spearmint *Mentha spicata*

SPEARMINT *Mentha spicata*

G C M H

other names garden mint, green mint,
Our Lady's mint, spire mint, lamb mint
plant family Labiatae (mint family)
height up to 3 feet (90 cm)
habit hardy perennial with extensive creeping
roots and bright green, aromatic spear-shaped
leaves; square stems are topped with slender
spires of tiny lilac, pink or white flowers from
summer to fall
habitat prefers full sun to partial shade and
average to moist, rich soil
zones 5–9

Spearmint can easily be recognized by its spear-shaped leaves. This is the common garden mint that cooks often refer to simply as "mint." It can become invasive if the roots are not contained. (See *Peppermint* on page 71 for advice on controlling.)

Spearmint was introduced to Northern Europe, including Britain, by the Romans, who brought it from the Mediterranean. John Josselyn, who first landed in New England in 1638, recorded spearmint being taken by the Pilgrim Fathers and other early settlers when they traveled to America.

Like all mints, spearmint helps promote digestion. This is one of the reasons why mint tea is served after meals throughout the Middle East, and why mint sauce or mint jelly makes such a good accompaniment to lamb. Mint, like parsley, is also a classic flavor-enhancer of boiled new potatoes. Mint sauces (among them pestos made from mint instead of basil) are excellent with pasta or as an accompaniment to beef, fish, or chicken.

John Gerard, in his *Herball* (1597), noted spearmint's popularity as a strewing herb: "The smelle rejoiceth the heart of man, for which cause they used to strew it in chambers and places of recreation." The volatile oil carvone provides the herb's distinctive aroma. A few drops of spearmint oil added to a bowl of steaming water creates an enjoyable steam inhalation. The essential oil of spearmint is also popular for use in aromatherapy.

Infusions of spearmint have traditionally been used to treat digestive disorders, but this use has not been proven. For medicinal use, peppermint is preferred over spearmint, both because it is somewhat stronger and because its benefits have been demonstrated through research (see page 71).

other species

Fuzzy gray-green apple mint (*M. suaveolens*) and green-and-gold ginger mint (*M.* × *gracilis* 'Variegata') are attractive garden plants. Their distinctive flavors make them good salad ingredients and they are pretty as a garnish.

Eau de Cologne mint (*M.* × *piperita* f. *citrata*) has a particularly strong fragrance. It is used in potpourri and cosmetics.

Corsican mint (*M. requienii*) is a minute, mat-forming and shade-loving form. Its tiny leaves are strongly peppermint-scented. This plant is delightful when grown between the paving stones on a shady path, as walking on it releases the refreshing aroma.

Pennyroyal (*M. pulegium*) is grown as an aromatic ground cover that can deter insects, including ants. Small lilac-pink flowers add color in midsummer. Pennyroyal has a coarse, pungent scent that makes it easily distinguishable from other mints. Though it may be useful as an ingredient in moth-repelling sachets, it is highly toxic and should not on any account be used medicinally or in cooking.

Apple mint *M. suaveolens*

Ginger mint *M.* × *gracilis* 'Variegata'

Eau de Cologne mint *M.* × *piperita* f. *citrata*

Corsican mint *M. requienii*

Pennyroyal *M. pulegium*

BEE BALM *Monarda didyma*

G C M H

other names bergamot, Oswego tea
plant family Labiatae (mint family)
height up to 4 feet (1.2 m)
habit hardy perennial with aromatic, pointed leaves covered with fine downy hairs; large red flower clusters top square stems in summer
habitat prefers full sun to light shade and rich, moist soil
zones 4–9

With its bright scarlet flowers, this plant makes an attractive addition to herb or flower gardens. Cultivars are available in a range of hues from white and pale pink to wine red and purple. However, in dry conditions, plants can be disfigured by severe cases of powdery mildew. To keep plants looking good all season, keep soil evenly moist (or seek out mildew-resistant

Bee balm *Monarda didyma*

cultivars). The flowers attract pollinating insects—hence the name bee balm—and in North America they attract hummingbirds, too.

The colorful flowers of this versatile herb are used to decorate salads, and both leaves and flowers are dried for potpourri. The leaves make a pleasant herb tea; this tea became quite popular during the era of the Boston Tea Party, when colonists were boycotting black tea from Britain. The leaves can also be used like spearmint as a refreshing addition to iced tea.

The alternative name bergamot comes from the similarity of its fragrance to true bergamot, bergamot orange (*Citrus bergamia*), which is the source of the distinctive flavor of Earl Grey tea. The bergamot oil used in aromatherapy is extracted from bergamot oil, not bee balm. Bee balm is also known as Oswego tea after the Oswego Indians, who lived along the Oswego River in what is now New York State and who used the plant medicinally.

Traditionally, an infusion of bee balm was given to new brides as a helpful tonic. It was thought to act as a gentle regulator of menstruation. It has also been used for digestive disorders, and by Native Americans for a range of conditions from colic to fevers. However, none of these uses has been proven.
Caution *Do not drink bee balm tea during pregnancy.*

other species
Other species of *Monarda* are known as horsemints, but are different from European horsemint, *Mentha longifolia*. The one most commonly called horsemint is *Monarda punctata*, with small flowers above showy pink bracts. Native Americans used it for fevers and indigestion. Wild bergamot (*M. fistulosa*) has lavender-pink flowers that resemble those of bee balm. Its leaves have a similar fragrance and flavor and can be used to make a minty tea. Native Americans drank infusions of it for similar uses to those for *M. punctata*. Both *M. fistulosa* and *M. punctata* prefer drier conditions than *M. didyma*.

Catnip *Nepeta cataria*

CATNIP *Nepeta cataria*
G M

other names catmint, catnep, catswort
plant family Labiatae (mint family)
height up to 3¼ feet (1 m)
habit hardy perennial with erect, branched stems and soft, serrated-edged aromatic leaves; whorls of small white, purple-spotted flowers from mid-summer to mid-autumn
habitat prefers sun and average, well-drained soil but tolerates partial shade and dry soil
zones 4–9

Cats are drawn to catnip like a magnet, and delight in sniffing it, chewing it, and rolling in it. Because cats behave with catnip as if they are in heat, it is believed that the main component of the volatile oil, nepetalactone, resembles a feline sexual pheromone.

The plant is not particularly attractive once rolled on, so grow it in pots out of cats' reach, surround it with a protective mesh fence, or grow so much of it that it prevails.

While catnip stimulates cats, it seems to have the opposite effect on humans. For many centuries the plant has been infused to make a tea which is considered calming. In ancient times, it was grown around Rome in large quantities specifically for this purpose. As well as being used for treating insomnia and nervous tension, catnip tea may also settle the stomach and help cases of flatulence and colic. It has been used for children and adults to combat the symptoms of colds and flu. None of these medicinal uses has been proven.

other species
There are over 250 species of catmint belonging to the same genus as catnip. Many of them have abundant lilac-blue flowers, which make them popular plants for flower gardens. The common *Nepeta* × *faassenii* reaches only 1 to 2 feet (30 to 60 cm). Taller types such as 'Six Hills Giant' and *N. sibirica* can top 3 feet (90 cm). All of these contain less nepetalactone than catnip, so they are less apt to be disturbed by cats.

Basil *Ocimum basilicum*

BASIL *Ocimum basilicum*
G C M H
other names sweet basil, St. Joseph wort,
French basil, true basil
plant family Labiatae (mint family)
height up to 2 feet (60 cm)
habit tender annual with many branches and
aromatic, bright green, pointed oval leaves;
small spikes of white flowers top the plant's
stems in summer

habitat prefers full sun and rich, moist, well-
drained soil
all zones (annual)
Given an open, sunny spot, basil is easy to
grow. One of the primary flavorings of
Mediterranean cuisines, it is the perfect
complement for tomatoes and is also used to
flavor vinegars, oils, salads, soups, and risottos
and provides the basis for the classic pesto
sauce. One of the most popular varieties grown

for cooking is *Ocimum basilicum* 'Genovese', which has large, dark green leaves with an especially intense flavor. Despite its Mediterranean associations, basil was originally an Indian herb. It did, however, reach the Mediterranean early. We do not know precisely when, but it was established by the time Galen, Dioscorides, and Pliny wrote about it in the first and second centuries AD. Today it is one of the most widely used herbs in the world.

Basil oil is used in aromatherapy, and can also be used with other dried herbs such as sweet marjoram and thyme in insect-repelling sachets. Infusions of basil leaves have been used to treat indigestion, and the plant's essential oil has been used to treat acne. However, neither of these uses has been proven, and medicinal use of basil is not recommended.

Caution *Because basil contains estragole, which animal experiments have suggested may be carcinogenic, Commission E recommends that basil should not be consumed during pregnancy, by breast-feeding mothers, by infants or toddlers, or over long periods continuously. However, it accepts its use for ordinary culinary flavoring.*

A 1987 article in Science *tried to put this in perspective by stating that 1 gram of basil was only* 1/28th *as carcinogenic as the ethanol in a can of beer. The American Pharmaceutical Association states, "Medicinal concentrations of this herb have never caused anyone any apparent harm," and the U.S. Food and Drug Administration lists basil as a safe food.*

Types of basil with lower estragole contents are considered safest. It is advisable to avoid the so-called "exotic" types of essential basil oil, as these have a high estragole content.

other species
Basil has different-flavored varieties such as *O. basilicum* 'Cinnamon', which has a marked flavor of cinnamon. Several varieties are known as lemon basil for their distinct lemon taste: These include 'Citriodorum' and 'Mrs. Burns' Lemon.' Forms with purple leaves include *O. basilicum* 'Red Rubin' and curly 'Purple Ruffles'. Bush basil (*O. minimum*), which is considered a separate species, has tiny leaves and forms tidy, small mounds.

Holy basil *(O. tenuiflorum)* is called kha prao tulsi in India, where it is considered to be sacred to the gods Vishnu and Krishna. Holy basil is used primarily for medicinal purposes rather than cooking. Its essential oil contains mainly eugenol, and its estragole content is much lower than that of *O. basilicum.*

EVENING PRIMROSE *Oenothera biennis*
G M
other names fever plant, night willowherb, tree primrose, common evening primrose
plant family Onagraceae (evening primrose family)
height up to 5 feet (1.5 m)
habit hardy biennial with a rosette of long, dark green crinkly leaves; sends up a leafy stalk topped by night-opening, fragrant yellow flowers in summer followed by interesting seedpods
habitat prefers full sun to partial shade and average to dry soil
zones 4–10

Evening primrose *Oenothera biennis*

The bowl-shaped flowers of this biennial herb open in the evening. They have an almost luminous yellow color. Evening primrose is a particular favorite in meadow gardens and naturalistic landscapes.

A North American wildflower, evening primrose was boiled and eaten by the North American Blackfoot tribe and was introduced to Europe in the seventeenth century. It is now in demand worldwide, and in the United States it is among the top ten best-selling herb supplements.

The reason for this is simple, although the herb's role is diverse. Evening primrose seed oil is the most extensively researched plant source of the essential fatty acid gamma-linolenic acid. Essential fatty acids—vital lipids that our bodies cannot make—have a key role in maintaining the functioning of membranes throughout the cells of the body and also lead to the formation of prostaglandins, which are needed for many areas of the body to function. Gamma-linolenic acid is a major constituent of human milk.

Studies have shown that evening primrose oil, applied externally, can be beneficial to eczema sufferers, particularly to ease itching. Research suggests that those inheriting atopic eczema may have an error in their essential fatty acid metabolism, which taking gamma-linolenic acid as evening primrose oil may circumvent.

Evening primrose oil is available as capsules for internal use. Used in this way, it may also be capable of guarding against coronary arterial disease. This is because essential fatty acids are instrumental in the transport of cholesterol. Studies have shown that gamma-linolenic acid can help to lower blood cholesterol levels, which may help prevent heart disease or a stroke.

One of the most popular uses of evening primrose oil capsules is for the relief of breast pain and tenderness linked to premenstrual syndrome. Some studies of the use of evening primrose oil have found an improvement for sufferers of rheumatoid arthritis. The American Pharmaceutical Association rates it relatively effective and safe when used in proper amounts.

Evening primrose oil has also been used in skin preparations and cosmetics, and to strengthen brittle nails.

Caution *Do not take evening primrose oil if you have epilepsy, as it has the potential to lower the seizure threshold.*

SWEET MARJORAM *Origanum majorana*
G C M H

other names knotted marjoram
plant family Labiatae (mint family)
height up to 2 feet (60 cm)
habit tender perennial usually grown as an annual, with aromatic, downy, gray-green oval leaves on reddish stems; clusters of small white to pink flowers in late summer
habitat full sun and average to rich, well-drained soil
zones 9–10

Sweet marjoram is a smaller plant than oregano (see opposite), with a more delicate scent and a milder, sweeter flavor. Its alternative name, knotted marjoram, comes from its small round flower buds, which resemble knots on the stems. It is used primarily as a culinary herb. Marjoram blends well with many other herbs and is a key ingredient in *herbes de Provence*. Fresh or dried marjoram is especially good with meat and green vegetables; small amounts of the fresh herb are good added to salads. It is also prized as a sausage ingredient.

The seventeenth-century English apothecary Parkinson recorded that dried 'swete margerome' was fashionably put into 'swete bags' or sachets to perfume linens and clothing. It is still popular as a dried herb for the home, especially in potpourris and aromatherapy.

An infusion has been used to treat colds and inflamed or irritated nasal passages.

Caution *Do not use marjoram oil during pregnancy or around small children.*

other species
Pot marjoram (*Origanum onites*) hails from Sicily; it found favor in England in the sixteenth century as a strewing herb. It has a

milder flavor than sweet marjoram and its leaves sometimes have a red color. Pot marjoram is slightly hardier (to zone 8) and prefers somewhat drier growing conditions.

OREGANO *Origanum vulgare*
G C M
other name wild marjoram
plant family Labiatae (mint family)
height up to 3 feet (90 cm)
habit hardy perennial with oval, aromatic leaves on purplish stems; clusters of pinkish purple flowers in summer
habitat full sun and well-drained to dry soil
zones 5–9

The genus name *Origanum* is from two Greek words: *oros* ("mountain") and *ganos* ("joy"), beautifully evoking Greek hillsides covered with bright oregano flowers and attendant feeding butterflies. There are some ornamental cultivars that are suitable for the flower garden. Though the flowers of common oregano are pretty and its leaves pleasantly fragrant, they are almost tasteless. For true oregano flavor, you must seek out Greek oregano (*Origanum vulgare* subsp. *hirtum,* also sold as *O. heracleoticum*); it looks similar but has clusters of white flowers.

Like other members of the mint family, oregano contains bitter diterpenes which promote digestion. The pungent leaves are used with meat dishes and in soups and salads. The peppery bite works particularly well with tomatoes, and oregano is an essential constituent of many tomato-based sauces and pizzas. If you want the true flavor of oregano in your food, it is worth growing your own. Commercial dried oregano is usually a blend and commonly contains "Mexican oregano" (*Lippia graveolens*), which is not even an *Origanum* species.

Oregano has long had a medicinal reputation. The ancient Greeks used it to treat poisoning and convulsions. A more recent use is taking an infusion for colds, coughs, or bronchial inflammations, but these uses have not been proven. Oregano oil is used in aromatherapy. However, most of the oregano oil that is commercially available is not even an *Origanum* species, but a thyme, *Thymus capitatus,* usually sold under the misleading name of "Spanish oregano."

Caution *While the amounts used for seasoning should pose no problem, do not take medicinal quantities of oregano during pregnancy and do not ingest the essential oil.*

Pot marjoram *Origanum onites*

Oregano *Origanum vulgare*

Parsley *Petroselinum crispum*

Parsley is a familiar sight in herb and vegetable gardens. Many varieties are available, but the most common are the curly variety (*Petroselinum crispum*) and the flat-leaved variety (*P. crispum* var. *neapolitanum*). Flat-leaved parsley has a more concentrated flavor, but the curly variety makes a more attractive garnish. Parsley is a key ingredient in *fines herbes* and *bouquets garnis*. It is commonly used in herb butters, sauces, dips and spreads, salads, soups, with potatoes, and with pasta and grains. For cooks who are lavish with garlic, parsley works well as a breath freshener, partly because of the leaves' high chlorophyll content. It is a very good source of vitamins C and A and iron.

An infusion makes a good skin tonic and a rinse for dry hair. Parsley has a diuretic effect, which professional herbalists use to treat kidney stones, urinary infections, and gout. However, parsley should not be used for self-treatment.
Caution *While parsley is safe in regular culinary amounts, large quantities should be avoided, as two of the compounds in its volatile oil, apiole and myristicin, can become toxic. The uterine stimulation caused by these compounds could bring about miscarriage, and women who are pregnant or trying to conceive should avoid eating excessive quantities of parsley. The herb also contains the furocoumarin psoralen, which may increase sensitivity to sunlight. Avoid parsley if allergic to other members of the carrot family.*

PARSLEY *Petroselinum crispum*
G C M H
other names garden parsley, persil, persele
plant family Umbelliferae (carrot family)
height up to 1 foot (30 cm)
habit hardy biennial grown as an annual with finely cut, dark green leaves; flat-topped heads of tiny greenish yellow flowers (usually only in second year)
habitat light shade to full sun and moist, fertile, well-drained soil
all zones (grown as annual)

ANISE *Pimpinella anisum*
G M
other names aniseed
plant family Umbelliferae (carrot family)
height up to 2 feet (60 cm)
habit Half-hardy annual with toothed, rounded basal leaves and finely cut upper leaves; flat-topped clusters of tiny, off-white flowers in summer, followed by ribbed seeds
habitat full sun and poor, well-drained soil
all zones (grown as annual)
Anise is attractive in the herb garden, but it requires a long and warm growing season to

produce ripe seeds. It also requires warmth (70°F/20°C) to germinate. Anise is the main flavor in a family of eastern Mediterranean spirits: ouzo, Pernod, and anisette. It is also used in cookies, to flavor candies such as aniseed balls, and in toothpaste and mouthwashes to mask any medicinal taste.

Anisette liqueur, originally flavored with the essential oil of anise, was traditionally taken to ease bronchitis and asthma. The plant contains compounds with an expectorant action and its volatile oils are antibacterial, so there is some basis to this practice. However, anisette liqueur is now usually made with synthetic flavorings. Commission E approves the use of anise seeds for coughs, colds, fevers, and congestion, as well as for inflammations of the mouth and pharynx. The Romans ate a cake made with anise seeds at the end of the meal to help prevent indigestion, and the dried seeds are still eaten to reduce flatulence and belching. Commission E lists anise for use in treating indigestion and loss of appetite.

Caution *While generations of people have used anise safely, a few individuals can be allergic to the anethole in its oil; anethole is also a component of fennel (see page 58). The*

concentrated form of anise's essential oil is too strong for it to be used safely, and it should not be used internally. Do not take more than ordinary culinary amounts of anise during pregnancy.

PSYLLIUM *Plantago afra*
M

other names fleaseed, plantago seed, ispaghula
plant family Plantaginaceae (plantain family)
height up to 16 inches (40 cm)
habit hardy annual with narrow leaves, usually in whorls; clusters of tiny globular flowers in late summer and early fall, followed by small shiny seeds
habitat open, full sun and well-drained soil
all zones (annual)

An unobtrusive, weedlike plant, this plantain relative is grown only for medicinal uses. Its small dark seeds in size, shape, and color strongly resemble the body of a flea—hence the old common name of fleaseed.

Both the seeds and the husks of psyllium have been used as reliable and safe laxatives for thousands of years. They are used in both conventional and herbal medicine as a source of natural fiber. If soaked in cold water and allowed to stand overnight, they will form a fluid mucilage. Alternatively, if hot water is added to them, they will more quickly form a thicker gel on cooling. These gels absorb and hold water and are minimally digested. As they pass along the intestine, they lubricate its walls and provide bulk to move the intestinal contents properly.

Psyllium is approved by Commission E for constipation and hemorrhoids, where a soft stool is required. It has become one of the most commonly used laxatives in the United States, as it is contained in many commercial preparations. Surprisingly, it is also approved for treating diarrhea because it absorbs excess liquid from loose stools. Commission E also approves its use for lowering cholesterol. Studies have shown that psyllium, like other high-fiber foods, lowers total cholesterol and LDL

Anise Pimpinella anisum

cholesterol (the so-called "bad" cholesterol) in the body.

other species

There are at least three closely related *Plantago* species known as psyllium. They are all used in the same way and, in commercial preparations, are sometimes marketed according to their individual names. *Plantago afra* (syn. *P. psyllium*) is normally just called psyllium, while *P. scabra* (syn. *P. indica*) is black psyllium and *P. ovata* is blonde psyllium or ispaghula.

The common lawn weed broadleaf plantain (*P. major*) has a long history as a healing plant, especially for pain relief. Although native to Europe and Asia, it acquired the names "Englishman's foot" or "white man's foot" for its wide oval leaves and the ease with which this vigorous weed sprang up in any place to which colonists unwittingly carried its seed. The leaves have been used to treat digestive problems, aches and pains, and for the relief of bites and stings.

TORMENTIL *Potentilla erecta*
M

other names cinquefoil, potentilla, red root, earthbank, English sarsaparilla
plant family Rosaceae (rose family)
height up to 1 foot (30 cm)
habit hardy perennial with whorls of toothed leaves on long stems; open bunches of small bright yellow flowers in summer, followed by small, strawberry-like fruits
habitat full sun to partial shade and well-drained soil
zones 4–9

This pretty little trailing plant has small yellow flowers, and might be suitable for a wildflower garden. The plant has a high tannin content (15 to 20 percent), making it extremely astringent. Consequently, it was used in the tanning of hides. Around half the tannins are catechin tannins, which after storage turn into "tormentil red" or "tanner's red" dye.

Cowslip *Primula veris*

This abundance of tannins makes tormentil a useful astringent for medicinal use as well. An infusion of the dried rhizome of tormentil, harvested in the spring, is a good mouthwash for inflammations of the mucous membranes, including sore throats and gums. Commission E approves this use and has also recognized its value for treating diarrhea.

other species

There are a number of similar small, yellow-flowering species of *Potentilla* found across the northern hemisphere including North America. Silverweed (*P. anserina*) is found as far north as the Arctic. Its roots were once gathered and eaten as a vegetable.

COWSLIP *Primula veris*
G M

other names keys-of-heaven, primavera
plant family Primulaceae (primula family)
height up to 10 inches (25 cm)
habit hardy perennial with a basal rosette of slightly wrinkled oval to oblong leaves; clusters of fragrant bright yellow flowers on slender stems in spring
habitat prefers light to partial shade and moist, rich soil; in the wild it grows in fields and pastures with alkaline soil
zones 5–9

Decorative in any garden, cowslips look good in spring borders and naturalize happily in grass or under trees. Traditionally the cowslip's flowers, hanging to one side of the stem, were thought to look like a bunch of keys, whimsically said to be those dropped by St. Peter from heaven.

The flowers are delicious in salads. They were traditionally used for making wine, though the quantities needed make that impractical today. Cowslips are increasingly rare and it is illegal in many countries to pick or remove them from the wild.

Commission E approves the use of cowslip as a treatment for coughs and bronchitis. Infusions made from the dried roots and flowers have an expectorant effect.

CHINESE RHUBARB *Rheum palmatum*
G M

other names da huang, turkey rhubarb, ornamental rhubarb
plant family Polygonaceae (dock family)
height up to 10 feet (3 m)
habit hardy perennial with thick rhizomes; huge, palm-shaped leaves have spiky edges; spires of small red flowers in summer
habitat full sun to partial shade and constantly moist, well-drained, fertile soil
zones 5–8

Chinese rhubarb is more attractive than the species grown for eating (*Rheum officinale*). It is often grown in damp woodland gardens for its imposing leaves and tall flower panicles. It thrives on a stream bank or other location next to water. In hot climates it requires some shade; in cooler climates it tolerates full sun as long as the soil never dries out. Some of the varieties, such as *R. palmatum* 'Atrosanguineum' and *R. palmatum* var. *tanguticum* are popular ornamental plants with tall flowering panicles.

The dried yellow rhizomes that give the herb its Chinese name da huang ("great yellow") have powerful purgative properties that stop the normal uptake of water from the bowel and accelerate movement along the intestine.

The rhizomes of Chinese rhubarb are powdered, then added to water to make an infusion. Although it has been approved by Commission E to treat constipation, Chinese rhubarb can bring sharp pains when taken as a laxative, and it is not suitable for long-term use. For home use, gentler laxatives such as psyllium are preferred.

Caution *Do not take Chinese rhubarb if you have any internal obstruction or possibility of appendicitis, and never take for longer than a few days without medical direction. Do not use at any stage of pregnancy or when breast-feeding, nor give to children under twelve years of age. Avoid regular use or taking large doses, as this could lead to dependence on laxatives and cause damage to the digestive system.*

ROSE *Rosa* spp.

G M H

other name brier, briar

plant family Rosaceae (rose family)

height up to 18 feet (5.5 m)

habit usually a hardy shrub with toothed leaves and thorns; flowers in summer may be white or a shade of red, pink, or yellow; may be single or in bunches; are often scented

habitat prefers full sun and well-drained, moist, fertile soil

zones vary with species and cultivar

The genus *Rosa* includes over a hundred species. The earliest garden roses are thought to have been hybrids or sports of species roses from Europe and the Middle East, and today there are over ten thousand cultivated varieties. Roses are probably the most beloved of all garden flowers, producing their beautiful blooms in a wide palette of colors and offering a wealth of delicious scents in gardens the world over.

An essential oil known as attar of roses is produced from the petals of roses (mainly from *Rosa* × *damascena* cultivars). This is an ingredient of many perfumes worn by women.

Around three hundred components have been identified in rose oil; it is one of the minor components, beta-damascone, at only around 0.14 percent of rose's volatile oils, that is responsible for much of the flower's smell.

Rosewater is a diluted form of attar of roses, which is first recorded as being made by the Persian Avicenna in the first century AD. Roses are invaluable for scenting the home and for decoration, in fresh or dried arrangements, and as staple ingredients of potpourris. Rose oil is used extensively in aromatherapy as a mildly sedative, anti-depressant and anti-inflammatory remedy, and rosewater, which has both soothing and mildly astringent properties, is much used in skin toners and creams.

Pliny recorded thirty-two medicinal roles for the rose in AD 77. Today, their use in medicine has almost died out but Commission E has approved the use of infusions of the petals of *R.* × *centifolia* and *R. gallica* for treating inflammations of the mouth and throat.

The ripe fruits, or hips, especially those of dog rose (*R. canina*) and rugosa rose (*R. rugosa*) have been found to contain more vitamin C

Gallica rose 'Charles de Mills'

Rugosa rose 'Roseraie de l'Haÿ'

Dog rose *Rosa canina*

Dog rose hips

than any other plant—twenty times more than oranges. Rose hips are used to make jellies or jams and dried for use in herbal tea blends. The seeds are cleaned out of the hips, and the pith of the hip is then boiled with sugar to produce rose hip syrup, which is used as a nutritional supplement, particularly for very young children. Rose hip products are promoted as preventives and treatments for colds and flu, but their efficacy is not proven.

Caution *Even vitamin C is not unequivocally benign: The body has the capability to flush out excess vitamin C, but high doses can cause diarrhea, and very high doses have even been linked on occasion to kidney or bladder problems. However, at the more modest doses that are usually taken, rose hip products are generally regarded as reasonably safe. This is especially so in the case of rose hip teas or syrups, in which the vitamin is not very concentrated.*

Rosemary *Rosmarinus officinalis*

ROSEMARY *Rosmarinus officinalis*
G C M H
other names incensier, sea dew
plant family Labiatae (mint family)
height up to 7 feet (2 m)
habit half-hardy perennial with narrow, dark green evergreen leaves up each stem; small, pale to dark blue tubular flowers in spring
habitat dry, sunny positions and well-drained to dry soil
zones 8–10

An evergreen shrub, rosemary is grown for its aromatic foliage and flowers. It would suit a mixed border or a sunny spot in an herb garden. In cold climates, grow rosemary in a large pot so you can overwinter it indoors. It will tolerate a light frost, but bring it indoors before hard frosts are expected. The hardiest rosemary cultivar is 'Arp'; it will survive outdoors in Zone 7 and sometimes even in sheltered portions of Zone 6. 'Prostratus' is a trailing cultivar ideal for a rock garden.

Rosemary's aromatic, pungent leaves are used fresh or dried in cooking, especially in marinades, stews, and with roast lamb, beef, or chicken. The leaves are somewhat tough, so you may wish to chop them before use—or use entire sprigs, which are easy to remove before serving. Rosemary blends well with many other herbs and is used in the *herbes de Provence* seasoning blend. It has some antimicrobial action and, in pre-refrigeration days, was placed with meat in an effort to preserve it.

The distinctive flavor of rosemary is due to the combination of volatile oils such as camphor with the bitterness of diterpenes. The diterpenes stimulate the gall bladder and upper intestine, making this herb a wonderful aid to digestion. Rosemary is approved by Commission E for treating indigestion and loss of appetite. It appears to ease flatulence and calm intestinal spasms. Another approved use is for treating rheumatism. Dilute the essential oil in a carrier oil to rub on sore joints, or add a few drops of oil or an infusion of leaves to a bath to help relieve rheumatic pain in muscles.

Rosemary is an invaluable herb for scenting the home—for instance, in a dried herb wreath or potpourri. Sprigs can be burned outdoors to help keep insects at bay. The essential oil is used in aromatherapy. An infusion makes an excellent hair rinse for dark hair, for dull or oily hair, or against dandruff.

Caution *Avoid ingesting the essential oil and any other internal medicinal use of rosemary during pregnancy. Rosemary essential oil stimulates circulation, so avoid using it for aromatherapy if you have high blood pressure.*

BLACKBERRY *Rubus fruticosus*
C
other names bramble
plant family Rosaceae (rose family)
height up to 13 feet (4 m)
habit hardy shrub with long, thorny stems and leaves made up of three to five leaflets joined at one point on the stalk; white or pale pink flowers in summer, followed by juicy dark berries in late summer and fall
habitat full sun to partial shade and average to rich, moist, well-drained soil
zones 5–9
Blackberries grow vigorously in most soils and situations; in some areas, gardeners consider them a weed. Cultivated varieties come in upright, trailing, and semi-upright forms; thornless varieties are also available. The trailing forms (sometimes called dewberries) require some form of support and are hardy only to zone 6. Upright cultivars may be hardy to zone 4 or even colder.

The blackberry has juicy, health-giving fruits packed with vitamin C. The berries are often picked in the wild. They can either be eaten raw or cooked in pies and fruit crisps or crumbles. Blackberries are popular for making jams, jellies, and wine. The leaves are often used in herbal tea blends.

The leaves of blackberry have a long history of medicinal use because of their high tannin content. Commission E approves their use in treating diarrhea and inflammation of the mouth and pharynx. An infusion is taken as a tea, or used as a mouthwash.

other species
Raspberry (*Rubus idaeus*) is used in the same way as blackberry. It is even more popular as a fruit and as a constituent of herbal teas, but its medicinal effects are less well attested.

Blackberry *Rubus fruticosus*

Raspberry *Rubus idaeus*

Sorrel *Rumex acetosa*

Yellow dock *Rumex crispus*

SORREL *Rumex acetosa*
G C
other names garden sorrel, common sorrel, green sauce, sour sauce, sour sabs
plant family Polygonaceae (dock family)
height up to 2½ feet (75 cm)
habit hardy perennial with large, long-stalked leaves; tiny reddish brown flowers clustered on tall stems from early summer followed by tiny hard fruits in fall
habitat full sun to partial shade and average to rich, moist soil
zones 4–8

Sorrel is primarily grown for use in the kitchen. To help keep it from becoming weedy, remove the flower stalks before they form seeds. The herb's sharp, sour taste (a result of its oxalic acid) led to sorrel's extensive use in Europe before lemons became common. It is still used raw in salads and cooked in soups and green sauces, especially for fish.

Sorrel has a diuretic effect. It has been used in the past to treat inflammations of the nasal passages and respiratory tract, but these uses are unproven. Medicinal use of sorrel is not advisable because it can sometimes cause allergic reactions.

Caution *Culinary and medicinal use of sorrel is best avoided by anyone who suffers from kidney problems, gout, or rheumatism, since there is a risk of crystal formation from the herb's high levels of oxalic acid.*

other species
Related species of sorrel have similar culinary uses. French or buckler leaf sorrel (*Rumex scutatus*), is a low, spreading plant. Sheep's sorrel (*R. acetosella*) is similar to kitchen sorrel, but can be more invasive.

YELLOW DOCK *Rumex crispus*
M
other names curled dock, curly dock, narrow dock
plant family Polygonaceae (dock family)
height up to 5 feet (1.5 m)
habit hardy perennial with thick, deep roots

and lancelike, long, wavy-edged leaves; small, green flowers in summer
habitat sun or partial shade and moist soil
zones 4–8
This dock is usually considered to be a weed, but its young leaves can be gathered in the early part of the year and lightly boiled or used raw in salads. They have a tartness that is similar to the plant's relative sorrel (see page 88) because both plants contain oxalic acid**.**

Yellow dock contains anthraquinones (emodin, chryosophanic acid, and physcion), which trigger waves of peristaltic movements in the bowel. As a result, the roots of yellow dock can be used as a mild laxative. It has also been used for inflammation of the nasal passages and respiratory tract. Neither of these uses has been proven, however. Yellow dock is taken as a decoction of the dried roots.

Caution *Yellow dock deserves the same caution as over-the-counter laxatives. Do not take yellow dock or any other laxative if you have an obstruction in the intestine or are at risk of appendicitis. Avoid regular use or large doses, which could give rise to laxative dependence or damage to the digestive system. Do not use yellow dock during pregnancy.*

Older leaves of yellow dock contain oxalic acid, which is harmful in large quantities, so avoid consuming them. For the same reason, avoid taking roots or leaves if suffering from kidney problems, particularly kidney stones or gout. (The roots also contain oxalic acid, though at much lower levels than the leaves.)

WHITE WILLOW *Salix alba*
G M
other names European willow, cricket-bat willow, common willow
plant family Salicaceae (willow family)
height up to 80 feet (25 m) or more
habit hardy tree, slender**,** long, pointed deciduous leaves with whitish undersides; pale green flowers in the form of catkins appear with the leaves in spring

habitat common beside watercourses; likes full sun and moist to wet conditions and most soils
zones 4–9
There are hundreds of species of willow growing around the world, varying greatly in size and appearance. White willow is a large tree with deeply fissured, gray-brown bark, ascending branches, and long, tapering leaves and catkins in spring.

There are records of willow being used as a painkiller in China from around 500 BC, and in first century AD Greece, the physician Dioscorides recommended it for lower back pain. In 1838 salicin was extracted from willow bark, and from this glycoside the main active component of the herb was first obtained; it was named salicylic acid after the genus name, *Salix*. It was this substance from which the pharmaceutical drug aspirin (acetylsalicylic acid) was later developed (see *Meadowsweet*, page 57). Because salicin has anti-inflammatory and analgesic properties, it can be used to reduce fevers and as a painkiller in a similar way to aspirin. Commission E approves using willow bark preparations for rheumatism and pain relief. Make a decoction of the bark and take ½ cup three times a day.

Willows have many other uses. The craft of willow weaving, to make baskets and larger structures, goes back many centuries. In Britain, willow is also used to make cricket bats.

other species
Native Americans used black willow (*Salix nigra*) and other willow species for medicinal purposes. Although white willow has long been the preferred medicinal species, crack willow (*S. fragilis*), purple willow (*S. purpurea*), and violet willow (*S. daphnoides*) contain more salicin.
Caution *Do not take willow preparations if you are sensitive to aspirin. Children under sixteen should avoid aspirin-related substances because of the risk of the rare condition known as Reye's syndrome, which can cause potentially lethal liver damage. Continuous use of salicylates can cause gastric bleeding.*

SAGE *Salvia officinalis*
G C M H
other names garden sage, broadleaf sage, true sage, Dalmatian sage
plant family Labiatae (mint family)
height up to 2½ feet (75 cm)
habit Hardy woody perennial or shrub with oblong, gray-green aromatic leaves on square, much-branched stems; small spikes of violet-blue, pink, or white flowers in summer
habitat full sun and average, well-drained to dry soil
zones 5–8

Salvia is a large genus, comprising many highly ornamental species. Common sage and over twenty related species grow in abundance on the dry mountainous slopes of Dalmatia on the west coast of the Balkans. Estimates have suggested that there are between five hundred and nine hundred species and varieties around the world.

Sage prefers hot, dry, sunny conditions. Evergreen in milder climates, it dies back to the ground where winters are cold. Berggarten sage (*Salvia officinalis* 'Berggarten') is a particularly good form, both for its flavor and appearance.

Sage *Salvia officinalis*

Its leaves are larger and more rounded than the species and overall growth is more compact. The burgundy-tinged leaves of purple sage (*S. officinalis* 'Purpurascens') are beautiful in gardens. Equally ornamental are 'Icterina', with leaves edged in creamy yellow, and 'Tricolor', whose green leaves are edged in cream with traces of purple. Both are good as seasonings but are hardy only to zone 7.

Sage provides a stimulating contrast to mild-tasting vegetables such as potatoes, but it is most commonly used in stuffings for roast poultry and pork. Here it provides more than just a different flavor, as the herb's bitterness (which comes from its diterpenes) makes it easier for people to digest fats.

The genus name *Salvia* derives from the Latin *salvere,* "to save," in recognition of the herb's healing role. When it was taken north to France its name became *sauge* and, with time, sage. In medieval times a proverb testified to herb's healing powers: "Why should a man die while sage grows in his garden?"

Sage has antibacterial, antifungal, antiviral, and astringent properties. The dried leaves can be used to repel insects around the home; and in the garden, the plant deters harmful insects. Sage can be included in dried herb wreaths and potpourris. An infusion makes a good rinse for dark, dry, or dull hair. The essential oil is used in aromatherapy. The herb's most abundant component is the ketone thujone, which is responsible for a significant part of sage's properties. Camphor (another ketone) is another of its many active components.

An infusion of fresh or dried leaves is used as a gargle for scratchy throats, sore throats, and tonsillitis; it can also be used as a mouthwash for canker sores. Taken internally, the tea stimulates the appetite and helps to soothe indigestion. These uses are all approved by Commission E.

Caution *Do not consume sage during pregnancy as it is a uterine stimulant. Large amounts of thujone are toxic, and although the heating of sage*

Clary sage *Salvia sclarea*

when making tea and using it in cooked dishes reduces the activity, it should not be taken to excess: internally, consumption should be limited to no more than ½ ounce (13 g) of sage leaves a day. Do not in any circumstances ingest the essential oil and, because this oil stimulates circulation, avoid using it for aromatherapy if you have high blood pressure.

CLARY SAGE *Salvia sclarea*
G C H
other names clary, clear eye
plant family Labiatae (mint family)
height up to 3 feet (90 cm)
habit hardy biennial with aromatic, oval, hairy leaves; small lilac-and-white flowers and showy lavender-purple bracts (leaflike structures) in spring and summer
habitat prefers full sun and well-drained soil
zones 4–9

Clary sage—especially the variety *Salvia sclarea turkestanica*—is a dramatic, colorful herb that makes a handsome border plant. Its tall panicles produce swathes of bright flowers. However, it is its distinctive and powerful scent that leaves the deepest impression. After the herb is handled the scent stays on the skin even after initial washing. Because of its persistence, the essential oil is used in perfumes as a fixative, and the flowers are used in potpourri and herbal sachets. The essential oil is also used extensively in aromatherapy, in preference to its close relative garden sage; although the herbs share many of the same properties, clary sage has lower toxicity. The name clary (clear eye) derives from its former use in treating eyes. It has been used medicinally as an infusion for flatulence and for the relief of menstrual cramps.

The fresh or dried leaves can be used to flavor food, in the same way as garden sage. Clary sage is also used commercially as a flavoring in, for example, beverages, baked goods, and candies.

Caution *Do not ingest the essential oil. Do not use clary sage, internally or externally, at any stage of pregnancy.*

ELDERBERRY *Sambucus canadensis* (North America)
EUROPEAN ELDER *Sambucus nigra* (Europe)
G M
other names elder, elderflower, Judas tree, country medicine chest, pipe tree
plant family Caprifoliaceae (honeysuckle family)
height *S. canadensis:* up to 12 feet (3.6 m)
S. nigra: up to 33 feet (10 m)
habit hardy tree with deciduous leaves divided into five to eleven leaflets; umbrella-like clusters of white scented flowers in summer, followed by bunches of black berries
habitat prefers full sun to partial shade and fertile, moist, well-drained soil
zones 4–9 (*S. canadensis*); 5–8 (*S. nigra*),
With their huge decorative flower heads, elderberries make handsome garden trees. There are several strikingly ornamental cultivars of the European species available, including *Sambucus nigra* 'Albovariegata', which has white-margined light green leaves and *S. nigra.* 'Aurea', with pale gold leaves.

Elderberries are high in vitamin C. The berries are cooked to make pies, jelly, and wine. In Britain, they are sometimes gently cooked with sugar to produce "elderberry rob," a thick winter cordial that acts against colds and soothes sore throats and coughs.

Elderflower champagne captures the essence of an early summer afternoon. However, the scent can have an edge to it, which the disparaging describe as being similar to that of a tomcat.

A tea made of the dried flowers is drunk to fight coughs, colds, and fevers. It brings out a sweat and helps to increase bronchial secretions. It may also be used as a gargle. These uses have been approved by Commission E. Another popular anticold tea is a mixture of equal amounts of elderflowers and peppermint.

Caution *Avoid ingesting the bark and leaves of the elderberry tree, as they have a purgative action so violent as to be unsafe. Nor should raw berries be consumed in any quantity: they also can have a strong purgative effect. The unripe berries of* S. canadensis, *which are more toxic than those of the European species, should be avoided altogether. Consume only the flowers and cooked ripe berries.*
other species
The blue berries of the blue elder (*Sambucus caerulea*), which grows in western North America, are cooked and eaten in the same ways as other elderberries.

European elder (*Sambucus nigra*) in spring

European elder (*Sambucus nigra*) in fall

Winter savory *Satureja montana*

Summer savory *Satureja hortensis*

WINTER SAVORY *Satureja montana*
SUMMER SAVORY *Satureja hortensis*
G C M
other names mountain savory, bean herb,
white thyme
plant family Labiatae (mint family)
height up to 16 inches (40 cm)
habit *Satureja montana*: hardy perennial with
dark green, narrow aromatic leaves; small spikes
of pale pinkish blue, pink, or white flowers
bloom in summer
S. hortensis: hardy annual with aromatic, small
narrow leaves on square, pale mauve stems;
small pale pink or white flowers scattered along
stems in summer
habitat *S. montana*: prefers full sun and well-
drained to dry soil
S. hortensis: prefers full sun and average, well-
drained soil
zones 5–8 (*S. montana*); all zones (*S. hortensis*)
(annual)
Winter savory is an aromatic perennial herb
that, with its mass of flowers from midsummer
on, deserves to be grown more widely outside
its native Mediterranean. The plants often

become straggly and need pruning, but they
respond well to this and can be shaped into a
low, compact hedge. Winter savory is evergreen
in mild climates but tends to be somewhat
short-lived.

The annual summer savory is equally
aromatic but wirier and less striking in
appearance. Its flowers, like those of winter
savory, are attractive to bees. It is easy to grow
from seed and makes a useful culinary herb.

The savories were listed among the garden
plants introduced by early settlers to North
America. In *The Winter's Tale* Shakespeare
mentions savory as being common.

Winter savory tastes rather like peppery
marjoram; summer savory is slightly sweeter
and milder. Both are used with meats and in
salads, bean dishes, stuffings, and salami and
other Italian sausages. Summer savory often
forms a part of a *fines herbes* mixture and is an
essential component of *herbes de Provence*. It has
been used to relieve diarrhea and may alleviate
gas pains and aid digestion, but these uses have
not been proven.
Caution *Avoid using both winter and summer
savory during pregnancy.*

Milk thistle *Silybum marianum*

MILK THISTLE *Silybum marianum*
G M

other names blessed thistle, St. Mary's thistle, Marian thistle, Our Lady's thistle
plant family Compositae (daisy family)
height up to 5 feet (1.5 m)
habit hardy annual with a rosette of spiny leaves; tall branching stem produces solitary purple thistlelike flowers in summer that become round, prickly seed heads
habitat full sun and well-drained soil
all zones (annual)

Producing a broad rosette of white-veined leaves, *Silybum marianum* is a handsome presence in the spring border, a contrast and complement to the slim verticals of daffodils and tulips. It also makes an attractive addition to flower arrangements.

According to the Doctrine of Signatures, the white marbling in the leaves was linked with milk production. Like many plants that were believed to assist women, it was put under the patronage of the Virgin Mary, which gave it a number of its alternative common names as well as its Latin species name, *marianum*. The seventeenth-century diarist and naturalist John Evelyn noted: "Disarmed of its prickles and boiled, it is worthy of esteem, and thought to be a great breeder of milk and proper diet for women who are nurses."

Milk thistle's present fame rests on another use, also noted in the seventeenth century, when the herbalists Gerard and Culpeper both wrote of its value in treating liver disease. In 1968 silymarin, a complex of flavonoids, was extracted from the seeds, and this has been found to be effective in protecting the liver from toxic damage. Commission E approves use of the dried plant and seeds in an infusion for treating indigestion.
Caution *Because of the serious nature of liver disease, do not self-treat this condition with milk thistle; consult a medical professional and take the herb only under direction.*

CHICKWEED *Stellaria media*
M H

other names starweed, winterweed
plant family Caryophyllaceae (pink family)
height up to 6 in (15 cm)
habit half-hardy annual with small light green leaves; small, starry white flowers for most of the growing season
habitat prefers partial shade and moist, fertile soil
all zones (annual)

Chickweed is a favorite food of chickens—hence its name. It is also one of the most widespread of weeds. Its frail looks are

Chickweed *Stellaria media*

deceptive; in mild climates it can be found growing throughout the year. In hot climates it dies out in summer and grows best in the cooler temperatures of spring and fall. Its leaves close up around tender shoots to protect them at night.

It is not only chickens that enjoy chickweed. Its taste of young peas makes it a pleasant addition to a salad. Lightly boiled, it can also be served as a vegetable, and is a source of vitamin C.

An infusion of the fresh flowering or dried herb can be added to a bath to treat the itching sensation of irritated, inflamed skin or eczema. The leaves can be used in a poultice. An infusion of chickweed has been used internally and externally to alleviate stiff joints and rheumatic pain. These uses are not proven.

COMFREY *Symphytum officinale*
G M

other names knitbone, boneset, bruisewort, slippery root, ass ear
plant family Boraginaceae (forget-me-not or borage family)
height up to 4 feet (1.2 m)
habit hardy perennial with large, rough, pointed leaves; white, pink, or blue bell-like flowers dangle from tall stems in summer
habitat full sun to partial shade and average, well-drained, moist soil
zones 3–8

Comfrey is a spectacular tall plant, but it can become invasive. It is difficult to remove from a spot once it is planted, as the smallest pieces of root will sprout. So choose your location carefully; it may be safest to grow comfrey in its own little bed. Bees love it, and its sequence of developing flowers as the stems unwind ensures a continuous supply of food for them.

Dried comfrey leaves (not the flowers or roots) can be used as a mulch in the garden. Leaves can also be used to make a liquid "manure tea" fertilizer that is high in potassium. Steep the leaves in water until they have decayed, then dilute with 20 parts of water to 1 part of tea before applying to garden plants.

Comfrey used to be thought of as a wonder plant that possessed healing properties, as well as being a high-protein food for humans and fodder for cattle. Then the hazard of its pyrrolizidine alkaloids, which can cause liver damage and possible cancer, placed an embargo on eating the plant.

However, comfrey remains highly valued for external use in treating wounds. The name comfrey derives from the Latin *confirmare*, meaning "to make firm," and the genus name *Symphytum* is from the Greek for "to unite." It has been used for centuries to encourage the healing of bruises and sprains, and these external uses are approved by Commission E.

The main component that makes comfrey a famed healing treatment is allantoin, which actively stimulates the growth of new cells. The tannins it contains assist healing by tightening the skin, while its mucilage soothes damaged tissue. Poultices can be made from the pulped fresh leaves or the crushed fresh root. (The hairy leaves can irritate, so the skin should be protected with thin clean cotton.)

The juice of the fresh plant or an infusion of the roots and leaves can be applied as a wash or added to a bath. The leaves can also be used in home-made salves, and in shampoos and rinses for dry hair. Comfrey is also a constituent of commercially available ointments.

Comfrey *Symphytum officinale*

Caution *Concern over the pyrrolizidine alkaloids it contains means that comfrey should not be taken internally or used on open wounds. Many countries (including Germany) have banned it for internal use. As a proportion of these compounds will be absorbed even through intact skin, even externally it should be used only in limited amounts and only for limited periods. Commission E has kept comfrey an approved herb for external use but advises that it should be used for no more than four to six weeks in a year. It should not be used during pregnancy or while breast-feeding, or on young children.*

COSTMARY

Tanacetum balsamita subsp. *balsamitoides*
G H

other names alecost, balsam herb, bibleleaf
plant family Compositae (daisy family)
height up to 3 feet (90 cm)
habit hardy perennial with oblong, silvery green leaves up to 8 inches (20 cm) long; clusters of daisylike flowers on long stalks in late summer
habitat prefers full sun or light shade and rich, well-drained soil
zones 4–9

Costmary was introduced to Europe from Asia, and in 1578 Henry Lyte wrote that it was "very common in all gardens." Today it has almost disappeared from Britain. In North America, however, where it was introduced in the seventeenth century, costmary has escaped to grow wild. It is often included in gardens of the Colonial era and collections of historic medicinal plants, as well as in herb gardens.

Costmary is used as a tangy salad herb but usually only in small amounts added as a flavoring. As its Latin species name indicates, costmary smells of balsam. This, plus its bitterness, led to its use for flavoring and preserving ale—one of its alternative names, alecost, means "spicy ale herb." In the past it was used to scent clothes. Dried leaves are still used in potpourri. The small flowers dry well for use in wreaths or dried arrangements.

FEVERFEW *Tanacetum parthenium*
G M H

other name featherfew
plant family Compositae (daisy family)
height up to 3 feet (90 cm)
habit hardy perennial with aromatic, deeply cut, medium green leaves; many small white daisy flowers in summer
habitat prefers full sun and well-drained soil
zones 4–9

Feverfew was first introduced to North America and Britain as an ornamental garden plant. It self-seeds prolifically, filling out corners with its masses of yellow-centered, white daisies. Flowers of double varieties look like small white pom-poms; the variety 'Aureum' has yellowish green leaves. Feverfew is very adaptable and easy to grow; it tolerates partial shade.

Costmary *Tanacetum balsamita* subsp. *balsamitoides*

Feverfew *Tanacetum parthenium*

As its name implies, feverfew was originally used against fevers. It also gained a reputation as a treatment for female conditions. According to Culpeper's sixteenth-century analysis, it "does a woman all the good she can desire of a herb." Importantly, he also noted that it was "very effectual for all pains in the head."

In 1978 a Mrs. Jenkins, the wife of a Welsh doctor, followed Culpeper's advice and found feverfew helpful against her migraines. The Migraine Trust picked up the story and clinical trials followed. Feverfew's effect on migraines has been linked to the sesquiterpene lactones it contains—in particular, parthenolide. Clinical trials and subsequent practice have found feverfew to reduce the frequency, severity, and duration of migraines. Rather than being made into an infusion, the fresh leaves are consumed directly; the customary dose is two or three fresh leaves a day. Leaves should first be wrapped in a slice of bread, as they can cause canker sores. Feverfew may also be taken in commercial forms such as tablets.

Feverfew makes a good filler flower for fresh arrangements, as well as a pretty dried flower. It is aromatic even when dried and repels insects, so it can be included in sachets.

Caution *Check with a medical practitioner before using feverfew to treat migraines. Use of feverfew is not recommended during pregnancy or lactation, nor is it appropriate for young children. Avoid using feverfew if you are sensitive to other plants in the daisy family; it may cause an allergic reaction, and contact with the fresh leaves may cause an allergic rash.*

DANDELION *Taraxacum officinale*
G M H

other names piss-a-beds, farmer's clocks, blowball
plant family Compositae (daisy family)
height up to 12 inches (30 cm)
habit hardy perennial with a basal rosette of deeply toothed leaves; hollow flower stems with solitary yellow flowers from spring to fall

habitat full sun to partial shade, any soil
zones 3–10

The name dandelion derives from the French *dent de lion,* and its former Latin name was *dens leonis.* Both mean "lion's tooth," and the jagged leaf edge is rather like a set of lion's teeth.

The dandelion is one of the stars of healthful herbs, yet it is a true weed. If you are growing it intentionally in a garden bed, it is important that you should regularly deadhead it, or you will find that seedlings are taking over the rest of the garden. Though dandelion will survive in most growing conditions, the roots are easiest to harvest where the soil is loose and rich in organic matter (humus).

Dandelion leaves are rich in vitamin A and an array of other vitamins and minerals. In salads its bitter leaves trigger the digestive system into action. To minimize bitterness, pick leaves before the plants bloom; the flavor is then somewhat like chicory greens. For a less bitter taste, the leaves can also be blanched by covering the growing plant with an upside-down flower pot to shut out the light. However, blanching leaves reduces their vitamin content.

Dandelion roots can be used like chicory roots to add distinctive flavor to coffee, or used alone as a caffeine-free coffee substitute. Scrubbed roots are dry-roasted and then ground (alternatively, they can be chopped finely before roasting). Roots of both dandelion and chicory contain the polysaccharide inulin.

Dandelion *Taraxacum officinale*

Thyme *Thymus vulgaris*

Wild thyme *Thymus serpyllum*

Dandelion and chicory also share the same bitter substance in their latex sap, lactucopicrin (also known as taraxacin, after dandelion's Latin name). German studies in the 1950s demonstrated that this substance stimulates the gall bladder into action and improves the digestion of a meal. Commission E approves the use of dandelion for treating urinary tract infections, liver and gall bladder complaints, indigestion, and loss of appetite. Make an infusion from the leaves and flowers or a decoction of the root and take a cupful up to three times a day.

An infusion of dandelion leaves makes a good skin cleanser and tonic. In an herbal bath it makes a good spring tonic. The boiled flowers produce a yellow dye.

THYME *Thymus vulgaris*
G C M H
other names common thyme, garden thyme, French thyme
plant family Labiatae (mint family)
height up to 1 foot (30 cm)
habit hardy perennial with small, pointed gray-green leaves; white to lilac-pink or lavender flowers in summer
habitat full sun to partial shade and light, dry, well-drained soil
zones 4–8

Common, or garden, thyme is often grown in herb gardens but is equally ideal for rock gardens, containers, and crevices in stone walls. Wherever it grows, its flowers attract bees. Thyme is evergreen except in cold climates. It is one of the earliest known culinary herbs and was probably introduced to Britain and northern Europe by the Romans. The strongly flavored leaves go well with most dishes, especially chicken and fish, and are much used in stuffings and soups and with grilled foods. Thyme is one of the best herbs for mixing with other herbs. It is often included in a *fines herbes* mixture and is a main ingredient of *bouquets garnis* and *herbes de Provence.*

Thyme flowers are attractive in miniature flower arrangements or modern "tussie-mussies." Thyme is aromatic in dried arrangements and can be included with other herbs in moth-repelling sachets. It can also be used to make a conditioner for dark hair.

Thyme's principal active constituent, thymol, was first recognized by the Berlin court apothecary in 1725. In the grim conditions of the field hospitals during the First World War, it was used as an antiseptic. Thymol and another component, carvacrol, have been found to be effective against a wide range of bacteria and fungi. Thyme has been used to treat wounds, and for inflammation of the mouth and pharynx. It is approved by Commission E for treating coughs and bronchitis: To soothe a cough, take 1 tablespoon of syrup 3 times a day. **Caution** *Do not ingest thyme's essential oil, as it is toxic. (The concentrations of compounds found in leaves are much less, so the amounts used in cooking or infusions are not harmful.)*

other species

The constituents of wild or creeping thyme (*Thymus serpyllum*) are similar to those of common thyme. The proportions of these constituents vary considerably over its twenty or more subspecies and varieties. Fundamentally it is similar to common thyme in its range of actions, although generally milder. However, its essential oil, often known as "serpolet oil," can cause allergic reactions.

Overall there are some 350 species in this Eurasian genus and a legion of forms that can give low-growing color to gardens. The classification of the species is complex, with lots of confusing synonyms and common names that can be the same for different plants. For example, another commonly grown species, *T. polytrichus* subsp. *britannicus* (syn. *T. drucei*), is also called wild or creeping thyme.

One particularly sweetly aromatic thyme is *T. × citriodorus,* lemon thyme (yellow and variegated forms of this are available). Its citrusy thyme flavor is good with fish and chicken, and in herbal teas. This species is also a favorite for use in potpourris, and its essential oil is used in aromatherapy.

LINDEN *Tilia cordata*

G M

other names lime, littleleaf linden
plant family Tiliaceae (lime family)
height up to 90 feet (25 m)
habit hardy tree with pointed, round, dark green, deciduous leaves; clusters of fragrant, pale yellow flowers in midsummer
habitat full sun to partial shade and moist, well-drained soil
zones 4–8

The littleleaf linden is an attractive shade tree with a broadly pyramidal form. It makes an attractive specimen tree in the average-sized lawn; it also works well as a street tree. The pleasing fragrance of its summer flowers is an added bonus. The Romans were great fans of the linden tree, planting it in their towns in the belief that it induced calm. In subsequent centuries it became traditional in Britain and France to plant linden trees around palaces, town squares, and village greens.

The scent of the flowers comes from the volatile oil constituent farnesol. These flowers are used to make a fragrant beverage tea. Drinking an infusion of fresh or dried linden flowers or a commercial linden tea is believed to help calm the nerves. Although these sedative effects are not proven, it has been used as a gentle but useful sleep inducer, sometimes mixed with hops and valerian.

A linden flower infusion induces sweating, which can be helpful in overcoming colds. It also may help reduce nasal congestion. The flower infusion is approved by Commission E for treating coughs and bronchitis.

other species

The flowers of large-leaved linden (*Tilia platyphyllos*) are also sometimes used for tea. Basswood, sometimes called American linden (*T. americana*), has much larger leaves and is hardy to zone 3. Its flowers can also be used for tea (1–2 teaspoons dried flowers to 1 cup hot water).

Linden *Tilia cordata*

NASTURTIUM *Tropaeolum majus*

G C M H

other names Indian cress
plant family Cruciferae (mustard family)
height up to 2 feet (60 cm)
habit tender annual with rounded leaves; large flowers ranging from bright yellow-orange to fiery red in summer
habitat full sun and average to poor, moist but well-drained soil
all zones (annual)

Nasturtiums are decorative, fast-growing plants that are ideal for containers or bright summer borders. For the best display, do not fertilize; richer soil leads to leaf growth at the expense of flowers. While most modern varieties remain under 2 feet (60 cm) tall, older types can be trained to climb up several feet or left to sprawl along the ground. Single colors are available, as well as the more common mixtures.

The flowers make a beautiful garnish, and both flowers and peppery leaves can be added to salads. The unripe seeds can be pickled like capers. The peppery taste is caused by a form of mustard oil (benzyl isothiocyanate). This constituent of nasturtiums has antifungal properties and inhibits the growth of bacteria and of viruses.

An infusion of nasturtium leaves is used against dandruff in hair lotions and shampoos. In folk medicine, nasturtium leaf infusions and washes have also been used to help ease painful muscles and to soothe minor skin rashes. Infusions of the leaves, taken internally, are approved by Commission E for treating coughs and bronchitis.

STINGING NETTLE *Urtica dioica*

G C M

other names nettle, common nettle
plant family Urticaceae (nettle family)
height up to 5 feet (1.5 m)
habit hardy perennial with pointed, egg-shaped to lance-shaped, toothed, leaves; stems and leaves are covered with stinging hairs; small light green flowers in dangling clusters in summer
habitat grows in wide range of conditions,

Nasturtium *Tropaeolum majus*

Stinging nettle *Urtica dioica*

especially full sun to partial shade and evenly moist to damp, rich soil

zones 3–9

Stinging nettle is a weed that likes disturbed soil and is a greedy feeder of nitrogen and other nutrients. It grows prolifically on sites where the ground has been disturbed by human habitation. The larvae of a number of butterfly species feed on its leaves.

People have always had a love-hate relationship with the stinging nettle. Its defensive stings (containing compounds such as histamine and formic acid—the substance in ant stings) can hurt, but its leaves are a good source of nutrients when cooked. When the greens are boiled or steamed, the sting disappears. Nettle soup is both delicious and nourishing. The fibers of stinging nettle stalks have a history of being used to make cloth from the Bronze Age to the beginning of the twentieth century. Nettle leaf tea makes a good hair rinse as a tonic for dry or dull hair, and as a dandruff-fighter.

The leaves have been used in an infusion as a mild diuretic to prevent and treat kidney gravel. The roots—best taken as a decoction— are even more diuretic in action. According to the American ethnobotanist James Duke, a serving of boiled or steamed nettles provides sufficient boron to reach the Rheumatoid Disease Foundation's advisory level for usefulness in treating arthritis. Commission E approves the use of the flowering nettle plant, taken as an infusion, to treat rheumatism.

The sting of fresh nettles has a history of use on swollen joints by arthritis sufferers, a process called urtication. The fresh plants are brushed on swollen joints, and the resulting sting is said to help relieve the pain and swelling. Some enthusiasts even keep a pot in their home or office for handy access to fresh shoots.

Caution *Although cooked nettle leaves are harmless, if you are suffering from a kidney condition, seek professional advice before using stinging nettle medicinally.*

Valerian *Valeriana officinalis*

VALERIAN *Valeriana officinalis*
G M H

other names all-heal, garden valerian, garden heliotrope, setewale

plant family Valerianaceae (valerian family)

height up to 5 feet (1.5 m)

habit hardy perennial with aromatic roots; leaves are made up of numerous slender, parallel leaflets (often toothed); loose, rounded clusters of tiny pink, pale lilac, or white flowers bloom in summer

habitat prefers full sun or partial shade with average to damp, well-drained soil

zones 4–9

The narrow profile and flexibility that fitted valerian for its original reedbed habitat mean it is also well suited to the blustery roadside verges where it is now so often found. It is frequently cultivated in informal borders or in herb gardens.

Cats have a fixation for the smell of the dried root, though many humans find this smell unpleasant. In the eighteenth century the English doctor William Cullen suggested that you could measure the quality of a sample of valerian by observing how much interest a cat took in it. In ancient times valerian had a reputation as a panacea. Its current role in the relief of insomnia was established in the eighteenth and nineteenth centuries: it became so popular that it has been dubbed "the Valium of the nineteenth century."

Insomnia is often linked with worry. Valerian acts as a mild sedative and is thought to promote both light sleep and deep sleep. Prescription sleeping pills can cause nightmares and a "hangover" malaise the following day, but studies show that these do not occur with valerian. Similarly, although the components in valerian have been found to bind loosely to the same receptors in the brain as commercial sleeping medications, valerian does not seem to cause the same problems of dependence. Though it is not clear which components in valerian are responsible for its action, it is approved by Commission E for treating nervousness and insomnia.

Valerian is taken as an infusion of the fresh or dried roots (harvested in the fall), as commercial capsules, or as a commercial tea. The essential oil from the root is used in aromatherapy. For a relaxing herbal bath, add a few drops of the oil to the water.

other species

Native North American species include swamp valerian (*Valeriana uliginosa*) in the east and mountain valerian (*V. sitchensis*) in British Columbia and the Cascade Range.

Caution *Those currently taking antidepressants or sedatives, or who have reduced liver or kidney function, should only take valerian under medical supervision. Large or long-term doses can cause headaches, stupor, or dizziness. In any case, to be on the safe side, drink no more than three cups of valerian tea a day.*

Vervain *Verbena officinalis*

VERVAIN *Verbena officinalis*
G M H

other names common verbena, European vervain, simpler's joy
plant family Verbenaceae (verbena family)
height up to 32 inches (80 cm)
habit hardy perennial with thin, square stems and unstalked, deeply cut leaves arranged in pairs; tiny pale mauve flowers in small, elegant spikes in summer
habitat prefers full sun and moist, well-drained soil
zones 4–8

Vervain has long been regarded with awe. Observers are impressed by the small perfect flowers and the stiff slender stems, and although less showy than some of its relatives, it is a graceful plant for an herb garden. It was used by the Romans as an altar plant, for which their term was *verbena*. The ancient Druids of Britain and France regarded it as a magical plant. It was even said to grow where Christ was crucified and was supposedly used to treat his wounds.

Vervain flowers dry well and can be used in herbal wreaths and dried arrangements, but the herb is grown mainly for its medical properties. Vervain was used traditionally for a wide variety of ailments. An infusion of the fresh or dried plant has been used for oral and upper respiratory ailments such as coughs and sore throats and to combat cramps and fatigue. However, none of these uses is proven and vervain has not been fully investigated scientifically.

Caution *Vervain should never be used at any stage of pregnancy.*

GINGER *Zingiber officinale*

G C M

other names true ginger, sheng jian (Chinese)
plant family Zingiberaceae (ginger family)
height up to 5 feet (1.5 m)
habit Tender perennial with large, pointed slender leaves on long reedlike stems growing from thick, aromatic roots; loose spikes of yellow-green flowers in summer
habitat partial shade and rich, deep, well-drained soil; prefers high humidity
zones 9–11

Ginger grows wild in tropical forests and can be cultivated outdoors in the kitchen garden in frost-free climates. Given the right conditions (bright light and high humidity) it can be successfully grown as an indoor or greenhouse plant. Container-grown plants rarely bloom. The portion used is the thick rhizome (a semi-underground horizontal stem).

It has been used in Chinese medicine for at least 2,500 years and as a foodstuff for much longer. It was reaching Roman markets in the Mediterranean 2,000 years ago. The Spanish introduced it to the Caribbean from the Far East. The root is widely used in cooking. The fresh root is crushed, grated, or sliced, especially in curries, pickles, and soups; the dried, powdered root is also used, especially in baking. Ginger-based drinks such as ginger ale, ginger beer, and ginger tea are simultaneously tangy and soothing.

Ginger *Zingiber officinale*

Ginger is a wonderful aid to digestion and is approved by Commission E for treating loss of appetite and indigestion. It has been demonstrated to stimulate the flow of gastric juices and encourage the release of bile, improving the digestion of fatty foods. It also helps to dispel flatulence. An infusion of a few slices of fresh ginger root works well.

Its volatile oil includes components—gingerols and shogaol—that can be helpful in relieving nausea and vomiting. Some trials have found it to be more effective than conventional medicines in combating post-operative nausea. Ginger is approved by Commission E for preventing travel sickness. It is also available in commercial capsules and powder.

Caution *Ginger has a good track record for safety. However, it is advisable to avoid medicinal amounts during pregnancy, as the potential side effects of ginger when used for morning sickness are still unresolved. If you have a heart condition, gallstones, or suffer from diabetes, consult a doctor before using ginger medicinally.*

Toxic herbs

Care must be exercised when using any herb for medicinal purposes, but there are some herbs whose effects are so strong that they can cause great harm. The herbs described on the following ten pages are toxic and could cause harmful effects or even death if used by amateurs. They are included here because they are popular garden plants, are used for crafts, or have important medicinal properties. However, none of the medicinal herbs described here should ever be taken internally except under close medical supervision, because the difference between the therapeutic dose and the harmful dose is very small. Though some of these plants are beautiful, they should not be grown where young children play unsupervised. They could cause poisoning if a child decided to sample them.

ARNICA *Arnica montana*
G M
other names leopard's bane, mountain daisy, mountain snuff, wolfsbane
plant family Compositae (daisy family)
height up to 1 foot (30 cm)
habit hardy perennial with long, oval hairy leaves; yellow, daisylike flowers in summer
habitat full sun and rich, well-drained soil
zones 5–8
Arnica is an attractive herb with hairy low-growing foliage and bright single yellow flowers. Being an alpine, it is suitable for rock gardens or raised beds, and will not tolerate hot summers. *Arnica montana* is a protected species in some countries because of over-collection from the wild.

In both Europe and North America, arnica was long considered an effective treatment for coughs and fevers; it was also used to treat angina, weak hearts, and the circulation of blood. It is recorded that the poet Goethe drank arnica tea to relieve his angina. However,

current advice is to avoid taking arnica internally at all. It can strongly irritate the mucous membranes of the upper gastrointestinal tract, causing burning pains, vomiting, and diarrhea. Its stimulating action may carry a risk of cardiac palsy. Overdosing can be fatal, and consequently the U.S. Food and Drug Administration classes arnica as an unsafe herb for consumption.

Arnica continues to be applied externally despite the hazards of internal consumption. It is approved by Commission E for external use in treating blunt injuries (bruises) and skin inflammations. The sesquiterpene lactones in arnica help to reduce inflammation and ease pain. Creams or ointments made from the flowers and rhizomes are used as anti-inflammatories and painkillers for strained muscles, minor joint pain, and bruises.
Caution *You should avoid using arnica externally if you have any sensitivity to other members of the daisy family, as contact dermatitis can occur. Avoid using arnica if you have broken skin, and avoid prolonged use. Never take it internally.*

WORMWOOD *Artemisia absinthium*
G H
other names absinthe, green ginger
plant family Compositae (daisy family)
height up to 3 feet (90 cm)
habit hardy perennial with gray-green, deeply lobed leaves; sprays of tiny, dull yellow flowers in summer
habitat full sun to light shade and average, well-drained soil
zones 4–8
Wormwood is an attractive border plant. Its mass of finely divided, aromatic fernlike silvery foliage provides dramatic contrast. The leaves are also used in floral arrangements.

Wormwood's bitter nature is recorded in its Latin species name *absinthium*, which means "absence of sweetness." Simply handling the dried herb will leave an extremely bitter taste on the fingers (wash your hands after handling the

Wormwood *Artemisia absinthium*

Deadly nightshade *Atropa belladonna*

fresh or dried herb). This is mainly attributable to sesquiterpene lactones such as absinthine. Wormwood was used to make absinthe, a destructive alcoholic drink popular in Paris in the late nineteenth century. Edouard Manet's painting "The Absinthe Drinker" hauntingly records its toxic and addictive effects, which led to the drink being banned. The absinthe available today uses substitute flavorings. Wormwood was also used to flavor vermouth (whose name, in fact, comes from the German word for "wormwood").

The same compound that makes wormwood toxic to humans, thujone, makes it useful for repelling insects. The dried leaves are a good choice for including in moth-repelling sachets. An infusion of the leaves can be used as an insecticide. In earlier times it was much used as a strewing herb. It also long had a use as an infusion for expelling parasitical intestinal worms, a function recorded in its name.

Branches of wormwood can be used in fresh or dried arrangements. Flowering branches are the most attractive and can be dried for use in herb wreaths.

Caution *Avoid internal use. The high levels of thujone in wormwood are toxic and can cause vomiting, stomach and intestinal cramps, headache, dizziness, and disturbance of the central nervous system, including epileptic fits in those who are susceptible.*

DEADLY NIGHTSHADE *Atropa belladonna*
M

other names belladonna, devil's cherries, naughty man's cherries, devil's herb
plant family Solanaceae (nightshade family)
height up to 5 feet (1.5 m)
habit hardy perennial with pointed, egg-shaped leaves up to 8 inches (20 cm) long; dangling, bell-shaped, palest purple flowers in summer are followed by bunches of purplish black berries
habitat grows often in hedges and woods, in full sun to partial shade and moist soil
zones not recommended for gardens

Deadly nightshade is an extremely poisonous plant. The berries are so lethal to children that Gerard's sixteenth-century advice still holds: "Banish therefore these pernicious plants out of your gardens and all places near to your houses where children do resort."

Deadly nightshade's generic name derives from Atropos, one of the three Fates in Greek mythology, whose duty was to cut the thread of life. Fashionable medieval Italian women used it in their eyes to dilate the pupils into large black pools. It was thought to make them look beautiful—hence the name "belladonna"—but they could see only a blur, and constant use damaged the eyes. This effect, caused by atropine, the most poisonous of the plant's alkaloids, is exploited today for medical eye examinations and surgery.

Some of the alkaloids in deadly nightshade inhibit the parasympathetic nervous system, which controls involuntary body functions such as the movement of the smooth muscle of the intestines. Because of this, they have been used—in controlled doses administered by doctors—as an anesthetic, and to treat irritable bowel syndrome and Parkinson's disease.
Caution *Even minor overdoses have effects ranging from hallucinations and delirium to respiratory failure and death. Children may find the shiny, dark berries tempting.*

LILY-OF-THE-VALLEY *Convallaria majalis*
G M H
other name May lily
plant family Liliaceae (lily family)
height up to 8 inches (20 cm)
habit hardy perennial with pairs of large, pointed oval dark green leaves; very fragrant bell-shaped white flowers in late spring to early summer, followed by round red berries
habitat partial shade and moist, humus-rich soil
zones 2–8

Lily-of-the-valley *Convallaria majalis*

Much loved for its sweet-scented white flowers, this low-growing, creeping plant makes good groundcover in the garden. The early Greek herbalists rated lily-of-the-valley highly. In about AD 400 Apuleius wrote that when Apollo made his son Aesculapius the god of medicine, he gave him the gift of lily-of-the-valley.

The flowers can be used fresh in small-scale flower arrangements and dried in potpourri. The volatile oil is used in perfume.

Lily-of-the-valley contains cardiac glycosides with an action similar to those of foxglove, and medical doctors have prescribed it to regularize heart rate. As a diuretic, it is also prescribed to reduce blood volume and lower blood pressure.
Caution *Use only under close medical supervision. Ingesting lily-of-the valley can cause delirium or death from heart failure and asphyxiation.*

THORN APPLE *Datura stramonium*
M
other names jimsonweed, devil's apple, Jamestown weed, stramonium, mad-apple
plant family Solanaceae (nightshade family)

Thorn apple *Datura stramonium*

height up to 7 feet (2 m)

habit half-hardy annual with large, jagged fetid-smelling leaves; large white to pale purple trumpet-shaped flowers in summer are followed by spiny, rounded fruits that are about the size of a golf ball

habitat prefers warm conditions in the open, in fertile soil

all zones (annual)

The oracle of Apollo at Delphi in ancient Greece and the Inca priests in South America are believed to have used thorn apple to assist prophecy by inducing visions. In the United States it is an abundant weed, growing in yards, roadsides, and waste places. The leaves smell unpleasant, but its trumpet-shaped flowers are large and showy. It was probably particularly common around the early Virginian settlement of Jamestown (Jimson), giving rise to its alternative name of jimsonweed.

Like its relatives henbane and deadly nightshade, thorn apple is strongly narcotic, and like them it also has valuable properties. The whole of the plant is poisonous because of the presence of the toxic alkaloids hyoscyamine, atropine, and scopolamine. Very small doses have an antispasmodic effect, so it has long been used to relax the gastrointestinal tract and the bronchial tract. In former times it was smoked to ease asthma.

More recently, the constituent scopolamine has been prescribed in time-release skin patches manufactured pharmaceutically for motion sickness. It reduces the muscle spasms that trigger vomiting. Thorn apple has also been used to control the spasms of Parkinson's disease. The narcotic effect of scopolamine has been exploited as a "truth serum."

Caution *Thorn apple is toxic and can be lethal at relatively small doses. Its effects range from hallucinations to heart irregularities and asphyxiation. Do not handle the plant with bare hands, since the toxic compounds could be absorbed through cuts or scrapes and may cause skin irritation.*

Foxglove *Digitalis purpurea*

FOXGLOVE *Digitalis purpurea*

G M

other names common foxglove, folksglove, fairy gloves, witches' gloves, dead men's bells, fairy bells

plant family Scrophulariaceae (foxglove or figwort family)

height up to 5 feet (1.5 m)

habit hardy biennial with large, stalkless, lancelike leaves; tall spikes of rosy purple to white bell-shaped flowers in summer

habitat prefers partial shade and moist, well-drained soil

zones 4–8

The foxglove is the most stately of woodland glade plants, and varieties in a wide range of delightful colors are grown in gardens around the world. Foxgloves are easy to grow from seeds but do not bloom until their second year.

Historically foxglove was applied to "scrofulous swellings"—tuberculosis of the neck lymph glands, also known as "the king's evil."

Foxglove, like lily-of-the-valley, contains cardiac glycosides, which encourage the heart to beat more strongly and slowly; they are particularly valuable in helping to regulate a fast, erratic heartbeat. The glycosides are also diuretic, assisting the production of urine and reducing blood volume and therefore blood pressure. The extracted component digitoxin in particular is used as a standard medical treatment. The common purple foxglove (*Digitalis purpurea*) is still grown as a source for this, as are Grecian foxglove (*D. lanata*) and straw foxglove (*D. lutea*).

Caution *All parts of the foxglove plant are toxic. Even at recommended dosages this herb can cause nausea, headache, stupor, perceptual confusion, and cardiac irregularities. Excessive doses can cause delirium or death from heart failure and asphyxiation. Use only under medical supervision.*

HENBANE *Hyoscyamus niger*
G M

other names black henbane, Jupiter's bean, hog's-bean, hen-bell
plant family Solanaceae (nightshade family)
height up to 32 inches (80 cm)
habit hardy annual with toothed, downy, sticky leaves; bunches of cream-colored flowers with purple veins from spring to autumn
habitat full sun and poor, dry, sandy soil
all zones (annual)

Henbane's flower, with its lacy pattern that leads to the bell-shaped dark velvet center, has a macabre beauty. It has had a colorful past, from being used by oracles to divine the future to being a main ingredient in the "flying ointments" and "love-philtres" of medieval witches. Historically it also had more mundane medicinal uses, such as easing toothaches.

As with its relatives deadly nightshade and thorn apple, henbane contains the toxic alkaloids scopolamine and hyoscyamine.

Henbane *Hyoscyamus niger*

Henbane's greater proportion of scopolamine makes it more sedative in action. This effect was recognized as long ago as the first century AD when the physician Dioscorides administered it to induce sleep.

Henbane exerts its action by countering the parasympathetic nervous system; the effect is to relax smooth muscles, particularly those of the gastrointestinal tract.

Caution *Henbane is very toxic, with effects similar to those of deadly nightshade and thorn apple, and it should be used only under medical supervision. Do not handle the plant with bare hands, as the toxic compounds could be absorbed through cuts or scrapes.*

OPIUM POPPY *Papaver somniferum*
G C M H

other names white poppy, mawseed, breadseed poppy
plant family Papaveraceae (poppy family)
height up to 4 feet (1.2 m)
habit hardy annual with toothed, wavy-edged blue-green leaves up to 10 inches (25 cm) long; white or lilac flowers in summer, followed by rounded capsules containing tiny dark seeds
habitat full sun and average to rich, well-drained soil
all zones (annual)

Opium poppy *Papaver somniferum*

Castor oil plant *Ricinus communis*

The opium poppy is a colorful annual that is invaluable for the border, fast-growing and upright with showy, short-lived flowers available in different shades. The flowers are followed by attractive globe-shaped seed capsules. The flowers make a spectacular addition to fresh flower arrangements (the ends need to be seared to keep the petals from falling off). The seedpods can be used for dried arrangements. The ripe seeds are used for baking, sprinkled on bread, cake, and cookies.

The effectiveness of the alkaloids in opium poppies is well known: They have been used as painkillers in many cultures for thousands of years. Unfortunately, they are also addictive and have devastated millions of lives and caused many deaths. As a result, the processing, sale, and even cultivation of the opium poppy are banned in many countries. Plants grown in cool climates contain reduced quantities of the alkaloids. Poppy seeds used in baking are not narcotic; they have no medicinal action and do not pose a health risk.

The alkaloids are contained in the latex sap of the plant. Opium is the dried sap; when dissolved in alcohol, the resulting tincture is known as laudanum. Doctors administered both opium and laudanum for centuries. In 1803 chemists extracted morphine, the first alkaloid to be singled out from a plant. Extraction of codeine and other alkaloids followed. Both morphine and codeine are sedative and painkilling; codeine is still used in medications to overcome the cough reflex.

Caution *For legal as well as safety reasons, use of the opium poppy should take place only under medical supervision. Opium and its derivatives are poisonous as well as addictive; overdosage can cause death from heart and respiratory failure.*

CASTOR OIL PLANT *Ricinus communis*
G M

other names palma Christi, castor bean, castor oil bush, kik
plant family Euphorbiaceae (spurge family)
height up to 17 feet (5 m)
habit evergreen shrub usually grown as a half-hardy annual; large palm-shaped leaves with five to nine pointed lobes; clusters of small green flowers with yellow stamens in summer, followed by red seed capsules
habitat prefers full sun and well-drained soil
zones 8–10

The castor oil plant is a striking-looking plant with large, palmlike leaves. It is a popular fast-growing ornamental, usually grown as an annual. The luxuriant leaves of some varieties, such as 'Carmencita' or 'Impala', are dark purple in color, making the plant effective as a focal point or background.

The oil pressed from the seeds of this plant provided generations of people around the world with a laxative. Its action is attributed to a fatty acid (ricinoleic acid in its different forms). The oil works as an irritant to stimulate evacuation of the bowels about two to six hours after taking the dose. As early as Roman times, Pliny the Elder described castor oil as a drastic purgative. It is technically classified as a cathartic (a strong laxative).

Castor oil is still the main laxative used in many parts of the world, though now not so regularly in the United States or Europe. However, it is often used in hospitals to clean out the bowels before surgery or X-ray investigation, and in cases of poisoning. Although it has been given to children, this should be avoided as its action is not gentle. Try instead one of the numerous less aggressive herbal alternatives (see page 120).

What is truly remarkable is that although the oil has such widespread use, the rest of the plant is extremely poisonous because it contains the protein ricin. Even the seeds from which the oil is pressed are dangerously toxic: Just a few, if chewed, can kill an adult. Ricin shot to public prominence during the Cold War when, in 1978, Russian espionage agents killed a Bulgarian defector in a London Underground station by inserting a minute amount into his leg from the tip of an umbrella.

Caution *Do not handle the castor oil plant without protective gloves, as it can cause skin irritation. Keep children away from the plant, especially its seeds.*

RUE *Ruta graveolens*
G M
other names garden rue, herb-of-grace, herbygrass
plant family Rutaceae (rue family)
height up to 3½ feet (1 m)
habit hardy perennial with blue-green leaves

Rue *Ruta graveolens*

deeply cut into small, rounded lobes; small mustard yellow flowers in summer followed by attractive small seedpods
habitat full sun to partial shade and average, well-drained soil
zones 4–9
Rue is a beautiful plant. Today it is grown in herb gardens and flower borders, not for its herbal action but for its attractive foliage. The cultivar 'Jackman's Blue' is often planted for the blue tinge of its leaf. The foliage is perennial in mild climates.

Rue is toxic, yet its generic name *Ruta* derives from the Greek word *reuo,* meaning "to release," as it was thought to free people from disease. In Britain and other Roman outposts it was one of the earliest garden herbs introduced by the invaders.

It has long been a medicinal plant and had a role as a witch-deterrent, since disease and evil were often synonymous to the medieval mind. It was even used to sprinkle holy water at High Mass and so received the name herb-of-grace. It was also used to repel insects (particularly fleas), and to treat snakebite. Another historic use for rue was to stimulate menstruation (and to attempt to induce abortions) and help overcome menstrual cramps.

Rue can cause skin irritation in sensitive individuals. It contains compounds (especially psoralen and other furocoumarins) that can cause photosensitization after contact with the plant, resulting in redness or rashlike blistering after exposure to the sun.

Caution *Avoid internal use of this toxic herb; it can cause vomiting, depression, liver and kidney damage, delirium, loss of consciousness, spasms, and in extreme cases death. Wear gloves when handling rue or working near plants, and avoid planting it where it may be brushed against, to avoid possible skin irritation.*

BLOODROOT *Sanguinaria canadensis*
G M

other names Indian paint, red root, red puccoon
plant family Papaveraceae (poppy family)
height up to 10 inches (25 cm)
habit hardy perennial with large, deeply lobed, blue-green leaves on long stalks growing from its red-brown rhizome; white flowers in spring
habitat woodland plant; full sun to partial shade and moist, rich soil
zones 3–9

This North American wildflower is valued for its early spring flowers. The snow-white blooms are short-lived and appear before the leaves have fully opened. Its beautiful leaves remain attractive through the summer in places where soils are consistently moist; plants go dormant if the soil dries out. Bloodroot makes an attractive addition to shady rock gardens and garden woodland walks. A double-flowered form is available.

Both bloodroot's common name and its Latin genus name *Sanguinaria* refer to the blood-colored sap present in its stems and roots. This was used by Native Americans as a war paint, and as a dye to color basketry and clothing—hence its alternative name of Indian paint. Settlers used bloodroot as an expectorant to clear chest congestion. In the nineteenth century it began to be used as a mouthwash. Two of its alkaloids (chelerythrine and sanguinarine) have been found to counteract plaque formation and the gum disease gingivitis and to fight bad breath. It is still found in some mouthwashes and toothpastes today, but most herbalists advise against swallowing any toothpaste that contains bloodroot.

Caution *Bloodroot should not be taken internally. The alkaloids in the plant are dangerously narcotic: small doses cause vomiting; higher dosages cause intestinal colic, and may even lead to collapse and death.*

Bloodroot *Sanguinaria canadensis*

Sassafras *Sassafras albidum*

SASSAFRAS *Sassafras albidum*
G

other names fennel wood, ague tree, cinnamon wood
plant family Lauraceae (laurel family)
height up to 70 feet (20 m)
habit hardy tree with bright green, scented leaves usually with three lobes (may also be mitten-shaped or pointed ovals); clusters of yellow flowers in spring
habitat full sun to partial shade and average to poor, moist but well-drained soil
zones 5–9

Sassafras is a fast-growing tree, grown for its aromatic foliage and attractive fall color. It is particularly effective in naturalized plantings. As it does not transplant well from the wild, plant only container-grown trees.

Sassafras is the perfect example of why it matters to examine the constituents of an herb and not just to rely on traditional uses. It was once among the most popular herbal flavorings in the United States for such products as root beer and toothpaste. Native Americans used it and pointed out this spicy-smelling tree to settlers as a remedy tree. Extracts from the root bark were formerly used for lowering blood pressure in older people; for treating urinary tract infections, rheumatism, colds, and flu; and as a specific treatment for syphilis.

However, not only is there no scientific evidence for most of these uses, but also in the 1960s the main component of the oils (safrole) was found to cause cancer. Consequently, the U.S. Food and Drug Administration has banned the use of safrole in flavorings; it has also prohibited use of the essential oil and interstate marketing of the bark for tea.

Caution *Avoid internal use of the plant or its essential oil. The essential oil is very toxic and causes kidney damage: A few drops could kill a child; a very little more could kill an adult.*

TANSY *Tanacetum vulgare*
G H

other name golden-buttons
plant family Compositae (daisy family)
height up to 3½ feet (1 m)
habit hardy perennial with aromatic, finely cut leaves; clusters of small, buttonlike yellow flowers in summer and fall
habitat full sun to light shade and well-drained soil
zones 4–8

Tansy is a vigorous spreader and therefore as a garden plant it needs controlling. *Tanacetum vulgare* var. *crispum* is a better garden plant, being less pungently scented and more compact, with decorative, fernlike leaves. Tansy has yellow, buttonlike flowers that retain their color well when dried, and are useful in dried herb displays and for adding color to potpourri. Sprigs of dried leaves can be used to deter ants or mice; the dried leaves can also be used in sachets as an insect repellent.

The gardener Thomas Tusser recorded that in the sixteenth century tansy was a popular strewing herb. The thujone, sesquiterpene

Tansy *Tanacetum vulgare*

lactones, and pyrethrins that help protect the plant from insect attack in the garden made it useful for controlling fleas in a trampled rush floor. It was used externally to control scabies and lice, and internally to kill intestinal worms. It was also used to relieve pain and to induce menstruation.

Caution *Tansy is toxic because of the high thujone content of its volatile oil. Poisoning proceeds very rapidly, causing vomiting, spasms, uterine bleeding, and kidney, liver, and heart damage; death can occur in only a few hours. Even for external use there are doubts about its safety, including a dermatitis risk. It should therefore be used only in moderation. It should not be used in aromatherapy. In some countries there are legal controls on the sale of the oil from tansy, and in others on the sale of the herb for medicines or food.*

ENGLISH YEW *Taxus baccata*
PACIFIC YEW *Taxus brevifolia*
G M

plant family Taxaceae (yew family)
height *Taxus baccata:* up to 80 feet (25 m); *T. brevifolia*: up to 65 feet (20 m)
habit *T. baccata:* hardy tree with short, dark green, shiny evergreen needles; pale yellow, small male and smaller female flowers on separate trees in spring followed by red fruits; *T. brevifolia:* hardy tree with slender, drooping branches, and leathery evergreen needles; pale yellow, small male and smaller female flowers on separate trees in spring, followed by green-brown seeds
habitat full sun to shade and rich, moist but well-drained soil
zones 6–7

English yew grows more slowly than other conifers but makes an ideal plant for hedges and topiary, as it responds to clipping by developing dense, fine-textured surfaces. The many ornamental cultivars include *Taxus baccata* 'Fastigiata', Irish yew (*T. baccata* 'Stricta'), and Aurea Group (syn. *T. baccata*

'Aurea'), which has golden yellow foliage. Pacific yew is smaller, with slender, drooping branches, scaly, red-purple bark and leathery leaves.

The Druids considered the yew to be immortal; since it is resistant to most pests and diseases, it nearly is. It is certainly one of the longest lived of trees, sometimes reaching ages of thousands of years. In Europe churches were often built beside already-old yews. In the past, herbalists used decoctions of yew leaves to kill tapeworms and to treat epilepsy, diphtheria, tonsillitis, rheumatic complaints, and menstrual problems. This was a dangerous practice because yew is extremely toxic.

However, modern medicine has put this plant to good use. The bark of the Pacific yew, and, to a lesser extent, the leaves and twigs of English yew, have emerged as the source of some of the most promising anticancer drugs to have been found in recent years. These drugs, paclitaxel (trade name Taxol) and docetaxel (trade name Taxotere), are used for the treatment of advanced ovarian cancer and advanced breast cancer, especially when standard treatment has failed.

The yew may yet yield more surprises. It has been found to contain ecdysterone, an insect hormone that controls molting. This compound may help protect the tree from insect attack and may find a role as an insecticide.

Caution *Avoid ingesting yew, and warn children to stay away from it (especially the berries). Yew is very toxic, causing heart failure and asphyxiation.*

English yew *Taxus baccata*   Pacific yew *Taxus brevifolia*

Herbs
for
Healthy
Eating

Why do we use herbs in food? In the past, some herbs—such as garlic—acted as preservatives as well as giving flavor. This double duty was useful in the days before refrigeration. Today the main reason for using herbs is to provide flavor that enhances food. Herbs also supply small amounts of vitamins and minerals for healthy eating, and some aid digestion. It is important to remember that not all plants classified as herbs are edible; some are even deadly poisonous (see pages 104–113).

CULINARY HERBS

A few culinary herbs are used all the time, others just occasionally. Some of the star performers are:

basil	garlic	parsley
bay	ginger	(curly and
celery	lemon balm	flat-leaf)
chervil	lemon basil	rosemary
chives	lemon thyme	sage
coriander	purple basil	spearmint
creeping	sweet	summer and
thyme	marjoram	winter savory
dill	onions	tarragon
fennel	oregano	thyme

Herbs occasionally used in cooking include:

angelica	eau de	lavender
anise	Cologne mint	licorice
apple mint	ginger mint	peppermint
bee balm	horseradish	rose
calendula	hyssop	sorrel

In addition to the culinary herbs listed below left, other herbs that are used as food rather than seasoning include greens of chickweed and dandelion (raw or cooked), stinging nettle greens (these lose their sting when cooked), elderberry flowers and berries, flax seeds, nasturtium flowers and immature seed pods, and wild strawberries. Chicory leaves, sometimes called endive, are eaten in salads. Roots of dandelion and chicory are sometimes roasted and brewed as a coffee-like beverage. Marshmallow, whose roots were made into the original marshmallow candy, also has edible shoots and roots.

Choosing a range of herbs assures a variety of textures and tastes that are pleasing to the eye as well as the palate. Celery is crisp and crunchy; feathery dill looks irresistibly light and fresh; purple-leaved forms of basil or sage add dramatic color as well as flavor to foods. Many herbs contribute an enticing fragrance. The distinctive scents of French tarragon, lemon balm, and the mints are good examples. Their delicious smells (produced by volatile oils in the herbs) do more than make food appetizing. They can actually improve digestion, because they initiate an anticipatory flow of digestive juices before a mouthful is eaten. Herbs can brighten a jaded palate, and stimulate appetite in invalids.

Herbs often bring a dish to life and boost the experience of eating. Strong herbs contrast nicely with bland staples. Sage works wonders on roasted potatoes, spearmint on bulgur, basil on mozzarella. When tart sorrel or pungent nasturtium is included in a salad, you do not need to use as much vinegar in a vinaigrette. The strong, sweet flavor of basil is so effective that a plain tomato salad needs no other herb accompaniment. Lemon balm brings a zingy freshness to a salad of early summer leaves.

Herbs are not just for taste, but also for health. Those who must cut back their use of salt will find that strong herb flavors can take its place as a flavor enhancer. For example, garlic

Flat-leaf parsley

Eau de Cologne mints

Rosemary

Chives

Garlic

Coriander

Oregano

Coriander

Thyme

Purple basil

Fennel

Tarragon

Apple mint

Creeping thyme

Spearmint

Bay

Purple sage

Sage

117

crushed into a salad dressing makes a delicious replacement for salt (see page 42 for other health benefits of garlic). If you do not like the smell of garlic on your breath, try chewing leaves of parsley or cilantro to cleanse your palate. Some herbs are rich in vitamins, though the amounts used for seasoning contribute only minute quantities. Parsley contains significant amounts of calcium, vitamin C, and vitamin A precursor (beta-carotene). (But parsley comes with a caution: If you are pregnant or trying to become pregnant, it is inadvisable to eat large quantities.) Sorrel also contains vitamin C. One of the best sources of vitamin A is dandelion; a handful of fresh leaves is sufficient to meet the daily dietary recommendation for an adult. The vitamin content of herbs is at its greatest when they are used fresh and raw, as in a salad, or added at the last minute. Cooking destroys much of the vitamin C.

Some herbs have a slightly bitter quality. As well as providing a further taste contrast, this aids digestion by stimulating the flow of bile from the gall bladder, important for digesting fats. Including chicory or its relatives Belgian and curly endive in a salad is therefore a smart as well as a tasty practice at the beginning of a rich dinner. Similarly, the slightly bitter volatile oils in sage also stimulate the flow of bile, and this makes sage an ideal accompaniment to fattier meats such as pork, goose, or duck. A number of herbs, including caraway and peppermint, contain volatile oils that help to calm the digestive tract.

PREPARING HERBS

If you grow your own herbs organically and they appear free from dirt, there is no need to wash them before use, and this helps greatly in preserving their freshness and crispness. If herbs are store-bought, wash them whole, shake off as much water as possible, and dry gently with kitchen towels before chopping. Time permitting, it helps to wash the sprigs in advance so that they can air-dry for a while after toweling.

Using a mezzaluna is an efficient way of rapidly mincing herbs such as cilantro (shown here) or parsley.

Use herbs as fresh as possible. It is not worth even trying to store basil, as it turns black so quickly. However, if parsley or cilantro must be stored for a day or two, trim the stalks and stand them in water in the refrigerator, covering the top loosely with a plastic bag so air can circulate. Chives can be kept in a loose plastic bag. Woody herbs like rosemary and thyme will last slightly longer and may be stored in an unsealed plastic bag in the refrigerator or in a jar of water at room temperature.

Chives and herbs with tender stems (such as cilantro) can be snipped easily with scissors. For herbs with woody or tough stems, pull off leaves before chopping. Herbs can be chopped in a food processor, but a practiced cook will find a good-quality chef's knife as quick as anything else for cutting up herbs. An all-purpose knife with an 8-inch (20-cm) blade works well. Keep the tip of the knife on the board and rock the handle up and down while moving the blade across the herbs. Or use a mezzaluna (see photo above), a half-moon curved blade with two handles that is used by working it in a rocking action in a slightly dished wooden bowl.

The recipes on the following pages illustrate some of the many ways to use herbs. Use them to expand your repertoire of culinary herbs, or as a basis for experimentation. All recipes serve four, unless otherwise stated. Unless dried herbs are specified, all herbs should be fresh.

Classic seasoning mixtures

FINES HERBES

Fines herbes means "fine herbs," or herb leaves chopped finely. The constants in this classic French seasoning mix are chervil, chives, and parsley. To these the cook can add a variety of other herbs, according to taste. Tarragon and thyme are the most common additions. Other possibilities include fennel leaves, marjoram, or summer savory, or you might like to try watercress *(Nasturtium officinale)*.

A classic dish with *fines herbes* is a simple omelet; use a tablespoon of finely chopped herbs for every two large eggs. *Fines herbes* may also be stirred into sauces or mayonnaise accompanying fish, or sprinkled on steamed vegetables such as green beans or carrots.

BOUQUET GARNI

A *bouquet garni* (literally, "garnished bouquet") is a small bundle of fresh or dried herbs, usually consisting of two or three parsley stems tied to a sprig of thyme and a bay leaf. Sometimes a sprig of sweet marjoram is added, or rosemary for a lamb dish. Dunk the bundle under the cooking liquid of stews or beans (and remove before serving) to infuse them with memories of summer and impart a degree of sophisticated flavor to blander meals. For a stronger-tasting *bouquet garni,* use the root of a parsley plant that has gone to seed in its second year, instead of the parsley stems. Dried *bouquets garnis* can also be tossed onto the barbecue fire to flavor grilled food (and to scent the air).

HERBES DE PROVENCE

Herbes de Provence is a mingling of dried herbs from the sun-baked hillsides of southern France, where the hot, dry climate ensures that the herbs will be strongly flavored. In addition to the common cooking herbs marjoram, rosemary, and thyme, the *herbes de Provence* mixture includes summer savory and lavender flowers. Sometimes fennel seeds and basil are also added. It is the dried lavender flowers that make the mix so distinctive. To make your own, combine equal proportions of the above herbs. This seasoning blend is traditionally sprinkled on chicken, lamb, pork, or fish before grilling; it also makes a good addition to a pasta sauce.

LEFT *Bouquets garnis* wrapped in cheesecloth, alongside ingredients.

LEFT BELOW The *herbes de Provence* seasoning mixture.

BELOW Roast pork with *herbes de Provence* (see page 134).

Herb-flavored oils and vinegars

Herbs added to oils or vinegars infuse them with their flavors; these flavors in turn are imparted to any dish made with the herbed oil or vinegar. Making a vinaigrette with such oils and vinegars brings a greater depth of flavors to a salad. Herb vinegars also offer convenience. They are handy for supplying the flavor of fresh herbs in the middle of the winter, and for adding herb flavors to salads and similar foods without any chopping. Flavored vinegars can also be used in pickling. The addition of spices such as dried chile peppers, plus celery, coriander, fennel, mustard, and other seeds adds visually as well as to the taste.

The acidity of vinegars helps to preserve them, so there is no need to worry about herbal vinegars spoiling, but it is possible that harmful organisms may develop in herbal oils. Extremely rarely, deaths have resulted from consuming herb-infused oils kept in warm conditions for prolonged periods. In herbal oils that are commercially bottled, this risk is removed by acidification of the oil.

Acidification can be done at home by putting a small amount of vinegar into the oil (2 or 3 parts vinegar to 100 parts oil) and shaking, before adding the herbs. The concoction initially emulsifies but, after the flavored oil is allowed to sit, it will clear. Keep herbal oils without acidification at room temperature for only a couple of days, and with refrigeration for no longer than a week.

HERB-FLAVORED OIL

Herbs that infuse oil well include thyme, basil, chervil, fennel (leaves and seeds), dill (leaves and seeds), rosemary, and marjoram. Adding garlic cloves produces a great flavor—even stronger if you crush the cloves lightly before adding them to the oil.

making herb-flavored oil

Clean, attractive bottle with stopper
Extra-virgin olive oil to nearly fill chosen bottle
1 to 4 sprigs chosen herbs
1 to 4 garlic cloves, crushed lightly
1 to 5 dried chile peppers (wear gloves when handling; chiles burn)
Small handful spice seeds

Pour the oil into the bottle. Add herb sprigs, garlic cloves, chiles, and spice seeds, to taste. Screw on a lid or cork the bottle. Use within a couple of days.

HERB-FLAVORED VINEGAR

Many herbs combine well with vinegar, adding a delicious flavor. Tarragon is the one most commonly used, but bay, thyme, fennel (leaves and seeds), dill (leaves and seeds), rosemary, basil, and marjoram are also good. Blueberries, cranberries, and elderberries will add color, as well as flavor, to red- or white-wine vinegar.

Putting bottles of vinegar containing herbs and spices on a sunny windowsill or outside in the sun for the first month after bottling will bring out more of the flavors. However, be aware that most herbs will turn pale and look less lively if left in bright light too long.

making herb-flavored vinegar

Clean, attractive bottle with stopper
White- or red-wine vinegar to nearly fill chosen bottle
1 to 4 sprigs chosen herb
1 to 3 garlic cloves, crushed lightly
Small handful spice seeds

Pour the vinegar into the bottle. Add herb sprigs, garlic, and spices, to taste. Alternatively, if you prefer a stronger flavor, you can pour warm—not boiling—vinegar over the herbs first, then funnel all into the bottle. Screw on a plastic cap or cork the bottle. Do not use a bottle with a metal cap, as the vinegar will react against it and turn black.

Olive oil with garlic
and thyme

Cranberries in
red-wine vinegar

Olive oil
with chiles

Bay leaves in
white-wine vinegar

Tarragon in white-
wine vinegar

VINAIGRETTE

In this recipe, alternatives to white-wine vinegar include red-wine vinegar, herb-flavored vinegars (see opposite), and balsamic vinegar. The olive oil can also be herb-flavored (see opposite). If the salad leaves are particularly tender and sweet, the proportion of olive oil to vinegar may be increased to 4 or 5 to 1. A basic vinaigrette can be made into a flavor-filled herbal vinaigrette by adding a handful of minced basil, chervil, cilantro, or other herbs.

Tearing, rather than cutting, the leaves of lettuce and other salad greens preserves the plant cells and thus more of the vitamin C content. Tossing the leaves with dressing right after tearing seals the leaves and further reduces vitamin loss. Dress the salad just before eating. If it is allowed to stand too long, the vinegar will wilt the leaves.

vinaigrette

1 garlic clove, crushed
1 tablespoon white-wine vinegar
3 tablespoons extra-virgin olive oil
Salt and fresh-ground black pepper, to taste

Add the garlic to the vinegar. Stir or whisk in the oil. Season with salt and pepper.

Dressings and sauces

Herbs can be blended with butter, plain yogurt, sour cream, or mayonnaise to make dressings and sauces for hot or cold food. Apart from the herb butter, which can be frozen, these sauces do not keep long but are quick to make.

herb butter

Herb butter makes an easy herb dressing for hot foods; the butter spreads the herbs as it melts. Choose herbs to match the food. Cilantro, chervil, thyme, chives, and parsley, individually, or in combinations, go well with grilled foods (especially corn-on-the-cob) or steamed vegetables. The butter must be very soft—but not melted—to start with or it will be difficult to mash in the herbs.
Makes about ¾ cup (175 g)

½ cup (1 stick, 113 g) unsalted butter, softened
1½ tablespoons snipped chives
1½ tablespoons minced parsley leaves
¾ tablespoon minced tarragon leaves
¾ teaspoon Dijon mustard
Salt and fresh-ground black pepper, to taste

In a small bowl cream together the butter, chives, parsley, tarragon, mustard, salt, and pepper. Let the mixture stand, covered, in a cool place for 1 hour or a little longer to allow the flavors to develop.

Serve immediately or roll into a log shape in wax paper and store for up to 4 days in the refrigerator. It also freezes well.

Serve the butter, a teaspoonful per portion, or to taste, with seafood, chicken, or meat.

herb mayonnaise

This makes an excellent dip for sticks of raw vegetables, also a good sauce for cold foods.
Makes about 1½ cups (340 ml)

Grilled corn-on-the-cob dressed with herb butter, and garnished with cilantro sprigs and lemon slices.

1 cup (225 ml) mayonnaise
¼ cup (13 g) snipped chives
½ cup (25 g) minced parsley leaves
1 tablespoon minced tarragon leaves

Combine herbs and mayonnaise in a small bowl. Chill in the refrigerator for at least 1 hour to allow the flavors to develop. It can be stored in the refrigerator for up to 4 days.

cilantro and mint sauce with almonds

Excellent with beef, chicken, fish, or cooked grains such as rice or bulgur.
Makes about 1 cup (225 ml)

½ cup (50 g) sliced almonds
1 cup packed (50 g) mint leaves
1 cup packed (50 g) cilantro sprigs
4 tablespoons sour cream
1 tablespoon honey
1 large garlic clove, coarsely chopped
Salt and fresh-ground black pepper, to taste

Dry roast the almonds in one layer in a small heavy skillet over medium heat, shaking frequently, until they are golden (about 4 minutes). Cool and grind finely in a food processor. Add the remaining ingredients and blend well.

sorrel sauce

The piquant flavor of sorrel sauce makes it a great accompaniment to fish, especially rich-tasting fish such as salmon. It is also good with white meat or bland vegetables such as potatoes. Makes about 1 cup (225 ml)

8 ounces (225 g) sorrel leaves
2 ounces (56 g) butter
½ cup (110 ml) heavy cream

Wash and drain the sorrel leaves, and chop them finely. Melt the butter in a medium saucepan over low heat. Add the sorrel and stir from time to time until it is melted to a puree (this may take 10 to 20 minutes, depending on the age of the leaves).

Remove the pan from the heat. Using a wooden spoon, force the puree, a little at a time, through a fine-meshed sieve. Discard any fibers left in the sieve. Put the sieved puree in a clean pan and return to a low heat. Stir in the cream. If necessary, you can store it in the refrigerator for a day or two. Reheat gently before serving.

spicy parsley sauce

Serve with grilled steak or hearty fish.
Makes about 2 cups (450 ml)

4 cups packed (200 g) flat-leaf parsley leaves
5 large garlic cloves, coarsely chopped
¾ cup (170 ml) extra-virgin olive oil
½ cup (110 ml) distilled white vinegar
½ teaspoon dried hot red pepper flakes

Blend the ingredients in a food processor. This sauce will keep up to a week in the refrigerator.

Tangy sorrel sauce complements poached salmon.

Pestos

"Pesto" comes from the Italian verb *pestare*, meaning to pound or grind. We have the cooks of Genoa to thank for this wonderful herb sauce. It is strictly made by pounding herbs in a mortar with a pestle, but these days a food processor or blender makes the job much less labor-intensive. Pesto is made from herbs mixed with garlic, nuts, olive oil, and often cheese. Classic pesto uses basil, but other herbs can be substituted. Although classic pesto calls for pine nuts, you can use other nuts such as the walnuts or pecans in the two recipes presented here. Use extra-virgin olive oil if possible. Parmesan cheese should be freshly grated; 1 cup grated Parmesan weighs about 3 ounces (80 g). Pesto is generally used as a sauce for pasta. This recipe makes enough for 1 pound (450 g) of pasta, which will serve three or four people. If the pesto is too thick, dilute with a tablespoon or two of the water the pasta was cooked in. It can also be used to season vegetables, rice, or grilled or broiled poultry, meat, or fish.

Cover the surface of the pesto as soon as it is made to prevent darkening. Plastic wrap is sufficient for a short time. A thin layer of olive oil—which is poured over the top and stirred into the pesto before serving—will preserve its color over a longer period. Pesto will keep in the refrigerator for up to a week.

basil pesto
Makes about 1½ cups (340 ml)

2 cups packed (100 g) basil leaves
4 medium garlic cloves, coarsely chopped
1 cup (125 g) shelled walnuts
1 cup (225 ml) extra-virgin olive oil
1 cup (80 g) freshly grated Parmesan cheese
¼ cup (20 g) freshly grated Romano cheese
Salt and fresh-ground black pepper, to taste

Puree the basil, garlic, and nuts in a food processor—or pound them using a mortar and pestle—to a coarse paste. Pour in the oil in a thin stream, keeping the machine running, or stirring as you go. Add the cheeses, salt, and pepper. Stir or process briefly to combine.

basil and pecan pesto
Makes about 1½ cups (340 ml)

2 large garlic cloves
½ teaspoon salt
2 cups packed (100 g) basil leaves
⅔ cup (150 ml) extra-virgin olive oil
½ cup (50 g) pecans
⅓ cup (25 g) freshly grated Parmesan cheese
Fresh-ground black pepper, to taste

Process all the ingredients until well blended.

cilantro and lime pesto
Makes about 1½ cups (340 ml)

2 cups packed (100 g) cilantro sprigs
1 cup packed (50 g) flat-leaf parsley leaves
½ cup (50 g) walnuts
⅔ cup (150 ml) extra-virgin olive oil
⅓ cup (25 g) freshly grated Romano cheese
½ teaspoon freshly grated lime zest
Salt and fresh-ground black pepper, to taste

Process all the ingredients until well blended.

Pounding basil, garlic, and pine nuts with a mortar and pestle.

dill and lemon pesto

Makes about 1½ cups (340 ml)

3 slices firm-textured white bread
1 large lemon
¾ cup packed (40 g) dill leaves
¾ cup packed (40 g) parsley leaves
2 teaspoons Dijon mustard
¼ teaspoon sugar, or to taste
½ cup (56 ml) extra-virgin olive oil
Salt and fresh-ground black pepper, to taste

Soak the bread in a small bowl with 3 tablespoons lemon juice and 3 tablespoons water for 5 minutes. Grate ½ teaspoon lemon zest. Squeeze any excess liquid from the bread and discard; place the bread in a food processor with the lemon zest and remaining ingredients, and blend well.

mint pesto

Makes about 1½ cups (340 ml)

⅓ cup (40 g) pine nuts
6 garlic cloves, coarsely chopped
3 cups (150 g) mint leaves
1 cup (225 ml) extra-virgin olive oil
2 tablespoons fresh lemon juice
Salt and fresh-ground black pepper, to taste

Process the pine nuts and garlic, or pound in a mortar. Add the mint leaves and process until a paste is formed. Pour in the oil in a thin stream, keeping the machine running, or stirring as you go. Add the lemon juice, salt, and pepper and blend thoroughly.

Penne, or any other form of pasta, is delicious served simply with basil pesto, olives, and a sprinkling of Parmesan cheese.

mint and ginger pesto
Makes about 1½ cups (340 ml)

2½ cups packed (125 g) mint leaves
1½ tablespoons peeled and grated
 fresh ginger
⅓ cup (40 g) roasted salted cashews
½ cup (110 ml) extra-virgin olive oil
1 large garlic clove, coarsely chopped
¼ teaspoon sugar
Salt and fresh-ground black pepper, to taste

Process all the ingredients together until they
are well blended.

Pizza with herb pesto and goat cheese (see page 133).

mixed herb pesto
Makes about 1½ cups (340 ml)

2 cups packed (100 g) flat-leaf parsley leaves
1 cup packed (50 g) basil leaves
2 tablespoons packed thyme leaves
2 tablespoons packed rosemary leaves
2 tablespoons packed tarragon leaves
1 cup (80 g) freshly grated Parmesan cheese
⅔ cup (150 ml) extra-virgin olive oil
½ cup (50 g) walnuts
2 tablespoons balsamic vinegar
Salt and fresh-ground black pepper, to taste

Process all the ingredients together until they
are well blended.

Dips and spreads

The easiest spread is just cottage cheese, goat cheese, or cream cheese mashed with a good sprinkling of minced herbs such as basil, chives, chervil, cilantro, or parsley. Proportions of 2 tablespoons of herbs to 8 ounces (225 g) of cheese make a good starting point, but vary them according to your taste. The mixture can be served with vegetable sticks of carrots, celery, and peppers; to serve with crackers, roll into a log shape in wax paper and then roll again in minced herbs. For a special effect, wrap the cheese spread into rolls in nasturtium leaves and garnish with nasturtium flowers.

Baked potato with cottage cheese and chives.

garlic, white bean, and sun-dried tomato salsa

Do not be alarmed by the amount of garlic in this recipe. The baking mellows its strong flavor to a creamy taste. If you do not have the other ingredients to make the dip, the baked garlic alone, squeezed on to French bread, is delicious. Serve with French bread or pita wedges.
Makes about 3 cups (675 ml)

1 head garlic, loose, papery outer skin removed
1 large lemon
1 can (15 ounces, 425g) cannellini or navy
  beans, well rinsed and drained
1 small jar (5 ounces, 140g) sun-dried tomatoes
  in oil, drained and chopped
1 tablespoon minced anchovy fillet
2 tablespoons pitted and sliced Niçoise or
  Kalamata olives
3 scallions, sliced finely
4 tablespoons minced flat-leaf parsley leaves
¾ teaspoon cayenne powder
2 tablespoons extra-virgin olive oil
½ teaspoon salt

Preheat the oven to 375°F (190°C). Wrap the garlic head in foil, sealing the edges. Roast until soft (about 1¼ hours). Cool slightly and peel each clove. Mash with a fork until smooth. Grate 2 teaspoons zest from the lemon and squeeze 2 tablespoons lemon juice. Place all the ingredients, except 1 tablespoon parsley, in a large mixing bowl and stir gently to combine. Transfer to a serving bowl and garnish with the remaining tablespoon of parsley.

tomatillo and avocado dip

A dip with a Latin flavor. Cilantro, used liberally in Mexican cuisine, is an acquired taste for some, but it adds excitement to dishes. Serve with tortilla chips.
Makes about 2 cups (450 ml)

1 pound (450 g) tomatillos (about 15),
  husked and rinsed
1 avocado, peeled and pitted
1 serrano chile (wear gloves when handling;
  chiles burn)
¾ cup packed (40 g) cilantro sprigs
1 tablespoon lime juice
1 teaspoon salt

Coarsely chop the tomatillos. Cut the avocado into pieces. Trim but do not seed the chile. Put all the ingredients into a food processor or blender and process until smooth.

Salads

Herbs are commonly used in salads to embellish a mixture of other leaves or vegetables, as in the recipes below. However, if wild "weeds" and other herbs not normally grown commercially are used, herbs can compose an entire salad.

salad of unusual herbs with basil croutons

Some of the herbs in this recipe cannot be bought in stores. Scout farmers' markets for them or grow them in your garden. If you do not have nasturtiums in your garden, watercress (*Nasturtium officinale*) can be substituted for the nasturtium leaves, as their flavors are somewhat similar. If you cannot find good-King-Henry, you can substitute lamb's-quarters (*Chenopodium album*), a common garden weed with a mild, almost nutty flavor. It is easy to recognize, with gray-green leaves that are almost diamond-shaped and roughly toothed; the undersides of the leaves have a whitish, mealy coating. Like good-King-Henry, it is a wild relative of spinach and can be eaten raw or cooked. The mildly sweet dressing used here sets off the sharp flavors of the arugula, dandelion, and sorrel.

For the croutons
¾ cup packed (40 g) basil leaves
3 tablespoons extra-virgin olive oil
4 thick slices firm-textured white bread
Salt and fresh-ground black pepper, to taste

For the dressing
1 tablespoon raspberry vinegar
¼ teaspoon sugar
Salt and fresh-ground black pepper, to taste
3 tablespoons extra-virgin olive oil

For the salad
1 cup (50 g) nasturtium leaves
1 cup (50 g) arugula leaves
½ cup (25 g) young dandelion leaves
½ cup (25 g) sorrel leaves
½ cup (25 g) good-King-Henry
1 head Boston lettuce, trimmed
2 tablespoons parsley
4 or 5 sprigs chickweed with flowers
4 or 5 nasturtium flowers
4 calendula flowers, petals only
Handful of black or green grapes (optional)

Make the croutons Preheat the oven to 350°F (190°C). Puree the basil and oil in a blender and season with salt and pepper. Cut the bread into ½-inch (15-mm) cubes and toss with the basil oil. Place in a single layer on a baking sheet and bake, shaking the sheet occasionally, until golden (10 to 15 minutes). Lightly season the croutons with salt and pepper.
Make the dressing In a large serving bowl whisk together the vinegar, sugar, 2 teaspoons water, salt, and pepper. Add the oil in a stream, whisking, until the dressing is emulsified.
Complete the salad Add the leaves to the bowl. Toss the salad well and garnish with the flowers, petals, grapes, and croutons.

herbed salad

1 small red onion
1 medium head romaine
1 small head frisée or curly endive
1 small head radicchio
4 medium carrots, peeled and grated
1 garlic clove, minced
⅔ cup packed (35 g) basil leaves, minced
¼ cup packed (15 g) flat-leaf parsley leaves, minced
3 tablespoons mixed herb leaves (such as thyme, dill, marjoram, or summer savory), minced
3 tablespoons white-wine vinegar
½ cup (110 ml) extra-virgin olive oil
Salt and fresh-ground black pepper
4-ounce (112-g) piece Parmesan cheese, shaved into slivers (optional)

A salad of unusual herbs: follow the recipe on the left, or experiment with your own combination of flavors.

Different herbs contribute their own flavors to a colorful mixture of tomatoes and yellow peppers.

Cut the onion in half lengthwise. Slice thinly crosswise and soak in salted ice water at least 15 minutes. Drain well.

Discard the coarse outer leaves of the salad greens. Tear the greens into bite-size pieces. Toss with the grated carrots and onion slices.

Mix the garlic and herbs. Add the vinegar, salt, and pepper. Whisk in the oil until it is well blended. Toss the salad with the dressing. Serve topped with slivers of Parmesan cheese.

tomatoes and yellow peppers with herbs

2 limes
½ teaspoon sugar
½ teaspoon salt
Fresh-ground black pepper, to taste
6 tablespoons extra-virgin olive oil
4 large ripe tomatoes
2 yellow peppers
½ bulb fennel
¾ cup packed (40 g) cilantro leaves, minced
¾ cup packed (40 g) flat-leaf parsley leaves, minced
⅓ cup (15 g) mint leaves, minced
3 scallions, finely sliced

Squeeze the limes. Into 3 tablespoons lime juice, stir the sugar, salt, and pepper. Whisk in the oil to make a dressing.

Slice the tomatoes and arrange on a platter. Cut the tops off the peppers, seed, and slice lengthwise. Arrange over the tomatoes. Remove the tough outer leaves of the fennel and slice into slivers. Scatter over the platter.

Drizzle 6 tablespoons of dressing over the salad. Mix the herbs and the scallions lightly with the remaining dressing and then mound on top of the salad.

Soups

stinging nettle soup

It may be hard to believe that something that stings as viciously as nettles could be edible, yet the plants lose their sting as soon as they are cooked. Stinging nettles are rich sources of several vitamins and minerals, including calcium. Nettles become tough and unpalatable as they get older so pick the greens before midsummer, wearing gloves, and take only the top few leaves. If a nettle bed is cut back to the ground, new tender stems will grow up and the young leaves can be used.

Stinging nettle soup garnished with a drizzle of light cream.

Large saucepan full of stinging nettle tops
   (about 1 pound, 450 g)
3 tablespoons unsalted butter or oil
3½ tablespoons all-purpose flour
4 cups (1 liter) vegetable broth or to taste
⅔ cup (150 ml) light cream (optional)
Salt and fresh-ground black pepper, to taste

Wearing rubber gloves, wash the stinging nettles, and drain. Cook the wet leaves down, without adding water, in a saucepan with a close-fitting lid over medium-low heat for 10 to 15 minutes. Drain off any liquid and add it to the broth. Bring the broth to a simmer. Coarsely chop the cooked greens.

Make a roux with the butter and flour, by melting the butter in a saucepan and stirring in the flour. Cook the roux for 2 minutes, then gradually stir in the hot broth; continue stirring until it reaches a sauce consistency. Season to taste. Mix in the cooked nettles, cool slightly, and liquefy in a blender or food processor. Thin to the desired consistency with more hot broth or cream, reserving some cream to drizzle on top of each serving as a garnish.

cucumber soup with mint

3 cucumbers
1 cup (225 g) plain low-fat yogurt
⅔ cup (150 g) sour cream
½ teaspoon mustard powder, or to taste
½ cup (25 g) mint leaves
Salt and fresh-ground black pepper, to taste
Cucumber slices and mint sprigs for garnish

Peel and seed the cucumbers. Finely dice half a cucumber and reserve. Coarsely chop the remaining cucumbers. In a blender puree the cucumber chunks, yogurt, sour cream, mustard, 1 tablespoon mint, salt, and pepper. Transfer to a serving bowl. Chill the soup at least 6 hours or overnight.

Mince the remaining mint leaves and stir into the soup with diced cucumber. Garnish the soup with cucumber slices and mint sprigs just before serving.

vegetable soup with fresh herbs

This is a variation on the classic Provençal *soupe au pistou*. The addition of the garlic-basil paste at the last minute transforms the taste.

3 large garlic cloves
1 cup packed (50 g) basil leaves
⅓ cup plus 2 tablespoons (100 ml) extra-virgin olive oil
⅓ cup (25 g) freshly grated Parmesan cheese
2 ounces (50 g) pancetta or unsmoked bacon, chopped (optional)
1 large onion, chopped

1 small fennel bulb, trimmed and cut into bite-size pieces
3 medium carrots, cut into chunks
¼ small head cabbage, cored and chopped
1 pound (450 g) plum tomatoes, coarsely chopped
5 sprigs flat-leaf parsley
2 sprigs thyme
1 bay leaf
3 cups (675 ml) chicken broth
1 can (15 ounces, 425 g) cannellini or navy beans, rinsed and drained
½ pound (225 g) green beans, ends trimmed, sliced
2 zucchini, ends trimmed, quartered lengthwise, then sliced
¼ pound (112 g) young dandelion leaves or baby spinach leaves, trimmed and washed
Salt and fresh-ground black pepper

Mash the garlic to a paste with ½ teaspoon salt. Put the garlic paste in a food processor, add the basil and blend until they are well combined. Scrape down the sides and, with the motor running, add ⅓ cup (75 ml) oil in a thin stream. Add the Parmesan and mix well. Season with pepper, to taste. Transfer to a small bowl and set aside.

In a large saucepan, heat 2 tablespoons oil over medium heat and add the pancetta. Cook 2 minutes before adding the onion. Cook 5 minutes, stirring occasionally, then add the fennel, carrots, and cabbage. Cook 5 minutes longer, stirring occasionally. Add the tomatoes, parsley and thyme sprigs, bay leaf, and broth, topping up with enough water to just cover the vegetables. Bring almost to a boil and simmer, uncovered, 15 minutes. Add the white beans, green beans, and zucchini and simmer until all are tender (about 5 minutes).

Discard the parsley and thyme sprigs and bay leaf. Tear the dandelion or spinach into bite-size pieces. Stir into the soup and season with salt and pepper, to taste. When you serve the soup, garnish each bowl with a spoonful of the basil-garlic paste.

Main courses

basil risotto

¼ cup packed (13 g) sage leaves, minced
2½ cups packed (125 g) basil leaves, minced
½ cup (40 g) freshly grated Parmesan cheese
5½ cups (1.2 liters) chicken broth
⅓ cup (75 ml) extra-virgin olive oil
2 medium onions, finely chopped
1½ cups (300 g) Arborio rice
¼ cup (56 ml) dry white wine
Salt and fresh-ground black pepper, to taste

Combine the sage and all but 2 tablespoons of the basil with the Parmesan and set aside. Bring the broth to a boil in a saucepan; reduce the heat and keep it at a bare simmer.

In a large heavy-bottomed skillet heat ¼ cup (56 ml) oil over medium-low heat and cook the onions, stirring occasionally, until softened but not browned (about 10 minutes). Increase the heat to medium and add the rice, stirring to coat it with the oil and onions. Add the wine and stir until absorbed. Stir in 1 cup (225 ml) of the hot broth and stir until absorbed. Keeping the mixture at a brisk simmer, continue to add broth, about ½ cup (110 ml) at a time, stirring constantly until absorbed. When the rice looks creamy (about 18 minutes), test for doneness, if necessary adding broth in smaller quantities until the rice is firm-tender.

Remove from the heat. Stir in the herb-and-cheese mixture, the remaining oil, salt, and pepper. Sprinkle the remaining 2 tablespoons of basil over the top.

pizza with herb pesto and goat cheese

If you do not want to make your own pizza dough, buy 4 prepared 7-inch (18-cm) pizza bases (available in supermarkets).

For the pizza dough
¾ cup (450 g) flour
1 package fast-acting yeast
½ teaspoon sugar
⅔ cup warm water
2 tablespoons olive oil
½ teaspoon salt

For the tomato sauce and pizza topping
1 tablespoon extra-virgin olive oil
2 cloves garlic, chopped
1 pound (450 g) ripe tomatoes, peeled, seeded and chopped
Salt and fresh-ground black pepper, to taste
½ tablespoon chopped oregano leaves
½ tablespoon chopped thyme leaves
½ tablespoon chopped basil leaves
12 ounces (340 g) goat cheese, sliced into 12 rounds
1½ cups mixed herb pesto (see page 126)
⅓ cup black olives

Make the pizza dough Combine the flour, yeast, and sugar in the bowl of a food processor and add the water. Turn the motor off and add the olive oil and salt. Process until the mixture forms a ball. Turn the dough out into a large oiled bowl, cover it with plastic wrap, and let it rise, in a warm place, until it has doubled in bulk (about 30 minutes). Punch the dough down and roll it out on a floured surface to make 4 7-inch (18-cm) rounds, with slightly raised edges.

Make the tomato sauce and topping Sauté the garlic in the oil until soft. Add the tomatoes, salt, and pepper. Simmer, stirring often, for 30 to 40 minutes, until the sauce is thick and concentrated. Add the chopped herbs.

Preheat the oven to 425ºF (220ºC). Lightly oil 2 large baking sheets and place 2 pizza bases on each sheet. Bake for 10 to12 minutes, until lightly browned. Remove from the oven and turn the heat up to 475ºF (250ºC). On each base, put a layer of tomato sauce, 3 rounds of goat cheese, and 3 tablespoons of mixed herb pesto; scatter a few olives on top. Return the pizzas to the oven until the cheese is golden and bubbling (5 to 7 minutes). Serve immediately.

roast pork with herbes de Provence
Serves 6 to 8

1 shoulder of pork, about 3½ pounds (1.3 kg)
3 tablespoons extra-virgin olive oil
Salt and fresh-ground black pepper, to taste
4 to 5 tablespoons *herbes de Provence* (see
   p. 119)

Preheat the oven to 350°F (190°C). Smear the surface of the pork joint with olive oil and season with salt and pepper to taste. Sprinkle a thick layer of *herbes de Provence* on a clean work surface. Roll the pork in the herbs, then place it in a roasting pan and dredge the top with more herbs. Transfer to the hot oven and roast, allowing 35 minutes cooking time per pound (1¼ hours per kilo). When you take the joint from the oven let it sit for 10 minutes before carving.

shrimp with mustard and dill
The feathery leaves of fennel can be substituted for the dill leaves in this recipe.

¾ cup (170 ml) Dijon mustard
½ teaspoon cayenne pepper
2 garlic cloves, minced
¾ teaspoon caraway seeds
¼ teaspoon turmeric
Salt, to taste
1½ pounds (675 g) raw medium shrimp,
  peeled and deveined
¼ cup (56 ml) vegetable oil
½ cup (25 g) snipped dill leaves

Mix the mustard, cayenne, garlic, caraway seeds, turmeric, and salt. Add the shrimp and combine well. Cover and chill for at least 1 hour and up to 6 hours.

   Shake the shrimp free of most of the spices. Heat the oil in a large deep skillet over medium-low heat. Cook the shrimp just until they become opaque and firm (3 to 4 minutes). Stir the dill into the shrimp during the last minute of cooking. Drain and serve.

Grains

brown rice with bay leaves
4 tablespoons extra-virgin olive oil
3 or 4 bay leaves
1 teaspoon salt
1¼ cups (350 g) brown rice

Heat the oil with the bay leaves in a large saucepan set over low heat. Pour 3¼ cups (730 ml) water into the pan, add the salt, turn up the heat and bring to a boil. Add the rice, cover tightly, and turn the heat back to low. Cook, without lifting the lid, until the rice is just tender (about 45 minutes). Discard the bay leaves before serving.

bulgur with parsley and mint (tabouli)
If you want to make this dish in advance, leave out the tomatoes until just before you plan to serve it. The other ingredients can sit overnight or even longer.

¾ cup (140 g) bulgur
½ red onion, finely chopped
⅛ teaspoon ground allspice
⅛ teaspoon cinnamon
2½ cups packed (125 g) flat-leaf parsley leaves,
  minced
¾ cup packed (40 g) mint leaves, minced
3 scallions, finely sliced
½ small cucumber, diced (preferably English, or
  remove seeds)
3 small ripe tomatoes, chopped
2 tablespoons fresh lemon juice
Salt and fresh-ground black pepper, to taste

Place the bulgur in a medium bowl and pour 2 cups (450 ml) boiling water over it. Let stand 1 hour. Drain well. Meanwhile, mix the onion with the allspice, cinnamon, parsley, and mint and let stand, covered, 30 minutes. Add all the other ingredients and toss together. Season with lemon juice, salt, and pepper.

Desserts and a drink

minted melon sorbet

1¾ cups (88 g) packed mint leaves
1 cup (250 g) sugar
1 small ripe honeydew melon
1 tablespoon fresh lemon juice

Mince 1½ cups (75 g) mint. Bring the mint, sugar, and 1 cup (225 ml) water to a boil, stirring constantly until the sugar dissolves. Simmer without stirring for 2 minutes. Strain the syrup through a fine sieve, pressing the mint to extract as much flavor as possible, and allow to cool completely.

Remove the rind and seeds from the melon. Coarsely chop enough flesh to measure 2½ cups (450 g). Place the melon, 1 cup (225 ml) syrup, remaining ¼ cup (13 g) mint leaves, and the lemon juice into a blender and puree until the mixture is smooth.

Freeze in an ice-cream maker, then transfer to the freezer in an airtight container to harden. Alternatively, place the mixture in the freezer in a shallow plastic container. Take it out of the freezer and turn it sides to middle with a metal fork every hour until it has frozen, then cover tightly. Half an hour before serving, transfer the sorbet to the refrigerator to soften slightly.

herbed strawberries

4 cups (450 g) strawberries, hulled and sliced
4 tablespoons minced nasturtium leaves or
  snipped dill leaves
3 tablespoons balsamic vinegar
2 tablespoons full-bodied red wine (such as a
  Cabernet or Rhône-style wine)
2 teaspoons sugar
½ teaspoon fresh-ground black pepper
Nasturtium blossoms, to garnish (optional)
1 cup (225 ml) plain yogurt, crème fraîche, or
  marscapone cheese, to accompany

Ginger lemonade garnished with lemon balm.

Stirring gently, combine the strawberries with the herbs, vinegar, wine, sugar, and pepper in a serving bowl. If you wish, garnish with nasturtium blossoms. Serve accompanied by a small bowl of yogurt, crème fraîche or marscapone.

ginger lemonade

Makes about 5 cups (1.1 liters)

2 large lemons
5 cups (1.1 liters) water
¼ cup (50 g) peeled and grated fresh ginger
2 tablespoons lemon balm leaves, whole
4 tablespoons honey, or to taste

Squeeze the juice from 1 lemon and cut the rind into coarse pieces. Boil the water and pour it into a heat-resistant bowl. Add the lemon rind pieces, the grated ginger, and the lemon balm leaves and steep, covered, for 20 minutes. Stir in the honey and lemon juice. Strain and chill. Slice the remaining lemon thinly to use as a garnish. Serve the lemonade over ice with one or more lemon slices.

The
Power
of
Herbs

Some people view herbs as a safer and "greener" alternative to conventional medicine. This idea is wrong on many counts. From regarding herbs as relatively harmless, it is only one step to dismissing them as ineffective—whereas in truth, herbs can be quite as powerful in their effect as modern drugs. As with any medicines, herbs can have undesirable side effects. Also, some that are extremely beneficial in small doses can be toxic in large doses. Herbs are the basis of many mainstream Western drugs, including digitoxin, aspirin, codeine, and morphine. At least 25 percent of all modern pharmaceutical drugs are herbal in origin.

So, great care is needed when deciding to use herbs to treat yourself and your family. This part of the book covers minor ailments that you can safely treat at home, applying herbs that you can grow yourself with methods that are simple and safe to use. The complaints dealt with are mild; if you experience any of the conditions described on pages 142 to 149 in a severe or prolonged form, you must seek attention from a qualified medical practitioner.

CAUTION

Before using any of these herbs for medicinal purposes, first read the entry on that plant in the directory (*Useful Herbs*, pages 38 to 113). Check the common names and plant descriptions to verify that you have the correct plant, and look for any specific advice on how to prepare the herb. Also take careful note of specific caution statements. Some herbs are recommended only for short-term use, some should be avoided by persons with specific medical conditions, and others may cause allergic reactions in some individuals. Herbal remedies should never be given to children or to pregnant or breast-feeding women without first checking with a qualified medical practitioner. You should also check first with your doctor if you are taking any medication or suffering from a medical problem or allergy.

For each problem, individual herbs are recommended in the appropriate form or preparation. Any additional details specific to the herb are described, along with the particular part of the plant (such as leaves, seeds, or bark) used for the remedy. Where no specific part is mentioned, you may use the whole plant.

Many of the herbs that have proven medical uses were deliberately omitted from this chapter for one or more of the following reasons. The conditions they treat may be such that they should first be seen and evaluated by a doctor; or the effects of the herb may be so potent that they are best prescribed or administered by a doctor or a qualified medical herbalist. In some cases the herb (or its mode of preparation, as with powerful essential oils) may have contraindications or unwanted side effects. In cases where the particular preparation is hard to do at home (for example, distilling an essential oil), it may be safer and easier to buy an over-the-counter form of the herb.

Many of the herbs mentioned in this chapter can also be purchased as ready-made tinctures, ointments, or creams at stores that sell herbs and herbal products.

COMMISSION E

Herbs have been used for millennia in folk medicine, but there are many popular and traditional uses of herbs that you will not find in this chapter. This is because there is little sound scientific proof, as opposed to anecdotal evidence, that they work.

The most reliable assessment of the evidence supporting medicinal uses of specific herbs is given in the conclusions of an expert panel of the German Institute for Drugs and Medical Devices. The panel is usually known simply as Commission E, and its work is respected worldwide. The Commission's conclusions stem from the most thorough and wide-ranging appraisal of the clinical research on herbs and their efficacy in treating ailments. Its approval of particular herb uses is noted in the text.

Herbal preparations

INFUSIONS

Making an infusion, the most common form of preparation, is a simple matter of preparing a strong tea from an herb and allowing it to steep for at least 10 to 15 minutes. You can make an infusion in a cup or in a teapot, but be sure that the vessel is covered while the herb is steeping in order to prevent the herb's essential oil—usually the medicinally active component—from evaporating. If you can smell the herb while it is steeping, you know that some of its essential oils are escaping.

To make a standard infusion, such as the infusion of peppermint leaves shown below, place 1 ounce (28 g) of fresh herb leaves or flowers, or ½ ounce (14 g) of dried herb in a pot and pour on 2 cups (450 ml) of just-boiled water. Let the herb steep for 10 minutes or, if its leaves are thick and leathery, up to 15 minutes. You can store the infusion in a covered container in a refrigerator for up to 24 hours.

dosage Recommended dosages vary from herb to herb, but to be on the safe side, avoid drinking more than three cups a day of any one herb.

DECOCTIONS

Decoctions differ from infusions in that the water containing the herbs is actively boiled. This method is used for tougher plant materials such as roots, barks, and berries that require a more robust extraction: In the photo at right, a decoction of the roots of licorice and ginger is being prepared. The higher heat increases the extraction of most of the medically useful substances, but it drives off more of the volatile components (the essential oils) than in the preparation of an infusion. For this reason decoctions are not suitable for tender herbs—such as the mints, or lemon balm—where the essential oils are the most useful component.

To make a standard decoction, place 1½ ounces (40 g) of fresh or ¾ ounce (20 g) of dried herbs in a saucepan with 3 cups (675 ml)

WHY WEIGH HERBS?

Measurements for herbs in the instructions in this chapter are given by weight (in ounces and grams) rather than volume. Though it may seem simpler to use a measurement such as 2 cups, this is not sufficiently accurate. An ounce of finely crumbled dry herbs is very different in volume from an ounce of dried whole leaves or bulky flowering tops. Measuring herbs by ounces or grams will be accurate regardless of whether the herbs are finely crumbled or still on the stem. Dried herbs are more concentrated than fresh herbs, so you need to check whether the amounts called for in any herbal preparation are dried or fresh. As a rule of thumb, use about twice as much fresh herb as dried. Herbs weigh very little: An ounce of most dried herbs is about two handfuls. So the infusions and decoctions described here use much more than you may be accustomed to in an herbal beverage tea.

of cold water. To extract as much of the active ingredients as possible, use chopped or cut herbs. Bring to a boil and simmer for 20 to 30 minutes or until the liquid has reduced by a third (to about 2 cups or 450 ml). Strain off the liquid and discard the herb. The decoction will keep in a clean covered jug or bottle in a refrigerator for two to three days.

dosage To be on the safe side, avoid drinking more than three cups a day of any one herb.

TINCTURES

Tinctures are solutions of herbal components in alcohol and can be made from tough or tender herbs. They are handy because they are concentrated, so only small amounts are needed. The alcohol readily dissolves the volatile oils from the herb, and since no heat is used to make the extract, less of the volatile components are lost. Tinctures are also useful if you want to store quantities of an herb for some time: The alcohol is a preservative, so once made tinctures can be kept in a dark sealed bottle for up to two years. Another advantage is that tinctures provide an easy method of carrying and preparing herbs when you travel. They can be used as alternatives to infusions when making washes and compresses (see entry on page 141). You should be aware that commercial tinctures are usually stronger than homemade tinctures, because manufacturers can press out the plant juices more efficiently. The doses suggested here are for homemade tinctures; if you purchase commercially made tinctures, be sure to follow the doses that are recommended on the product label.

Tinctures are simply made by letting the herb soak in alcohol for a period of time to extract the active ingredient. To make a standard tincture, cover 10 ounces (280 g) of fresh herbs or 5 ounces (140 g) of dried herbs with 1 quart (1 liter) of 35 to 40 percent alcohol (70 to 80 proof). Vodka is ideal because of all the spirits it has the least flavor; however, if you want to mask the taste of bitter herbs, use rum or brandy. Store the mixture in a sealed container for two weeks, then strain through a muslin bag and squeeze out the liquid. Discard the herb and pour the tincture into a sterilized, dark glass bottle for storage in a cool dark place. The tincture will keep for up to two years.

dosage Take 1 teaspoon two to three times a day, preferably diluted in a glass of water or fruit juice. Tinctures contain only a relatively small amount of alcohol, but if you prefer not to ingest even that, most of the alcohol can be evaporated: Simply add 10 teaspoons (50 ml) of water just off the boil to a 1 teaspoon (5 ml) dose of tincture and allow the liquid to cool before drinking it.

SYRUPS

Syrups have a dual purpose. They are a way of making herbal preparations soothing to the throat or more palatable. They also provide a method of keeping herbs longer, because honey and unrefined sugar are preservatives.

To make a standard syrup, gently heat 2 cups (450 ml) of an herbal infusion or decoction with 1 pound (450 g) of honey (about 1⅓ cups) or 1 pound (450 g) of unrefined sugar (about 2 cups), stirring until the honey or sugar has dissolved. Cool and strain into sterilized dark glass bottles or jars sealed with cork stoppers; do not use screw tops in case the syrup ferments (which could cause a screw-top jar to explode). If stored in a cool, dark place syrups should keep for about six months.

To make onion syrup, use a mechanical or electric juicer to extract the juice from 1 pound (450 g) of onions. Add the onion juice to a syrup made from heating 4 ounces (112 g) of honey (⅓ cup) and ¾ pound (340 g) of sugar (3 cups) in 2 cups (450 ml) water.

dosage Take 4 to 5 teaspoons daily.

OINTMENTS

An ointment is a soft, oily or fatty substance that contains the dissolved components of some healing material. Unlike creams, ointments do not contain added water. Consequently, ointments are used to form a surface layer on top of the skin; they can also act as a protective barrier. An ointment is an excellent means of applying St.-John's-wort, chamomile, calendula, and most of the other herbs listed for skin conditions on pages 147 and 148.

To make a standard ointment, melt 1 ounce (28 g) of beeswax and 1 cup (225 ml) of olive oil together with 5 ounces (140 g) of chopped fresh herbs or 2½ ounces (70 g) of dried herbs in a double boiler or a glass bowl set over a pan of boiling water. Heat gently for a couple of hours, stirring frequently, or place the glass bowl in a low oven for 3 hours. Remove from heat and strain the mixture through muslin into a jug. Then quickly pour the ointment into sterilized screw-top jars; wait to tighten the lids until the ointment is cool.

The ointment will keep for up to three months if stored in a cool place in dark glass jars or in a dark location.

application Apply to the affected area two or three times a day.

CREAMS

Creams are emulsions of water and oil or fat that, like ointments, contain the dissolved components of a healing substance. Unlike ointments, creams do not create an impervious layer; they are partly absorbed into the skin, and let the skin breathe and sweat. Most of the herbs listed for skin conditions (see pages 147 and 148) can be applied as creams.

To make a standard cream, melt 5 ounces (140 g) of emulsifying wax, 2½ ounces (70 g) of glycerine, and 5 tablespoons (70 ml) of water together with 3 ounces (80 g) of chopped fresh herbs or 1½ ounces (40 g) of dried herbs in a double boiler or a glass bowl set over a pan of boiling water. (If using dried herbs you may have to add up to 2 teaspoons more water to get the right consistency.) Heat gently for 2 hours, stirring frequently, then remove from heat and strain the mixture through muslin into a bowl. Stir the strained mixture slowly until it is cold.

If the mix is too stiff, work in more water until it is a thick but creamy consistency. Place the ointment into sterilized screw-top jars using a flat knife or narrow spatula. The ointment will keep for up to three months if stored in a refrigerator, preferably in dark glass jars.

application Apply to the affected area two or three times a day.

POULTICES

A poultice is a warm, moist quantity of herbs applied directly to an affected area of the body and held in place with a cloth. Suitable herbs are those used for skin problems and for aches and pains (see pages 147–149).

To make a standard poultice you do not need exact measurements. Just take a quantity of fresh or dry herbs that will cover the affected area in a thick layer. Place these in a saucepan, add just enough boiling water to cover the herbs, and simmer for 2 to 3 minutes. Allow the herbs to cool slightly, squeeze out the excess water, and place the warm plant mass directly on the skin. Wrap a clean cloth or bandage firmly around the herbs to hold them in place.

application Apply to the affected area every few hours as necessary.

WASHES AND COMPRESSES

Washes are strained herbal infusions or decoctions that are used for localized pain relief; they can be very soothing when applied to sore skin. Follow the instructions on page 139 for making a standard infusion or decoction. You can also make a wash by diluting 1 tablespoon (14 ml) of an herbal tincture with 2 cups (450 ml) of water. A wash is most soothing when applied cold. Immerse the affected area in it, or apply the wash frequently with a soft cloth.

Compresses are soft cloths soaked in an herbal wash and held securely against the skin to soothe it or to relieve pain. They, too, are particularly soothing when they are cold, so resoak the cloth frequently to keep it cool and reapply as necessary.

Digestive disorders

CONSTIPATION

The seeds and husks of psyllium are an excellent remedy, recommended by "standard" doctors as well as herbal practitioners. First soak the seeds or husks in water, then add a small pinch to a glass of water—at least ½ cup (4 fluid ounces or 110 ml), and drink. Or grind the seeds and husks into a powder and add 1 teaspoon (5 g) to 1 cup (8 fluid ounces or 225 ml) of water. While taking psyllium, be sure to drink plenty of extra water or fruit juice regularly.

Infusions of crushed flax seed can also be helpful. An infusion of the dried powdered roots of Chinese rhubarb makes a strong laxative, to be tried only after milder treatments have failed.

CAUTION

A very few people have experienced allergic reactions, ranging from sneezing to asthma, after taking psyllium. Discontinue treatment if this happens to you.

All of these herbs are approved by Commission E for treating constipation. In addition, some herbalists recommend an infusion or decoction of dandelion root.

DIARRHEA

Herbal treatments include infusions of the leaves of agrimony, blackberry, or of the leaves and flowers of lady's mantle. A decoction or tincture of the rhizome of tormentil can also be used. Because of its ability to absorb liquid, psyllium is a good treatment for diarrhea, too; see *Constipation*, left, for how to prepare it. These uses are all approved by Commission E.

NAUSEA

An infusion of ginger is an excellent remedy for mild nausea and motion sickness; it is approved by Commission E for this. Slice or grate a chunk of fresh ginger root (rhizome) roughly half an inch (13 mm) thick; pour over a cup (225 ml) of just-boiled water and allow to steep for at least 15 minutes, preferably longer. Drink this tea to relieve feelings of sickness, or, to prevent motion sickness, take it three to four hours before traveling.

The husks and seeds of psyllium contain high levels of fiber-rich mucilage that expands to form a gel when soaked in water. The glass vessels shown here contain (from left to right) psyllium husks; gel from husks; gel from seeds; and seeds. This invaluable herb has both a laxative and an antidiarrheal action.

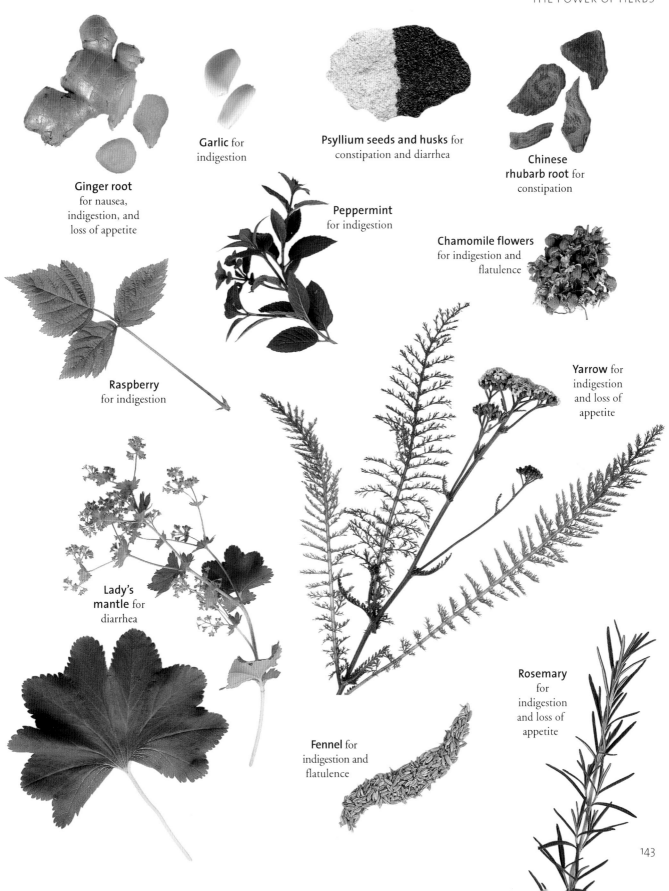

Garlic for indigestion

Psyllium seeds and husks for constipation and diarrhea

Chinese rhubarb root for constipation

Ginger root for nausea, indigestion, and loss of appetite

Peppermint for indigestion

Chamomile flowers for indigestion and flatulence

Raspberry for indigestion

Yarrow for indigestion and loss of appetite

Lady's mantle for diarrhea

Rosemary for indigestion and loss of appetite

Fennel for indigestion and flatulence

143

INDIGESTION

This condition includes a host of digestive complaints including acidity and "upset stomach." An infusion of peppermint leaves is a renowned calming treatment for indigestion. Infusions can also be made from the leaves of lavender, rosemary or lemon balm, both the leaves and the dried flowering branches of horehound or yarrow, and the crushed seeds

of dill, anise, fennel, milk thistle, or coriander. Use the leaves and crushed roots when making infusions of chicory. Cut or crushed raw onion (added to a salad, or sandwiched between two slices of bread), is very helpful, as is ginger root (prepare as for *Nausea* on page 142). Lemon balm is particularly useful for indigestion triggered by tension and anxiety. All these herbs are approved by Commission E for treating digestive complaints.

A famous account of an herbal cure for indigestion is to be found in Beatrix Potter's story *The Tale of Peter Rabbit*, where Peter's mother gives him chamomile tea after he has gorged himself in Mr. McGregor's garden. You too might like to try an infusion of chamomile (preferably annual or German chamomile, shown above). Infusions of the following herbs may also provide some

relief: spearmint (shown above), bee balm, and the seeds or leaves of celery. Another remedy often recommended is raw garlic: this is easier to get down if it is finely sliced and eaten with slices of apple; or you can chop it and scatter over a salad. If you want to avoid having the smell on your breath, chew some parsley afterward.

Bitter herbs such as centaury, chicory and dandelion stimulate the flow of gastric juices; this has given them a reputation for improving digestion if they are taken ahead of a meal.

LOSS OF APPETITE

Many of the herbs used to treat *Indigestion* (see left) are prepared in the same ways to treat loss of appetite. The most widely recommended include yarrow, onion, chicory, coriander seeds, centaury, lavender, horehound, anise, rosemary, and ginger root. In addition to and including these, Commission E approves an infusion of sage leaves (shown below) to stimulate the appetite. You can also try infusions of tarragon leaves, or celery seeds and leaves, or decoctions of dandelion root.

FLATULENCE AND BLOATING

Again, some herbs for indigestion, prepared in the same ways, can help to relieve flatulence and the feeling of bloating. Commission E approves fennel for treating these afflictions. You can also try infusions of chamomile (both species), dill seeds, peppermint, spearmint, or bee balm.

CANKER SORES

Sage can help speed the healing of canker sores in the mouth. Make an infusion and use it as a mouthwash. You can also try using an infusion of agrimony in the same way.

Respiratory tract problems

COLDS, MILD FLU, AND SINUS CONGESTION

While in the past sorrel and yellow dock were used to relieve congestion of the nasal passages arising from infection, today the most popular herbs for tackling colds and flu are echinacea and garlic. Echinacea has been approved by Commission E for both boosting immunity and reducing the severity of symptoms. Commission E also approves infusions of the flowers and leaves of meadowsweet, peppermint leaves, the seeds of anise and the flowers (only) of the European elderberry (below: peppermint leaves, a glass of peppermint tea, and a jar of dried elderberry flowers). These herbs can also soothe the irritation in nasal passages (rhinitis) caused by hay fever and other allergens. Annual chamomile also receives Commission E's approval for treating these ailments, though some people who are allergic to related ragweed and chrysanthemums may find that they react to chamomile as well. Raw onion may also bring relief. Eat the onion finely chopped or crushed (scattered over a salad or sandwiched between two slices of bread). Or extract the juice using a mechanical or electric juicer and either drink it as it is or prepare a syrup.

You can also try infusions of the leaves of sweet marjoram, sorrel, or oregano.

COUGHS AND BRONCHITIS

Mild irritation of the throat or bronchial tubes, and coughs as well, are eased by many of the same herbs that are used for colds and allergies.

STEAM INHALATIONS

Herbal inhalations may be effective in clearing congestion. Make an infusion of thyme, rosemary, or chamomile. Allow it to steep for a few minutes, then pour it into a bowl. Alternatively, add 1 to 2 teaspoons of an herbal tincture (a tincture of rosemary is shown above) to a bowl of hot water. If you wish, add a couple of drops of eucalyptus oil. Sit with your head over the bowl (preferably with a towel covering both head and bowl) and breathe in the steam through your nose. You may have to emerge from the towel from time to time, but try to persist for 5 to 10 minutes. When you have finished the steam inhalation, stay in a warm room for at least 15 minutes to allow the airways time to clear.

The most highly recommended of these are onion, meadowsweet, annual chamomile, anise seeds, and European elderberry flowers, all used as specified at left. Various other herbs are also approved by Commission E for coughs and bronchitis. Horseradish can be taken as an infusion of the fresh or dried root: Chop the fresh root before steeping, or use cut or ground dried roots. Or you can simply chop or grate fresh horseradish roots and spread the resulting paste on bread or some other bland food. Finely grated horseradish or freshly pressed juice can also be drunk if diluted with a liquid such as wine. You can also try an infusion of linden flowers or thyme.

To soothe dry coughs, try an infusion of marshmallow, made using the chopped leaves or the roots. You can also make a soothing syrup

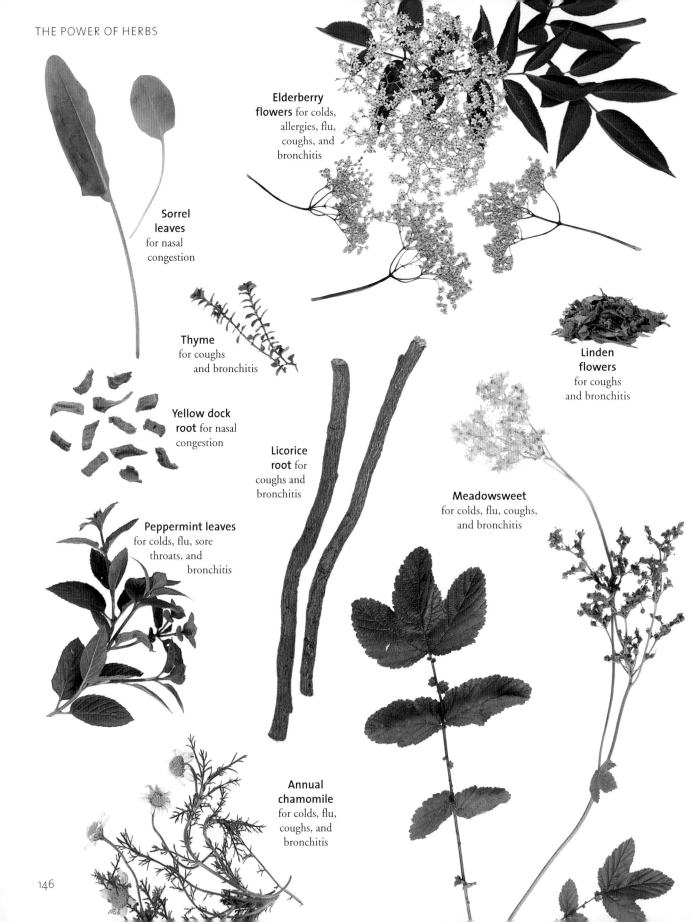

Sorrel leaves for nasal congestion

Elderberry flowers for colds, allergies, flu, coughs, and bronchitis

Thyme for coughs and bronchitis

Linden flowers for coughs and bronchitis

Yellow dock root for nasal congestion

Licorice root for coughs and bronchitis

Meadowsweet for colds, flu, coughs, and bronchitis

Peppermint leaves for colds, flu, sore throats, and bronchitis

Annual chamomile for colds, flu, coughs, and bronchitis

out of a marshmallow infusion. Cowslip, licorice, oregano, and thyme can aid the relief of congestion. Oregano and thyme can be taken as infusions, licorice as a decoction of the root. Or you can try an infusion of cowslip flowers or a decoction of the roots.

Some herbalists recommend infusions of oregano for coughs. Garlic, eaten raw, is thought to be helpful. Other herbs that may soothe a cough include infusions of vervain leaves, or celery seeds or leaves, or decoctions of elecampane root.

SORE THROATS

A number of herbs are recommended to soothe sore or scratchy throats. You can make an infusion of calendula flowers (shown below) or of rose petals (particularly those of *Rosa* x *centifolia* and *R. gallica*) or the flowers and leaves of annual chamomile. Other options include infusions made from the leaves of peppermint, witch hazel, sage, or blackberry, or from crushed anise seeds. You can drink these infusions, but they are also very soothing when used as gargles. Onions can be eaten raw or prepared as a syrup. All of the above uses are approved by Commission E.

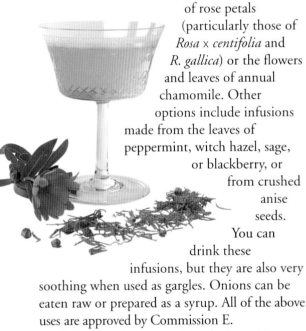

Other infusions you might find soothing are lady's mantle, perennial chamomile, tormentil, or thyme. Or you can try the traditional combination of ginger, garlic, and lemon. Crush a medium-sized garlic clove, grate a piece of ginger root of about the same size, and squeeze the juice of a lemon. Mix them all together with 1 teaspoon of honey, add 1 cup (225 ml) of warm water, and stir. You can drink up to three cups a day while the symptoms last.

Skin problems

RASHES AND OTHER SKIN IRRITATIONS

Various soothing herbs may provide some relief for irritated or itchy skin.

Witch hazel is recommended to soothe rashes and other skin irritations: use the bark for tinctures and ointments, and the bark and leaves for an infusion that you can apply as a cool wash. A soothing cream can be made from the flowers of St.-John's-wort, or an infusion or tincture of the flowers can be used as a wash. An infusion of annual chamomile also makes a soothing wash or can be used as a compress. The flowers of calendula can be used as a tincture (above left), a cream (above right), or an ointment. The gel found in fresh aloe leaves is very soothing to any form of skin irritation; cut the fleshy leaf (right) in half along its length to extract the gel. Poultices made from decoctions of agrimony or crushed seeds of flax may also provide some relief. Commission E approves all of these uses.

Chickweed is helpful for many types of skin irritation, particularly to relieve itching. Make a poultice or, for larger areas, try strewing handfuls of the fresh or dried herb in a bath or basin of warm water and soaking the affected area. Ointments and creams made from chickweed are also soothing to irritated skin. Also worth trying is a poultice made from the chopped root and leaves of marshmallow. Infusions of plantain, lady's mantle, cleavers, or nasturtium make good washes that may help to soothe skin irritations. This use of plantain is approved by Commission E.

Warts, another common skin complaint, can be treated with regular applications of raw garlic, sliced or crushed. You can also try applying the gel from fresh aloe leaves.

MINOR BURNS AND SUNBURN

Most of the herbs recommended on page 147 for skin irritations may also be used to soothe burns. Aloe, calendula, witch hazel, St.-John's-wort, and annual chamomile are all approved for this use by Commission E.

Note that for burns (including sunburn), you should apply herbal preparations at a cool temperature; hot poultices are not suitable. Cold water or cold compresses should be applied to burns immediately and for at least 15 minutes.

You might find it handy to freeze infusions of calendula, witch hazel, St.-John's-wort, or chamomile and store them as ice cubes in the freezer, ready to apply to small burns.

After the cold treatment, ointments or creams made from the same herbs, or the gel from aloe leaves, can be applied to provide ongoing relief.

CUTS AND WOUNDS

Several herbs can be helpful for minor wounds and scratches. Calendula, witch hazel, St.-John's-wort, and annual chamomile are all approved for this by Commission E; use as described under *Rashes and Other Skin Irritations*, on page 147. Some herbalists also recommend raw garlic (sliced or crushed), aloe gel, or an infusion of thyme used as a wash, but these uses are unproven.

Thyme for cuts and wounds

Nasturtium for skin irritations

Lady's mantle for skin irritations

Cleavers for skin irritations

Garlic for cuts, wounds, and warts

Aloe vera for rashes, minor burns, sunburn, cuts, and wounds

Chamomile for rashes, minor burns, sunburn, cuts, and wounds

Aches and pains

JOINT PAIN
Good herbs for treating joint pain include rosemary and stinging nettle. Both are approved for this use by Commission E. Prepared as infusions, they can be applied directly to the affected joint in the form of washes or compresses. A nettle infusion may also give some relief when drunk as a tea.

BRUISES AND SPRAINS
For bruises and sprains, comfrey (below), applied directly to the injury, may help to reduce pain and inflammation. Make a poultice from the leaves, press the juice from the leaves and roots, make an ointment from an infusion of the leaves and roots, or mash the fresh roots. These external uses are approved by Commission E. Witch hazel is also often recommended to soothe bruises: you can apply it as a tincture or ointment made from the bark, or make a cool wash from an infusion of the bark and leaves.

ACHING MUSCLES
An infusion of nasturtium leaves, used as a wash, may provide some comfort for aching muscles. A decoction of bay leaves added to a bath may also soothe aches. Chickweed, added to a bath or applied to a localized area as a poultice, may also be helpful.

VARICOSE VEINS
You can ease the pain or throbbing of varicose veins with an infusion of witch hazel, which you can apply as a cool wash or compress. This use has been approved by Commission E. Yarrow (right) is also sometimes recommended: wash the affected area with a cool infusion, or apply an ointment. Drinking an infusion of yarrow may also help ease the pain.

Nervous tension and insomnia

Herbal preparations are particularly good for relieving nervous tension and for calming the mind and body to make sleep easier. Infusions of lavender, lemon balm (right), fresh hop flowers (below), and the root of valerian are all approved by Commission E for these uses. Infusions of catnip and of annual and perennial chamomile also have calming effects. See also the recommendations for relaxing baths in *Herbs at Home,* page 163.

Herbs
at
Home

From the days of the earliest settled communities, herbs have been employed not only as seasonings and medicines, but also for a range of other uses around the home. The strong and pleasing scents of herbs such as lavender, sweet marjoram, chamomile, rosemary, thyme, the mints, and roses sweeten our rooms, our clothes, and our bathwater. Herbs like calendula, fennel, lady's mantle, yarrow, and (again) roses, make decorative additions to flower arrangements. The therapeutic qualities of these and other herbs also contribute to their value as oils for massage and as cosmetics for skin and hair care.

Herbs for refreshing and sweetening rooms

We might be inclined to balk today at the medieval practice of strewing herbs around our living rooms. However, there are plenty of ways to use herbs as air fresheners that fit well with tidier modern practices.

FLOWER ARRANGEMENTS

Many herbs are obvious candidates for flower arrangements. Fragrant roses growing in the garden beg to be cut and brought indoors. The sunny, round flowers of calendula come in varied shades of yellow and orange. Feverfew's abundant, dainty white daisies make excellent filler flowers. The tousled mops of bee balm may be red, lavender, or shades of pink, depending on the variety. Yarrows have flat-topped flower clusters and come in many wonderful shades of yellow, gold, and rose to brick red, as well as the basic white.

The pink flowers of Joe Pye weed and its relatives can anchor a large, late-summer bouquet. The varied purples of different types of lavender look best in smaller arrangements. Cutting these flowers will not diminish your outdoor display; for most plants, cutting stimulates the production of more blooms.

Other herbs such as dill, fennel, lady's mantle, and meadowsweet offer a more subtle beauty. Their leaves and flowers bring delicacy and grace to fresh flower arrangements while acting as a foil to bright flower colors. If you strip dill or fennel of all but the top leaves and plunge the cut stem ends into boiling water for 20 seconds, they will last 10 days or more. Try combining either one of these in an arrangement

The chartreuse flower sprays of lady's mantle set off the soft pinks and creamy whites of carnations, alliums, and lilies.

with deep carmine-pink cosmos flowers. Lady's mantle's delicate green flower sprays blend surprisingly well with almost all other flowers. They provide a stunning contrast to orange marigolds and combine beautifully with a cool, creamy display of white roses, white foxgloves, and masterwort (*Astrantia*). Refresh lady's mantle daily with a long cold drink and it will last at least a week. The frothy white flowers of meadowsweet have a pleasing sweet vanilla scent, and its leaves release a contrasting sharp pungency when crushed.

Aromatic leaves can be used as greenery, though you will have to rub the leaves gently to enjoy their fragrance. Feathery southernwood is perhaps the most pungent. Mints last well in arrangements; the variegated leaves of ginger mint and the fuzzy grayish leaves of apple mint are particularly attractive. Leaves of lady's mantle are not aromatic, but their beautiful, bold shape enhances any arrangements.

NOSEGAYS

A ready-made nosegay or posy of flowers and herbs is always a welcome gift. It will be all the more of a pleasure if it is designed to be long-lasting. Originally carried to ward off bad odors, or even the plague or evil spirits, such nosegays (also called "tussie mussies") can be as simple or as complicated as you like. They are especially delightful when made with fresh scented herbs and flowers from the garden. Choose flowers that are not quite at full bloom, and cut the stems to "hand-holding" length, about 6 inches (15 cm) long. If sap seeps from their stems, singe the ends by holding them over a candle flame, and then soak in cold water

The simplest method of drying herbs is just to hang bunches upside down in a warm, dry, well-ventilated place.

overnight. Build the nosegay outwards, beginning with an odd number of perfect buds—rosebuds, perhaps, or lilac. Around the buds evenly space smaller blooms that dry well (see below) such as lavender or chamomile. Around these arrange a ring of leaves, wrapping the foliage stems around the flower stems. Secure—but do not crush—the stems with florists' wire. Finish off with a plain ribbon wrapped around the stems. Another option is to wrap stems in a doily or tissue paper cut in a circle; either can be secured with ribbon.

Alert the recipient that the nosegay can be hung upside-down to dry. Of course, nosegays can be made up of purchased dried flowers and herbs, but these do not have quite the same initial charm and freshness of scent.

DRIED HERBS AND FLOWERS FOR THE HOUSE

Because so many herbs dry well, dried herb arrangements, and rings, wreaths, and potpourri including herbs are all very popular. (For a few herbs, the drying process sometimes even accentuates their aroma.) You can use them as a source of sweet smells in midwinter, releasing

153

delicate scents of summer to bring back memories of warmer days. Some plants may be chosen purely for decoration, but scented plants such as lavender and rose, shown here, are the most important. Scented herbs whose foliage works well with dried arrangements include bay, costmary, eucalyptus, rosemary, thyme, and sage. Herb flowers that keep their color well when dried include feverfew, tansy, and calendula. For basic information on how to harvest and dry herbs and flowers, see *Growing and Preserving Herbs,* pages 38–39.

A few special techniques are used to preserve flowers for craft uses. If the flowers will be used in potpourri, remove the leaves to help them dry faster. If only the petals will be used, remove the petals from the flower heads before drying. Rose petals, the staple of most potpourri, should be laid out on trays or screens. Dry flowers away from light to preserve as much color as possible.

If the flowers are to be used in a vase or in hanging arrangements, it is best to wire them with florists' wire before drying them, since they will be too brittle to be easily wired once they are dry. First, cut off most of the flower's stem, leaving only about 1 inch (2.5 cm). Form a false stem by poking a length of wire cut to about 10 inches (25 cm) horizontally through the base of the flower. Then bend the wire back and secure it, coiled around itself, just below the head of the flower.

Other techniques for drying involve immersing the herb in drying powders such as borax (or clean sand mixed with borax), or more expensive but faster-acting silica gel powder. (If you purchase silica gel crystals, these can be crushed with a rolling pin.) These methods are useful for fussy or delicate blossoms such as calendulas. The amount of time needed will depend on the size and type of flower. For example, calendulas need up to two weeks in borax to dry completely.

To store whole dried flowers for later use, wrap them carefully in tissue paper, place carefully in shoe boxes, then label. Flowers and petals for potpourri should be stored in labeled, airtight containers away from light.

Rose petals laid out on a screen to dry. All but the thickest petals will dry in about a week.

HERB RINGS AND WREATHS

Decorative rings or wreaths can be lovely at any time of year. One of the simplest can be made by wrapping long strands of flowering hop vines into a ring. The fresh vines are very flexible (except when they are cold); secure the strands by wrapping them around each other. Hang the hop wreath on a door or wall, unadorned or accented with dried flowers such as dark red dahlias tucked between the strands.

A ring of herbs—made either of fresh, short-stemmed herbs (whatever is in season) or your favorite dried herbs—can be used as the centerpiece of a table decoration. You can place a single candle, or a group of three, in the middle, but be careful to keep the flames well away from any flammable dried foliage.

For a ring of fresh herbs, make a base from a circle of florists' foam, or of sphagnum moss packed inside a "sausage" of ½ inch (1.5 cm) mesh chicken wire. Set the base in a round plastic container and soak with water. Cut small branches or stems of herbs, about 6 inches (15 cm) long, and set them in the foam or moss, securing them with florists' wire or hairpins if necessary. Set on a table and keep the foam or moss moist, taking care to protect the table from moisture when watering.

For a dried herb ring, start with a ring-shaped base of straw or moss purchased from a garden center. You can make your own by winding pliable willow or grapevine stems around a wire hoop, or by bending heavy-gauge wire into a circle. For the background of your wreath, choose a plant that you have plenty of and that dries easily—perhaps rosemary, yarrow, or wormwood or a related *Artemisia* species. (Be sure to wash your hands after working with wormwood.) Cut a dozen or more stems about 6 to 8 inches (15 to 20 cm) long and tuck the cut ends into the base or weave these between stems or wires to cover the ring. (Alternatively, you can start with dried herbs for the wreath's background.) Then use dried flowers and herbs singly or in small bunches as accent plants at intervals around the ring. It usually looks best to limit your colors to three or so.

HERB BALLS AND "TOPIARY"

Hanging herb balls like the one shown on the right can be made in various ways. The simplest method is to pierce a hole through a purchased sphere of florists' foam and thread a ribbon through for hanging. Push dried (or wired) flower and herb stems into the florists' foam to cover the whole surface. To avoid breaking the more delicate stems, you can use a thick wire or ice pick to make a preliminary hole before inserting. To make a topiary "tree" like the one shown here, or some other shape, purchase a block of floral foam and cut it to the desired shape by slicing with a strand of florists' wire held taut between your hands. You can make more elaborate shapes using a wire base sold by garden centers for training topiary plants; these are harder to cover, however, as each stem or small bunch of flowers and herbs must be secured in place with florists' wire.

POTPOURRI

Today, potpourri is usually a loose mixture of dried ingredients. The crinkly

Various methods of displaying potpourri. The set of shelves shows glasses holding potpourris of (clockwise from top left): Dried roses with bay leaves, and hop and chamomile flowers; a mixture of bee balm flowers with chamomile flowers and elecampane root; rose petals with ornamental grass heads and mixed sweet herbs; a spicy mixture of rosemary, French lavender, mallow, and clary sage with aromatic wood shavings. The basket (bottom) also holds rose petal potpourri.

petals, foliage, and spices, with the addition of a few small dried flower and seed heads, are pretty as well as fragrant. Displayed in shallow bowls or elegant glass containers, potpourri can form a stunning centerpiece to a table or sideboard.

In former times, moist potpourri was more common: Flower petals were layered with spices and salt (the word "*pourri*," meaning "rotted," clearly applies to this method). This did little for the appearance of the petals, but the fermentation produced a strongly aromatic "cake." It was not meant to be seen but was placed in a pretty, lidded potpourri jar. The lid might have had holes to allow the aroma to escape, or it might have been left unpierced and removed only when the room needed refreshing. If you want to replicate this effect, gather roses and other fragrant flowers such as lavender as soon as morning dew has evaporated in the warm air. Lay them out on trays or screens and leave them in an airy place for a day or two so that they lose some of their moisture. Layer the partially dried petals and flower heads in a wide-mouthed jar with a scattering of powdered spices—perhaps a mixture of cloves, allspice, and nutmeg; top every couple of inches with a dusting of sea salt. When the jar is full, screw its lid tight and place it in the dark for a week or longer, until it forms a somewhat solid cake. Break the potpourri into pieces (and, if desired, add more spices and one of the fixatives listed on page 157) before filling your potpourri jars.

Most dry potpourri mixes include strongly scented petals from rose varieties such as the damasks (*Rosa × damascena*), the apothecary's rose (*R. gallica*), the musk roses (*R. moschata*), and cabbage roses (*R. × centifolia*), plus flowers such as lavender. Also good for scent are bee balm and chamomile flowers. Whole or powdered spices such as cloves, coriander seed, and sandalwood are also an important ingredient of potpourri. For example, scattering a teaspoonful of cinnamon powder and another of crushed cumin seed gives a warm spice aroma. Aromatic leaves are often included; delicate leaves such as sweet marjoram and sage may crumble into small pieces, but rosemary and bay leaves hold their shapes well. Potpourris almost always include a few drops of essential oils to enrich and strengthen the aroma.

FIXATIVES FOR POTPOURRI

Because herb and flower scents are volatile, they soon disperse, but you can make them last longer by adding fixatives to bind them. Powdered orris root is the fixative most commonly used in potpourri today. It is made from the rhizomes of the Florentine iris (*Iris germanica* var. *florentina*). You can grow your own if you are patient. It does not smell particularly good when harvested, but after a couple of years the dried roots develop a sweet violet fragrance. Gum benzoin, a powdered tree resin (*Styrax* spp.) is also sometimes used. Other fixatives include frankincense (*Boswellia* spp., spicy fragrance), myrrh (*Commiphora* spp., sweet and spicy), sandalwood (*Santalum album* or *Pterocarpus santalinus,* sweet and woodsy), vetiver root (*Vetiveria zizanoides,* earthy), and tonka bean (*Diypteryx odorata,* vanilla-scented). Recipes can be varied by adding other fixatives instead of or as well as the main ones.

GENERAL METHOD FOR POTPOURRI

Put the dried flower petals and scented herbs into a mixing bowl. Put the fixative into a separate bowl, and add a few drops of an essential oil. Mix by hand. Pour the oiled fixative over the petals and mix thoroughly, gently turning the petals. (Or, if you want to make a layered potpourri like the one shown below left, mix each ingredient separately with the fixative.) Put in a sealed airtight container and keep in a dark spot for six weeks to two months. Shake the container from time to time. Once the mixture has sat for the recommended time, put some into a pretty bowl. Reseal the container to keep any remaining for future use.

The quantities given in the recipes below can be multiplied in proportion to the amount of the base ingredients. If the fragrance fades after several years, the mixes can be revitalized with a few drops of essential oil. You can vary the herbs used or experiment by making mixes with your own favorite herbs and fragrant flowers.

ROSE AND LAVENDER POTPOURRI

4 ounces (112 g) dried rose petals (and a few whole small buds, if possible)

1 to 2 ounces (28 to 56 g) dried lavender flowers

1 ounce (28 g) dried lavender leaves

1 teaspoon dried lemon thyme leaves

½ teaspoon orris root powder

½ teaspoon powdered cloves

5 to 8 drops rose essential oil

2 drops lavender essential oil

SPICY HERB POTPOURRI

3½ ounces (100 g) dried bay leaves

2 ounces (56 g) dried calendula flowers

1 ounce (28 g) dried eucalyptus leaves

½ teaspoon orris root powder

½ teaspoon powdered cloves

8 drops rose essential oil

3 drops bergamot oil

Antique apothecary's measures are good for displaying dried flowers or potpourri. At left is a layered display of dried lavender flowers, rose petals and buds, sunflower seeds, and the decorative seed heads of grasses. At right are rose petals, a spicy potpourri of aromatic wood shavings scented with essential oils and a bergamot-based potpourri.

HERB SACHETS, BAGS, AND PILLOWS

It used to be common practice to place sachets—small bags perfumed by herbs—between layers of clothes to give them a pleasing fragrance. Lavender-based mixtures have long been the most popular for this. Historically, sachets also served the more practical function of deterring musty smells or insect attack. Southernwood, wormwood, and related artemisias, which contain the toxic oil thujone, were often included in moth-repelling mixes. Other herbs that can be used in bags as insect repellents include chamomile, mints, basil, feverfew, tansy, and sage.

Traditionally sachets and bags like the ones shown on the left were made of scraps left over from dressmaking, so they could be squares, circles, or other shapes. Circles of a lightweight, pretty material such as organdy or calico around 10 inches (25 cm) diameter are the easiest to use as they require no stitching. They can simply be secured with a rubber band and a decorative ribbon, looped for hanging. For a small rectangular drawstring bag, cut two pieces of material 3½ inches (9 cm) by 5 inches (13 cm). For a flatter sachet cut your cloth 5 inches (13 cm) square. In either case, place the wrong sides of the two pieces of material together and sew around three sides, using a ½ inch (1.5 cm) seam allowance. Fill with your chosen potpourri mix, then tie the top of the rectangular bag closed with a narrow ribbon. For the flatter sachet, sew up the final side by hand.

Fabric and ribbons for making herb bags, with the dried lavender flowers and rose petals that will be used to fill them.

Pillows stuffed with hop flowers, alone or with other relaxing herbs, can help promote restful sleep.

The hop-stuffed pillow was popularized as a sleeping aid by Britain's King George III. Herb pillows are still a pleasant alternative to sleep-inducing chemicals. Any pretty pillow or cushion cover, perhaps antique or home-made, can serve as the outer case for a pillow filled with hops or other herbs. Hop scent is not long-lasting, so it makes sense to design the pillow to make it easy to change the herb stuffing often. Enclose the herbs in an inner case made of a double thickness of cambric, muslin, or other tough lining material. For extra comfort enfold the herbs in a layer of 4 ounce (112 g) polyester batting, cut to fit inside the lining and sewn up on three sides. Fill with any preferred mix of dried herbs and potpourri flowers (avoiding anything too lumpy or hard) until comfortably firm, then hand-sew the remaining side. For sleep pillows, hops are the best choice, though you can also include other herbs with relaxing aromas, such as chamomile or lavender flowers or rose petals.

INCENSE AND SCENTED CANDLES

It is significant that of the three gifts thought worthy of the baby Jesus, two were scented tree resins. In ancient times both frankincense and myrrh were used as fumigants, producing a strong-scented smoke that was thought to purify the air and drive away evil. To achieve a traditional camphorous smell, light some dry sprigs of rosemary over a metal tray, then immediately blow out the flame, allowing the rosemary to smolder and scent the air. (This procedure must be carried out at a safe distance from flammable furnishings.) Or, to avoid being driven indoors at the end of a barbecue, place sprigs of rosemary, bay, or lemon balm on the barbecue embers. They will scent the air and help keep away midges and mosquitoes.

In the 1960s and 1970s, the "hippies" revived the practice of burning incense in the home. Incense (sometimes in the form called "joss-sticks") is still popular, as are scented candles. If you make your own candles, you can experiment with adding scents using essential oils. Choose a fragrance that appeals to you, or select one for its supposed effects from the list on page 162. But do not be tempted to put in many drops of oil or you will lose all subtlety.

A mix of scented petals from 'Charles de Mills', 'Fragrant Cloud', and 'Crimson Glory' roses. The candles are scented with rose oil.

Using essential oils

Essential oils are usually extracted from plants by a process of steam distillation. This process is difficult to do at home, as it requires specialized equipment, painstaking labor, and huge quantities of plant material. For example, it takes about 440 pounds (200 kg) of fresh lavender flowers to produce 2½ pounds (1 kg) of lavender essential oil. Obviously, most people find that the best course is to buy commercially produced essential oils.

Be careful when shopping for these, however. People buying herbal essential oils for use in the home and in aromatherapy (see page 161) might reasonably believe them to be "natural"—that is, made from the plant written on the label. However, the chemical and perfume industries often adulterate the oil by blending it with synthetics (a method which is allowed by the International Organization for Standardization for essential oils). For example, lemon balm has a low yield on distillation, so

An aromatherapy burner, with lavender essential oil.

commercial lemon balm oil is often mostly synthetic components. To be sure that an herbal essential oil is close to the real thing, you should always buy a reputable aromatherapy brand. Also, it is worth checking that the label carries not just the common name, such as lemon balm, but the Latin species name as well—in this case, *Melissa officinalis*.

Essential oils are used in a wide variety of ways. To scent a room, they can be added to candles or burned in a special aromatherapy burner (see photo above). Or, simplest of all, a few drops can be added to a small bowl of hot water, kept warm over a candle (or, if you prefer, on a radiator or a hot plate). Heat increases the rate at which the scented oil vapor is released. These oils can even be added to furniture polish—for many older people, the warm lemon- or lavender-and-beeswax smell and shine of well-polished furniture brings back childhood memories.

Essential oils can be added to unscented lotions and shampoo, to body and massage oils, or to a bath. When using essential oils in the bath, add five to ten drops after the bath is filled, not while the water is running, so that the oils stay on the water surface. Good oils for bathtime relaxation are lavender, marjoram, rose, yarrow, chamomile, and valerian. Some oils, such as eucalyptus, peppermint, rosemary, and basil, are more powerfully aromatic than others, so you may find that you prefer fewer

CAUTION

Essential oils are concentrated—use them with care. Do not take essential oils internally. Keep them away from the eyes to prevent irritation. Do not use them undiluted on the skin. Unless otherwise specified, dilute them in carrier oils (see page 161) before use. Keep them away from children. Be careful not to spill undiluted essential oil, as the vapor can be overpowering, especially for young children and pets. Always check that you are not allergic to a particular oil before using it, even in the bath. To test for allergy, add 2 drops to ¼ cup of water. Blend, then rub a little of the solution on your inner arm. If after half an hour or so there is no reaction, you can use it safely. However, you should still not use to excess or for undue periods of time, or allergic sensitivities and other reactions may develop. Essential oils are flammable and should be stored in a cool, dark place.

drops of these than of other oils. Alternatively, you can dilute them in a carrier oil before adding to the bath. Try to ensure that there is no draft, or the vaporized essential oil molecules will be blown away instead of forming a scented envelope over the bath. Essential oils can damage the surface of plastic bathtubs, so rinse off fully after use.

CARRIER OILS

Essential oils are often mixed into a "carrier" oil before use. When the essential oil is being used as a cosmetic or for massage, sweet almond is the preferred carrier oil, as it is least apt to be allergenic. Other good carrier oils include sunflower, grapeseed, walnut, hazelnut, olive, evening primrose, and jojoba oils. Make sure that any oil you intend to apply to the skin has been produced naturally and ideally has been cold-pressed rather than subjected to a heat treatment, which alters the chemical balance and the smell. Such oils turn rancid more quickly, so purchase in small quantities and store unused oils in the refrigerator. If they solidify, they will return to liquid form when they warm to room temperature.

To dilute an essential oil, measure out the carrier oil, and pour into a glass bottle. Carefully add the essential oil or oils by dropper to produce a 1 to 3 percent solution of essential oil in carrier oil (1 to 3 parts essential oil to 100 parts carrier oil). A simple way to produce this dilution is to use up to four drops of essential oil per tablespoon (14 ml) of carrier oil. (That is equivalent to up to 24 drops per half-cup, or 110 ml, of carrier

From left to right: grapeseed oil, to be used as a carrier oil; rose oil diluted in sweet almond oil; lavender essential oil; bergamot oil in a grapeseed oil carrier; citronella essential oil.

oil—the proportions shown in the beakers at left). If in doubt, keep to a low concentration. A minority of commercially available essential oils such as bergamot and other citrus oils, lemongrass, and some spice oils should not be used in a solution above 1 percent, since they can cause irritation. Be very careful when you are using essential oils with children: Consult a qualified professional who has experience with children, and use a dilution a quarter of the adult strength.

Some oils have been found to harmonize well in combinations. For example, lavender is one of the best mixers, happily producing balanced scents with any of a range of other oils including chamomile, fennel, basil, rose, calendula, peppermint, rosemary, tea tree, yarrow, and sage. As you collect more oils, follow your own nose: Change the oils and blends you use to suit your moods and needs.

MASSAGE OILS AND AROMATHERAPY

Aromatherapy is a method of using essential oils to enhance mental and bodily functions— by inhaling the vapors from the oils, by using a special aromatherapy diffuser, or by applying the oils to the body by massage. Adding a few drops of an herbal essential oil to a carrier oil can make a pleasant massage oil—a particularly relaxing way to enjoy aromatherapy.

ESSENTIAL OILS AND THEIR PROPERTIES

You can use your favorite scented oils for massage for the pleasure of their scent. Particular oils are used in aromatherapy because they are said to have specific effects, so you may also wish to experiment with some of the oils listed below to test their benefits for yourself. For more information on properties of specific herbs, see Useful Herbs, pages 38–113.

ANGELICA helps relieve fatigue, anxiety, and nervous tension.

BAY (also called bay laurel) is said to relieve anxiety and melancholy.

CALENDULA is known as the "skin saver" for its healing properties and its value as a comforter for "mature" skin.

CORIANDER, distilled from the seeds, relieves muscular aches and helps with sleep and nervous exhaustion.

FENNEL, distilled from the unripe seeds, also relieves stress and nervous tension. It is delicious in the bath.

LAVENDER engenders relaxation and a sense of well-being by balancing the emotions and promoting restful sleep. It is also supposed to help ease breathing and promote healing of the skin.

PEPPERMINT and gentler **SPEARMINT** are for energy and mood brightening as well as mental clarity. As an additional benefit, the mint vapors from the bath may help ease a stuffy nose.

PERENNIAL CHAMOMILE has a fruity aroma; it helps promote restful sleep and eases anxiety.

ROSE (or "rose absolute," from *Rosa* x *centifolia* flowers) is the traditional "mood" or aphrodisiac oil, but it is also calming and promotes restful sleep.

ROSEMARY has a pungent smell; it brightens moods and helps mental clarity, memory, and alertness.

SWEET BASIL, with its slightly licorice aroma, works like rosemary to brighten moods and help mental clarity, memory, and alertness.

SWEET MARJORAM is said to "comfort the heart" and so relieve stress and muscle tension.

THYME is an aid to concentration and memory, and helps relieve fatigue.

CAUTION

Some essential oils—including wormwood, pennyroyal, St.-John's-wort, and tansy—are toxic and should never be used for massage. There are many oils, including rosemary, thyme, sage, hyssop, clary sage, basil, fennel, bay, comfrey, lemon balm, and marjoram, that should not be used in early pregnancy. Some doctors consider it better not to employ aromatherapy massage at all during the first half of pregnancy. If you are pregnant, have allergies, or have a serious medical condition, always consult a qualified medical practitioner if you want to use essential oils for aromatherapy. Consult, too, if you have circulation problems, epilepsy, are on medication, or have a psychiatric condition. For example, rosemary, thyme, and sage should particularly be avoided by those with elevated blood pressure. Seek advice from a professional aromatherapist and your doctor for your particular circumstances. Do not use essential oils on young children unless with the advice of a qualified medical practitioner. (Chamomile and lavender are normally thought safe for young children if diluted to one-quarter strength, but you should always check with your doctor.) Always dilute essential oils before using them for massage.

Herbs for beauty

Herbs have always been used for hair and skin care. If you want to look good, though, your first priority should be the pursuit of good health. Follow the commonsense rules: Avoid becoming overtired or stressed, eat a balanced diet, and get adequate rest. Control your intake of caffeine drinks and alcohol, and quit smoking. Within this holistic approach, lotions with herbal essential oils can be used for cleansing, nourishing, toning, and moisturizing the skin.

HERBS FOR THE BATH

Instead of using purchased essential oils in the bath, you can use herbs gathered from the garden. Small herb-filled bags like the ones shown above right (made the same way as sachets, described on page 158) can be used to perfume the bathwater. Simpler yet, you can just make a strong infusion or decoction of herbs and add that to your bath. For an infusion, pour half a kettle of boiling water over four or five cups of selected, coarsely chopped herbs and allow to steep for 20 to 30 minutes. Strain before adding to the bath. Decoction is a better method for spices and stems or bark. Use the same proportions as for the infusion above, but add the spices or bark to cold water, bring to a boil,

and simmer for 10 minutes or so before allowing to cool. Strain and use, or transfer to a pretty bottle. Bottled infusions and decoctions will keep for a few days in the refrigerator. Add a cupful of the scented water to each bath.

Infusions of rosemary or stinging nettle are effective in relieving aching muscles and joints, as are comfrey and chickweed.

A decoction of white willow bark (above) is also good for aches and pains. For a tonic bath use a combination of comfrey and parsley, or calendula and mint. To give you a "lift" before an evening out, make your own mixture from basil, bay, calendula, fennel, rosemary, sweet marjoram, sage, and thyme. When relaxation is the priority, choose rose, lavender, fennel, chamomile, or bay. To combine restfulness with luxury and a delicious scent, add to any of these some fresh, heavily perfumed rose petals; you can go further and add orange peel, flowers, or leaves as well. For the most decadent bath of all, scatter a few drops of rose oil and a handful of rose petals over the surface of the water.

Simple natural preparations can offer a degree of luxury. This bathroom shelf holds rosemary rinse, for dark hair; almond and honey soap; aloe vera soap; chamomile rinse for fair hair; and lavender essential oil.

SKIN CARE

It is important to treat your skin type appropriately. For oily skin, steam cleansing is very beneficial. Sit over a bowl of steaming water to which one or two drops each of lavender and yarrow oils has been added; place a towel over your head to help contain the steam. This treatment helps reduce problems with blocked pores. Once it has been cleansed, oily skin will benefit from rinsing with an infusion of mildly astringent herbs such as chamomile and chervil; these tighten the skin and close up pores. Another good toner for oily skin is a face splash made from a cooled infusion of lady's mantle leaves. (If you have particularly sensitive skin, you can rinse with cold, soft water after a minute or two.)

flower-water skin toner

This toner uses gently stimulating and antiseptic purchased flower waters. It is suitable for all skin types.
Makes 2 cups (450 ml)

1 cup (225 ml) rosewater or lavender water
1 cup (225 ml) distilled witch hazel
3 drops of rose or lavender essential oil (to match the choice of flower water)

Put into a dark glass bottle, and store in a cool spot. Use within six months. Shake the bottle to mix before each use.

cucumber and lavender cleansing milk

The combination of cucumber and lavender provides a soothing, gentle action that makes this cleansing milk invaluable for oily and normal skin types.

½ cup (110 ml) buttermilk
1 section of cucumber (about 3 inches or 10 cm long)
5 drops lavender essential oil

Peel the cucumber, then liquefy in a blender. Pour into a bowl; add the buttermilk and lavender oil and fold in. Let the mixture stand for two hours, strain and bottle it, and then refrigerate. Use within a week.
Caution *Those with highly sensitive skins may find that cucumber causes a reaction; test on a small, unobtrusive part of the body first.*

rose moisturizing cream

A pleasant, fragrant cream for dry or normal skin. The mixture of almond oil with lanolin and sunflower oil makes it useful soothing chapped or weathered skin.

4 tablespoons lanolin
2 tablespoons sunflower oil
4 tablespoons almond oil
1 teaspoon borax
4 tablespoons rosewater
5 drops rose essential oil

BENEFICIAL HERBS FOR SKIN

Infusions of the following are beneficial for the skin. For preparation, see page 139. Cool to lukewarm before using.

CALENDULA LEAVES AND FLOWERS
soothing and healing

LEMON BALM LEAVES
soothing and astringent

DANDELION LEAVES AND ROOTS
a cleansing tonic

MARSHMALLOW ROOTS AND LEAVES
emollient and healing

PARSLEY LEAVES
gently astringent, help prevent thread veins

STINGING NETTLE LEAVES, SEEDS AND ROOTS
cleansing, toning, help improve circulation

Melt the lanolin in a double boiler over low heat. Gently heat the sunflower and almond oil together in another saucepan. Add the oils to the lanolin and stir to combine. Take the pan off the heat. In a third pan, warm the rosewater and dissolve the borax in it. Then slowly add the rosewater and borax to the oil mixture, beating until cool. As thickening sets in, mix in the rose oil. Transfer the cream to an attractive, clean small pot or jar. Wait until the mixture has cooled thoroughly before tightening the lid. Use within a few days.

Caution *Before using, test a small, unobtrusive patch of your skin for any allergy to lanolin.*

HAIR CARE

Herbal applications are particularly appropriate for hair care, as is demonstrated by the large number of herbal hair products available commercially. When infusing herbs in water, use either clean rainwater or boiled and then cooled water; this is particularly important if your tap water is heavily chlorinated. For an "instant" herbal shampoo, prepare an herb infusion or decoction (see page 139) from any of the herbs given below, to suit your hair type, and add an equal volume of a baby shampoo. (Herbal shampoos are best used within a few days, so make only small quantities at a time—perhaps 1 cup of infusion.) Place in a container, cap securely, and shake to mix. Pour on to pre-wetted hair and shampoo as usual.

rosemary rinse

An excellent general conditioner, traditionally used for brown hair, making it softer, fuller, and more manageable. It can add luster to dull hair and also acts against dandruff and other dry scalp problems. Thyme and sage are also good general conditioners for darker hair. They can be substituted for rosemary in this recipe.

Method Pick a handful of rosemary and rub it between your hands for 10 seconds or so to help release the oils in the leaves and petals. Put the rosemary in a jug, pour on 2 cups (450 ml) of boiling water, and allow it to cool. The liquid will be pale green. Or, if you want a stronger concentration, make a decoction by simmering the rosemary in water for 10 minutes. The water will then turn a rich reddish color (see page 163). This decocotion is frequently recommended by herbalists as a scalp stimulant.

chamomile rinse

The traditional natural enhancing rinse to bring out the highlights in blond hair. Calendula flowers can also be added.

Method Make an infusion by steeping a handful of chamomile flowers in 2 cups (450 ml) of water for 15 minutes. Strain and allow to cool, then use as a conditioning hair rinse. Leave on the hair for 12 minutes or so, and rinse away with warm soft water.

BENEFICIAL HERBS FOR HAIR

The following herbs can be used in shampoos, or as rinses and conditioners. Prepare as infusions, following the directions on page 139.

FOR GREASY HAIR
calendula flowers, lavender, peppermint, rosemary, southernwood, yarrow, lemon balm

FOR DULL HAIR
calendula, stinging nettle, southernwood, rosemary, sage

FOR DRY HAIR
stinging nettle, marshmallow, comfrey, sage, parsley

FOR DANDRUFF
stinging nettle, nasturtium, rosemary

GLOSSARY

Terms in **bold** refer to other entries in the glossary.

Abortifacient A substance that could induce abortion or miscarriage.

Adaptogen A substance that helps the body adapt to different conditions and thus may increase tolerance to environmental or internal stress. Ginseng is a well-known example.

Adrenaline See **Epinephrine**.

Alcohols A class of compounds made up of carbon, hydrogen, and oxygen. Ethanol is the familiar alcohol made by fermentation of sugars and found in beers, wines, whiskey, and other spirits. In plants, alcohols are often constituents of essential oils; these include geranol, menthol, nerol, citronellol, cedrol, and benzyl alcohol. They sometimes have antiseptic and/or antiviral properties.

Aldehydes A class of compounds derived from alcohols. Plant aldehydes are components of essential oils. Examples include neral, citronellal, and benzaldehyde. The names are often the same as that of the related alcohol except that they end in -al rather than -ol.

Alkaloids A group of complex substances occurring in various plants and having diverse effects on the body. All contain nitrogen as well as carbon, hydrogen, and oxygen, and their names end in -ine. The name comes from "alkaline-like." Many are toxic and some cause hallucinations or are addictive, but a number of alkaloids are used medicinally. Examples of alkaloids are quinine, morphine, atropine, nicotine, caffeine; also the highly poisonous strychnine and coniine.

Analgesic A pain reliever, such as aspirin or morphine.

Annual A plant that completes its life cycle in one growing season.

Anthraquinones Anthraquinone is a yellow crystalline solid used in making dyes. Some anthraquinone compounds occur as **glycosides** in plants such as rhubarb and senna. These are strong irritants and can have a powerful laxative effect.

Antibody A type of blood protein manufactured in response to the presence of a foreign substance, such as a virus. An effective antibody renders the body immune to the disease borne by the invader.

Anticoagulant Acting to prevent or retard clotting (for example, of blood).

Antioxidant A substance that counters **oxidation**; examples are vitamins A, C, and E. Antioxidants also counter the harmful effects of **free radicals.**

Antispasmodic Preventing or arresting **spasms.**

Astringent A material that causes a tightening of tissues (by binding to surface proteins). Examples are witch hazel extract, rosewater, and chamomile tea (all of which contain **tannins**).

Atherosclerosis The build up of fatty deposits in artery walls. This is the most common form of arteriosclerosis, or "hardening of the arteries."

Azulenes A group of chemicals that are found in the essential oils of certain plants. The "parent compound" is a violet-blue liquid; its molecules have an unusual double-ring structure. The azulenes in plants are derivatives of this compound. The most important of them is chamazulene, also blue, which is responsible for many of the herbal properties of chamomile.

Biennial A plant that flowers and dies in its second growing season.

Carbohydrates A large group of different substances containing carbon, hydrogen, and oxygen. Plant carbohydrates are made by photosynthesis and include sugars and **polysaccharides** such as starch and cellulose.

Carcinogenic Tending to cause the formation of cancerous cells.

Carminative Able to calm the digestive tract and promote the expulsion of gas.

Carrier oil An oil into which an **essential oil** is mixed, so as to dilute it, before use.

Cathartic Causing dramatic evacuation of the bowels.

Cellulose A **polysaccharide** consisting of long chains of glucose units, cellulose is the chief constituent of plant cell walls. It is an important component of dietary fiber.

Chronic Describing a condition lasting for a prolonged period.

Cirrhosis A form of **chronic** liver disease involving the formation of fibrous cells in the liver that impair the organ's function. Its various causes include hepatitis and the poisoning that can result from long-term alcohol abuse.

Colic Waves of pain affecting the digestive tract.

Commission E An expert panel of the German Institute for Drugs and Medical Devices. This panel is respected worldwide for its thorough and wide-ranging appraisal of the clinical research on herbs and their efficacy in treating ailments. Its approval of particular herb uses is noted in the text of this book.

Coumarin A white crystalline substance with a scent similar to that of vanilla. Coumarin is the compound that is responsible for the smell of new-mown hay and sweet woodruff (*Galium odoratum*). Natural and synthetic forms are used extensively in perfumes. Coumarin compounds occur in many plants and are antibacterial and anticoagulant in action. In large quantities coumarin is toxic; it is used as rat poison.

Cream Emulsion of water and oil or fat that contains the dissolved components of a healing substance (see page 141).

Cystitis A condition in which the bladder is inflamed, causing painful urination. It normally arises from bacterial infection.

Decoction An extract made by boiling (see page 139).

Diuretic Stimulating urination.

Doctrine of Signatures An ancient theory according to which each plant was held to bear a sign that identified which part of the body it could be used to treat.

Emetic Inducing vomiting.

Emollient Softening or soothing, especially to the skin.

Enteric-coated Describing capsules or tablets that are coated so that they do not dissolve until they have passed through the stomach.

Enzymes Chemicals (proteins) that act as catalysts, helping to speed up biological processes without being changed themselves.

Epinephrine The hormone that prepares the body for action—the classic "fight or flight" response—in emergencies. It increases the heart and breathing rates and raises the blood sugar level. Also called **adrenaline**.

Essential fatty acids A special class of **fatty acids** vital to the body's proper functioning. These cannot be made by the body, so must be supplied in the diet. Examples are linoleic acid (found in linseed oil) and linolenic acid (found in linseed oil and evening primrose oil).

Essential oils The name given to the **volatile oils** secreted by aromatic plants (such as lavender and rosemary) that give each plant its characteristic smell or taste. Essential oils usually owe their fragrance to **terpenes** or **terpenoids** and small amounts of **alcohols**, **esters**, **aldehydes**, and other compounds.

Esters Compounds containing alcohols attached to fatty acids. They are present in essential oils, and often pleasantly scented.

Estrogens Female sex hormones.

Expectorant A substance that triggers the coughing up of mucus from the respiratory tract.

Fatty acids The major constituent of natural fats and oils. Fatty acids are made up of carbon, hydrogen, and oxygen in varying proportions. A fat is saturated when its molecules hold the maximum amount of hydrogen; monounsaturates have less hydrogen and polyunsaturates the least. See also **essential fatty acid**.

Flavones Crystalline compounds occurring in some plants. They are typically yellow (*flavus* is Latin for "yellow") and can be bitter or sweet. Some have **diuretic**, antiseptic, anti-inflammatory, or **antispasmodic** effects; some are also used in dyes.

Flavonoids A group of pigments found in many flowers and fruits, containing a **flavone** structure in their molecules. Different flavonoids are responsible for many bright colors in plants. Flavonoids can deter a range of insects from a plant, while at the same time attracting specialist insects. Some flavonoids are bitter, while other closely related molecules can be very sweet.

Free radicals Chemicals formed in the body as part of its metabolism and defense against bacteria. Excessive production of free radicals is believed to create conditions that may lead to degenerative diseases including heart disease and cancer.

Furocoumarins Compounds related to **coumarin** that are found in umbellifers (e.g., angelica) and in certain essential oils (e.g., bergamot). They can cause photosensitive reactions in sunlight.

Glucosilinates Compounds found only in plants of the mustard family (Cruciferae), responsible for the high resistance to disease and insect attack of some cruciferous plants. Glucosilinates can irritate the skin or cause blisters. This action was used therapeutically in "mustard plasters" to increase blood flow to an area.

Glycosides A large group of compounds in which a simple sugar molecule is joined to another molecule. The sugar is usually glucose (in which case the compound is called a glucoside), but many other sugars are found in glycosides. The compounds responsible for foxglove's action on the heart (digoxin and digitoxin) are glycosides.

Hemorrhoids Veins that protrude from the anal wall or within the rectum.

Hydrocarbon An organic compound containing hydrogen and carbon, but no oxygen. **Terpenes**, for example, are hydrocarbons.

Hypertension High blood pressure.

Hypotension Low blood pressure.

Infusion An extract obtained by soaking, normally in hot water (see page 139).

Inulin A **polysaccharide** found in certain plants, especially members of the daisy (Compositae) and bellflower (Campanulaceae) families, where it acts to store energy for the plant (a role usually carried out by starch). It is present in burdock, dandelion, and chicory as well as elecampane (*Inula*), for which it was named. The compound itself has a sweet taste but is not digested or absorbed. It may have a positive effect on the populations of beneficial bacteria in the intestines.

Ketones A class of compounds chemically similar to **aldehydes**. The names are often the same as that of the related alcohol, except that they end in -one rather than -ol. Some (e.g., carvone) are useful in herbal medicine, but many are toxic.

Mucilages Slimy gels obtained from plants such as marshmallow and slippery elm (*Ulmus rubra*). Mucilages may have a soothing effect on inflamed tissues and are used in some cosmetics.

Mucus Slippery material secreted by cells of mucous membranes that line the soft tissues of the body, such as the gut and respiratory tract. In healthy individuals it moistens and protects the mucous membranes.

Ointment A soft, oily or fatty substance that contains the dissolved components of some healing material (see pages 140–41).

Oxidation A chemical process in which a substance combines with oxygen, causing a reaction. As examples, combustion is the oxidation of paper or wood; rust is the oxidation of iron.

Pathogen A disease-causing agent, such as a virus or bacterium.

Perennial A perennial plant is one that lives for at least three seasons.

Phenolic acids A group of naturally occurring acids found in certain plants, where they may act as a defense against some pests and diseases. These acids are **antioxidants.**

Placebo An inactive substance used as a control when assessing the activity of another substance; a dummy pill.

Polysaccharides Compounds (**carbohydrates**) that consist of a number of small sugar units linked together. Polysaccharides serve diverse roles in plants. Starch, for example, stores energy for plants (and supplies energy to animals that feed on the plants), while cellulose plays a structural role.

Poultice A moist pack, often composed of herbal material, that is applied to the skin (see page 141).

Prophylactic An agent that acts to prevent disease.

Pyrethrins Compounds found in certain species of chrysanthemum (*Pyrethrum*). The pyrethrins and their synthetic equivalents (pyrethroids) are highly toxic to insects (including, unfortunately, honeybees) and relatively nontoxic to people and other animals (though extremely toxic to fish); hence their extensive use as an insecticide.

Pyrrolizidine alkaloids A group of toxic alkaloids found in certain plants, such as tansy and ragweed (*Senecio jacobaea*), where they may act as a deterrent against grazing by some animals. Herbs containing pyrrolizidine alkaloids should never be taken internally, as they can damage the liver.

Resins The solid or semisolid dried saps of certain woody plants, such as myrrh (*Commiphora* spp.).

Saponins Plant glycosides that froth when mixed with water. These are the compounds that give soapwort (*Saponaria officinalis*) its name and its ability to clean delicate fabrics. There are two main types. The triterpene saponins, or triterpenoids, (found in cowslip roots and some other plants) generally act as strong **expectorants**. The steroidal

saponins (found in licorice and some other plants) can act like human steroid hormones, and can be stimulant, anti-inflammatory, and **diuretic**.

Sedative Having a soothing or calming effect.

Serotonin A compound that transmits information (nerve impulses) in the brain, functioning in memory and sleep.

Sesquiterpene lactones Biologically active compounds found in plants belonging to the daisy family (Compositae). They often cause an allergic skin reaction and should be avoided if there is any sensitivity or tendency to strong allergic reactions.

Spasm Involuntary muscular contraction, especially one resulting in cramp or convulsion.

Tannins A group of compounds (particularly tannic acid) found to some extent in all plants. Tannins occur in high amounts in the bark of trees, but also in leaves and other parts of plants. They are acidic and are used medicinally for their **astringent** effect. Tannins are also used commercially in dying fabric, inks, the production of wine and beer, and even in photography.

Terpenes A group of important **hydrocarbons** found in plants. Terpenes are the main constituent of most **essential oils**. Examples are limonene (responsible for the scent of lemons), pinene (found in pines), and camphene (in camphor). One important group of terpenes are the carotenes, pigments that give carrots their orange color; they play a limited role in photosynthesis and are an important source of vitamin A. Terpenes are classified according to the number of hydrocarbon units in their molecules: Monoterpenes, sesquiterpenes, diterpenes, triterpenes, and tetraterpenes.

Terpenoids Derivatives of **terpenes**. Camphor (used as a treatment for colds, and as an insect repellent) and menthol (used as an antiseptic, in inhalants and as a flavoring) are examples of terpenoids.

Thujone A compound found in certain species of *Artemisia*, especially wormwood. Thujone may help these plants avoid being eaten by animals. It is the main active principle of wormwood. Chemically, it is a monoterpene. It also has similarities with the structure of tetrahydrocannibinol, which is the active component of cannabis. Thujone is addictive and in large quantities toxic.

Tincture A concentrated solution of herbal components in **alcohol** (see page 140).

Transpiration The release of water by evaporation from leaves.

Vitamin One of a group of substances that are required in small quantities for the vital function of the body. Vitamins cannot usually be synthesized by the body, so they need to be obtained from food.

Volatile oil An oil that readily evaporates; a component of an herb's **essential oil**.

Waxes Substances found in many plants that have properties similar to beeswax. Structurally, they are esters made up of large-molecule fatty acids combined with alcohols.

Xanthones A group of compounds (**flavonoid glycosides**) found in many plants. Xanthones are credited for the antiviral effect of some herbs, such as St.-John's-wort.

FURTHER READING

Blumenthal, Mark (ed.). *The Complete German Commission E Monographs: Therapeutic Guide to Herbal Medicines.* Newton, Mass.: Integrative Medicine Communications, 1998.

Bown, Deni. *Encyclopedia of Herbs & Their Uses.* New York and London: Dorling Kindersley, 1995.

Bradley, Peter (ed.). *British Herbal Compendium.* Bournemouth, Dorset: British Herbal Medicine Association, 1992.

Brandies, Monica. *Ortho's Guide to Herbs.* Columbus, Ohio: Ortho Books, 1997.

Brown, Donald, J. *Herbal Prescriptions for Better Health.* Roseville, Calif.: Prima Publishing, 1997.

Chevallier, Andrew. *Encyclopedia of Medicinal Plants.* New York and London: Dorling Kindersley, 1996.

Culpeper, Nicholas. *Culpeper's Complete Herbal and English Physician* (reprint of the 1649 edition). Glenwood, Ill.: Meyerbooks, 1987.

Duke, James. *Handbook of Biologically Active Phytochemicals & Their Activities.* Boca Raton, Fla.: CRC Press, 1992. *The Green Pharmacy Herbal Handbook.* Emmaus, Pa.: Rodale Press, 1997.

Evans, William Charles. *Trease & Evans Pharmacognosy.* 14th edition. St. Louis Mo.: W. D. Saunders, 1996.

Fleming, Thomas (ed.). *PDR for Herbal Medicines.* 2nd edition. Montvale, N.J.: Medical Economics Company, 2000.

Foster, Gertrude B. *Park's Success with Herbs.* Greenwood, S.C.: Park Seed Company, 1980.

Foster, Steven and James Duke. *A Field Guide to Medicinal Plants and Herbs of Eastern and Central North America.* 2nd edition. New York: Houghton Mifflin, 2000.

Garland, Sarah. *The Complete Book of Herbs and Spices.* London: Frances Lincoln, 1979; Pleasantville, N.Y.: Reader's Digest, 1979.

Grieve, Maud. *A Modern Herbal.* New York: Dover Publications, 1978.

Griffiths, Mark. *The Royal Horticultural Society's Index of Garden Plants.* New York and London: Macmillan, 1994.

Griggs, Barbara. *Green Pharmacy: The History and Evolution of Western Herbal Medicine.* Rochester, Vt.: Healing Arts Press, 1997.

Harbourne, Jeffrey. *Introduction to Ecological Biochemistry.* San Diego, Calif.: Academic Press, 1997.

Healing Power of Herbs. Pleasantville, N.Y.: Reader's Digest Books, 1999.

Kowalchik, Claire and William H. Hylton (eds.). *Rodale's Illustrated Encyclopedia of Herbs.* Emmaus, Pa.: Rodale Press, 1998.

Landsberg, Sylvia. *The Medieval Garden.* London: British Museum, 1996.

Lust, John B. *The Herb Book.* Sini Valley, Calif.: Benedict Lust Publications, 1974.

Magic and Medicine of Herbs. Pleasantville, N.Y.: Reader's Digest Books, 1986.

Medical Advisor: The Complete Guide to Alternative & Conventional Treatments. Alexandria, Va.: Time Life, 2000.

National Audubon Society Field Guide to North American Wildflowers, Eastern Region. New York: Knopf, 2001.

National Audubon Society Field Guide to North American Wildflowers, Western Region. New York: Knopf, 2001.

Ody, Penelope. *Complete Medicinal Herbal.* New York and London: Dorling Kindersley, 1993.

Pierce, Andrea *et al. The American Pharmaceutical Association Practical Guide to Natural Medicines.* New York: William Morrow, 1999.

Rose, Jeanne. *375 Essential Oils & Hydrosols.* Berkeley, Calif.: Frog Ltd, 1999.

Schar, Douglas. *Echinacea: The Plant that Boosts Your Immune System.* Berkeley, Calif.: North Atlantic Books, 1999.

INDEX

Page numbers in **bold** refer to principal references. Page numbers in *italic* refer to illustrations

A

aches and pains 149, 163
Achillea ageratum see mace, English
A. millefolium see yarrow
Aconitum napellus see monkshood
agrimony (*Agrimonia eupatoria*) **40–41**, *40*
  growing 20
  medicinal uses 142, 144, 147
air fresheners 152
Alcea rosea see hollyhock
Alchemilla mollis see lady's mantle
allergies 145
Allium cepa see onions
  A. sativum see garlic
  A. schoenoprasum see chives
almonds, cilantro and mint sauce with 122
aloe (*Aloe vera*) **43**, *43*
  growing 20
  medicinal uses 147, 148, *148*
Althaea officinalis see marshmallow
Americas 12, 13, 14
Anethum graveolens see dill
angelica (*Angelica archangelica*) 22, **45–46**, *45*
  essential oil 162
  growing 20, 26, *26*, 32
  harvesting *36*
Angelica atropurpurea see masterwort
  A. sylvestris 46
anise (*Pimpinella anisum*) 10, **80–81**, *81*
  growing 21
  medicinal uses 144, 145, 147
Anthriscus cerefolium see chervil
aphids 30, 31
Apium graveolens see celery
apothecaries 12–13, *13*
appetite, loss of 144
apple mint (*Mentha suaveolens*) **73**, *73*, 153

Armoracia rusticana see horseradish
arnica (*Arnica montana*) **104**
aromatherapy 160–62
artemisias 22, 48–49
  companion planting 31
  drying 37
  in the home 155, 158
Artemisia abrotanum see southernwood
  A. absinthium see wormwood
  A. annua see wormwood, sweet
  A. dracunculus see tarragon
  A. pontica see wormwood, Roman
  A. vulgaris see mugwort
arugula: salad of unusual herbs 128
aspirin 15, 89
Assyria 10
Atropa belladonna see deadly nightshade
atropine 15
Avicenna (Ibn Sina) 11
avocado and tomatillo dip 127
Ayurvedic medicine 10, 15

B

basil (*Ocimum basilicum*) **76–7**, *76*
basil and pecan pesto 124
basil croutons 128
basil pesto 124
basil risotto 133
baths 163
bush basil (*Ocimum minimum*) 77
culinary uses 116
essential oil 160, 161, 162
freezing 37
growing 19, 21, 24, 25, 27
harvesting 36
in the home 158
mixed herb pesto 126
vegetable soup with fresh herbs 132
basswood (*Tilia americana*) 99
baths 160–61, 163
bay (*Laurus nobilis*) 22, **65**, *65*
  baths 163
  brown rice with bay leaves 134
  essential oil 162
  growing 20, 24, 25, 35

in the home 154, 159
medicinal uses 149
potpourri 156, *156*
Bayer 15
beauty care 163–65
bee balm (*Monarda didyma*) 14, 22, **74**, *74*
  growing 21, 24, 26, 34
  in the home 152
  medicinal uses 144
  potpourri 156, *156*
  for wildlife 25
Beech, Dr. Wooster 14
bees 25, *25*
bergamot (*Monarda fistulosa*) 74, 161, *161*
blackberry (*Rubus fruticosus*) **87**, *87*, 142, 147
bloating 144
bloodroot (*Sanguinaria canadensis*) 14, **111**, *111*
boneset (*Eupatorium perfoliatum*) 14, **56**, *56*
  growing 20, 26
  for wildlife 25
borax, drying 154
botanic gardens 14
bouquet garni 119, *119*
boxwood (*Buxus sempervirens*) 14, 18, *18*
bread, basil croutons 128
bronchitis 145–47
bruises 149
bulgur with parsley and mint 134
burners, aromatherapy 160, *160*
burns 148
butter, herb 122
butterflies 25
Buxus sempervirens see boxwood

C

calendula (*Calendula officinalis*) 10, 22, **50**, annefanne*50*
  baths 163
  drying 154
  essential oil 161, 162
  growing 20, 24, *33*
  herb gardens *19*
  in the home 152, 154
  medicinal uses 147, 148
  skin care 164
cancer 6
candles 159, *159*, 160
canker sores 144

cannellini beans: garlic, white bean and sun-dried tomato salsa 127
caraway 118
carrier oils 161
cashews: mint and ginger pesto 126
castor oil plant (*Ricinus communis*) **109–10**, *109*
catnip (*Nepeta cataria*) 22, **75**, *75*
  growing 21
  medicinal uses 149
celery (*Apium graveolens*) **46–47**, *47*
  culinary uses 116
  growing 20
  medicinal uses 144, 147
centaury (*Centaurium erythraea*) **50–51**, *51*, 144
chamomile, annual (*Matricaria recutita*) **68–69**, *68*
  growing 20
  medicinal uses 144, 145, *146*, 147, 148, *148*, 149
chamomile, perennial (*Chamaemelum nobile*) 22, **51–52**, *51*
  baths 163
  companion planting 31
  drying 37
  essential oil 160, 161, 162
  growing 20, 24, 26
  hair rinse 165
  in the home 152, 153, 158
  medicinal uses *143*, 144, 147, 149
  potpourri 156, *156*
  skin care 164
Charaka Samhita 10
cheese: pizza with herb pesto and goat cheese *126*, 133
Chelsea Physic Garden, London 14
chervil (*Anthriscus cerefolium*) 12, **46**, *47*
  freezing herbs 37
  growing 19, 20, 24, 26, 32, *33*
  skin care 164
chickweed (*Stellaria media*) **94–95**, *94*
  baths 163
  culinary uses 116
  medicinal uses 147, 149
chicory (*Cichorium intybus*) **52–53**, *52*

culinary uses 116, 118
growing 20
medicinal uses 144
Chinchona see Peruvian bark
Chinese medicine 15
chives (*Allium schoenoprasum*)
    10, 22, *42*, **43**
    companion planting 31
    freezing herbs 37
    growing 20, 24, *24*, 25, 32
    herb butter 122
    herb mayonnaise 122
    knot gardens 18
    storing 118
Christianity 11
Cichorium intybus see chicory
cilantro *see* coriander
    cilantro and lime pesto 124
    cilantro and mint sauce with
        almonds 122
    culinary uses 118, *118*
    storing 118
    tomatoes and yellow
        peppers with herbs 130
cinnamon 10
citronella oil *161*
clary sage (*Salvia sclarea*) 21,
    91, *91*, *156*
cleavers, medicinal uses
    147–48, *148*
colds 145
Columella 10
comfrey (*Symphytum
    officinale*) **95–96**, *95*
    baths 163
    growing 21, 35
    medicinal uses 149
    for wildlife 25, *25*
Commission E 138, 142, 144,
    145, 147, 148, 149
companion planting 31
compresses 141
coneflower, pale (*Echinacea
    pallida*) 7, 55
coneflower, purple *see*
    echinacea
conservation 6–7
constipation 142
containers, growing herbs in
    24–25, *24*, 28
Convallaria majalis see lily-of-
    the-valley
Convention on International
    Trade in Endangered
    Species (CITES) 6–7
coriander (*Coriandrum
    sativum*) 12, **53**, *53*
    companion planting 31

essential oil 162
growing 19, 20, 32
medicinal uses 144
see also cilantro
Corsican mint (*Mentha
    requienii*) 73, *73*
costmary (*Tanacetum
    balsamita* subsp.
    balsamitoides) 21, 28, **96**,
    96, 154
cottage gardens 19
coughs 145–47
cowslip (*Primula veris*) 21, 26,
    82, **83**, 147
creams 141
croutons, basil 128
crown rot 31
Crusades 12
cucumber: cucumber and
    lavender cleansing milk
    164
    cucumber soup with mint
        132
culinary herbs 23, 115–35
Culpeper, Nicholas 13–14
cut flowers 23
cuts 148
cuttings 35

D
damping off 31
dandelion (*Taraxacum
    officinale*) **97–98**, *97*
    culinary uses 116, 118
    growing 21
    medicinal uses 144
    salad of unusual herbs 128
    skin care 164
dandruff 165
Datura stramonium see thorn
    apple
deadheading 28
deadly nightshade (*Atropa
    belladonna*) 15, **105–106**,
    105
decoctions 139–40, 163
desserts 135
diarrhea 142
diatomaceous earth 29
digestive disorders 142–44
Digitalis purpurea see foxglove
dill (*Anethum graveolens*) 10,
    12, 22, **44–45**, *44*
    culinary uses 116
    dill and lemon pesto 125
    freezing herbs 37
    growing 19, 20, 25, 32
    in the home 152–53

medicinal uses 144
    shrimp with mustard and
        dill 134
dips 127
diseases 29, 31
distillation 11, *11*, 12
division 34, *34–35*
dock, yellow (*Rumex crispus*)
    88–89, 145, *146*
dog rose (*Rosa canina*) **84–85**,
    85
downy mildew 31
drainage 29
dressings 122–23
drugs 6, 15, 138
drying 37, 153–54, *153*

E
Eau de Cologne mint
    (*Mentha* x *piperita* f.
    citrata) 73, *73*
Ebers papyrus 10
echinacea (*Echinacea purpurea*
    and *Echinacea angustifolia*)
    7, 20, **54–55**, *54*
Echinacea pallida see
    coneflower, pale
Eclectic School 14
Egypt, ancient 10
elder, blue (*Sambucus
    caerulea*) 92
elder, European (*Sambucus
    nigra*) **92**, *92*
elderberry (*Sambucus
    canadensis*) **92**, 116, 145,
    146
elecampane (*Inula helenium*)
    64–65, *65*
    companion planting 31
    growing 20
    medicinal uses 147
    potpourri *156*
ephedra (*Ephedra sinica*) 10
essential oils 11, *11*, 12,
    160–62
eucalyptus (*Eucalyptus
    globulus*) **55**, *55*, 154, 160
Eupatorium perfoliatum see
    boneset
    E. purpureum see Joe Pye
        weed
evening primrose (*Oenothera
    biennis*) **77–78**, *77*

F
fennel (*Foeniculum vulgare*)
    12, 22, **58–59**, *58*
    baths 163

essential oil 161, 162
freezing herbs 37
growing 20, 32, *33*
in the home 152–53
medicinal uses *143*, 144
fertilizers 28
feverfew (*Tanacetum
    parthenium*) 19, **96–97**, *96*
    companion planting 31
    growing 21, 24, 32
    in the home 152, 154, 158
Filipendula ulmaria see
    meadowsweet
fines herbes 119
fixatives, potpourri 157
flatulence 144
flax (*Linum usitatissimum*) 22,
    67, *67*
    culinary uses 116
    growing 20, *33*
    medicinal uses 142, 147
flea beetles 30
flower-water skin toner 164
flowers:
    deadheading 28
    drying 153–54
    flower arrangements 23,
        152–53
    harvesting 36
foliage 22
food, culinary herbs 115–35
formal gardens 18
foxglove (*Digitalis purpurea*)
    15, **107–108**, *107*
    growing 20, 26
    in the home 153
frankincense 157, 159
freezing herbs 37
frost 27, 28

G
garden design 18–19
gardening 18–35
garlic (*Allium sativum*) 10, 12,
    42–43, *42*
    culinary uses 116–18
    garlic spray (pesticide) 29
    garlic, white bean, and sun-
        dried tomato salsa 127
    growing 20
    medicinal uses *143*, 144,
        147, 148, *148*
    vegetable soup with fresh
        herbs 132
George III, King of England
    159
germander (*Teucrium
    chamaedrys*) 14

ginger (*Zingiber officinale*) 10, **103**, *103*
   ginger lemonade 135
   growing 21, 25
   medicinal uses 142, *143*, 144, 145–47
   mint and ginger pesto 126
ginger mint (*Mentha* x *gracilis*) **73**, *73*, 153
ginseng, American (*Panax quinquefolius*) 7
Glycyrrhiza glabra see licorice
goat cheese, pizza with herb pesto and *126*, 133
goldenseal (*Hydrastis canadensis*) **62**, *62*
grains 134
Greece 10
growing herbs 18–35
gum benzoin 157

H
hair care 165
Hamamelis virginiana see witch hazel
hardiness, growing herbs 27
harvesting herbs 36, *36*
hay fever 145
hedges, herb 18, 28
henbane (*Hyoscyamus niger*) **108**, *108*
herb bags 158, 163
herb balls 155, *155*
herb gardens 18, *18*, *19*
herbal remedies 6, 23, 137–49
   history 10–15
   preparations 139–41
herbals 13–14
herbes de Provence 119, *119*
   roast pork with *herbes de Provence* 134
history 9–15
hollyhock (*Alcea rosea*) 44
holy basil (*Ocimum tenuiflorum*) 77
hops (*Humulus lupulus*) **61**, *61*
   growing 20, 35
   herb gardens *19*
   medicinal uses 149
   pillows 159
   potpourri *156*
   wreaths 155
horehound, white (*Marrubium vulgare*) 20, **68**, *68*, 144
horsemint (*Monarda punctata*) 74

horseradish (*Armoracia rusticana*) **47**, *47*
   growing 20, 29, 35
   medicinal uses 145
Humulus lupulus see hops
Hydrastis canadensis see goldenseal
Hyoscyamus niger see henbane
Hypericum perforatum see St.-John's-wort
hyssop (*Hyssopus officinalis*) 14, **64**, *64*

I
Ibn al Baytar 11
incense 159
India 10, 11
indigestion 144
indoor herb gardens 28
infusions 139, 163
inhalations, steam 145
insects: pests 29–30
   repellents 158, 159
insomnia 149, 159
International Union for the Conservation of Nature 6
Inula helenium see elecampane
ipecac (*Psychotria ipecacuanha*) 14
iris, Florentine (*Iris germanica* var. *florentina*) 157
Islam 11
ispaghula (*Plantago ovata*) 82

J
Japanese beetles 30
Jardin du Roi, Paris 14
Joe Pye weed (*Eupatorium purpureum*) **56**, *56*
   growing 20, 26
   in the home 152
   for wildlife 25
joint pain 149

K
knot gardens 14, 18, *18*

L
lady's mantle (*Alchemilla mollis*) **41**, *41*
   growing 20, 26, *27*
   in the home 152, *152*, 153
   medicinal uses 142, *143*, 147–48, *148*
   skin care 164
Laurus nobilis see bay
lavender (*Lavandula angustifolia*) 22, **66**, *66*

baths 163
companion planting 31
cucumber and lavender cleansing milk 164
drying 154
essential oil 160, 161, *161*, 162
growing 20, 24, 26, *26*, 34
herb gardens *19*
in the home 152, 153, 158
knot gardens 14, 18, *18*
medicinal uses 144, 149
potpourri 156, *156*, 157, *157*
skin care 164
for wildlife 25
lavender, French (*Lavandula stoechas*) 66
lavender, spike (*Lavandula latifolia*) 66
laxatives 142
leaf miners 30
leafspot diseases 31
leaves: drying 37
   harvesting 36
Leech Book of Bald 11
lemon: dill and lemon pesto 125
   ginger lemonade 135
   medicinal uses 147
lemon balm (*Melissa officinalis*) **70**, *70*
   culinary uses 116
   essential oil 160
   ginger lemonade 135
   growing 20, 24, 26
   harvesting 36
   in the home 159
   medicinal uses 149
   skin care 164
   for wildlife 25
lemon thyme (*Thymus* x *citriodorus*) 99
lemongrass oil 161
licorice (*Glycyrrhiza glabra*) **59**, *59*
   harvesting 36
   medicinal uses 145–47, *146*
light, indoor herb gardens 28
lily-of-the-valley (*Convallaria majalis*) 20, **106**, *106*
lime and cilantro pesto 124
linden (*Tilia cordata*) 99, *99*, **145**, *146*
linden, large-leaved (*Tilia platyphyllos*) 99
Linum usitatissimum see flax
lungwort, medicinal uses 13

M
mace, English (*Achillea ageratum*) **40**, *40*
Malva moschata see musk mallow
marjoram, pot (*Origanum onites*) 21, 78–79, *79*
marjoram, sweet (*Origanum majorana*) 10, **78**
   baths 163
   essential oil 160, 162
   growing 21, 24, *24*, 25
   in the home 152, 156
   knot gardens 14
   medicinal uses 145
Marrubium vulgare see horehound, white
marshmallow (*Althaea officinalis*) **44**, *44*
   culinary uses 116
   growing 20, 26
   medicinal uses 145, 147
   skin care 164
massage oils 161
masterwort (*Angelica atropurpurea*) 46, 153
Matricaria recutita see chamomile, annual
mayonnaise, herb 122
meadowsweet (*Filipendula ulmaria*) 13, **57**, *57*
   growing 20, 26, *27*
   in the home 152, 153
   medicinal uses 15, 145, *146*
mealybugs 30
medicinal herbs *see* herbal remedies
Melaleuca alternifolia see tea tree
Melissa officinalis see lemon balm
melon sorbet, minted 135
Mentha see mint
   M. × *gracilis see* ginger mint
   M. × *piperita see* peppermint
   M. × *piperita* f. *citrata see* Eau de Cologne mint
   M. pulegium see pennyroyal
   M. requienii see Corsican mint
   M. spicata see spearmint
   M. suaveolens see apple mint
mezzaluna 118, *118*
Middle Ages 11–13
mildew 31
milk thistle (*Silybum marianum*) 21, **94**, *94*, 144

mint (*Mentha*) 12, 22, **72–73**, *72–3*
  baths 163
  bulgur with parsley and mint 134
  cilantro and mint sauce with almonds 122
  cucumber soup with mint 132
  culinary uses 116
  drying 37
  growing 21, 24, 25, 26, 28, 34, 35, *35*
  harvesting 36
  in the home 152, 153, 158
  mint and ginger pesto 126
  mint pesto 125
  minted melon sorbet 135
  for wildlife 25
moisturizing cream, rose 164–65
Monarda didyma see bee balm
  M. fistulosa see bergamot
  M. punctata see horsemint
monasteries 11–12
monkshood (*Aconitum napellus*) 15
morphine 15
mountain valerian (*Valeriana sitchensis*) 102
mugwort (*Artemisia vulgaris*) 13
muscles, aches and pains 149
musk mallow (*Malva moschata*) 44
mustard 12
  shrimp with mustard and dill 134
myrrh 157, 159

N
nasturtium (*Tropaeolum majus*) 14, **100**, *100*
  culinary uses 116
  growing 21, 27
  herbed strawberries 135
  medicinal uses 147–48, *148*, 149
  salad of unusual herbs with basil croutons 128
Native Americans 14
nausea 142
Neanderthal man 10
Nepeta cataria see catnip
  N. × *faassenii* 75
  N. sibirica 75
  N. 'Six Hills Giant' 75
nervous tension 149

nettle, stinging (*Urtica dioica*) **100–101**, *100*
  baths 163
  culinary uses 116
  medicinal uses 149
  skin care 164
  stinging nettle soup 131–32, *131*
nosegays 153, *153*

O
Ocimum basilicum see basil
  O. minimum see basil, bush
  O. tenuiflorum see holy basil
Oenothera biennis see evening primrose
oils: carrier oils 161
  distillation 11, *11*, 12
  essential oils 160–62
  herb-flavoured 120, *121*
  massage oils 161
ointments 140–41
onions (*Allium cepa*) 10, 12, 43
  growing 20
  medicinal uses 144, 145, 147
  onion syrup 140
opium poppy *see* poppy
oregano (*Origanum vulgare*) **79**, *79*
  growing 21, 25
  medicinal uses 145, 147
  for wildlife 25
Origanum majorana see marjoram, sweet
  O. onites see marjoram, pot
orris root 157

P
pain relief 149, 163
Panax quinquefolius see ginseng, American
Papaver somniferum see poppy
Paracelsus 13
parsley (*Petroselinum crispum*) 10, **80**, *80*
  baths 163
  bulgur with parsley and mint 134
  companion planting 31
  culinary uses 118
  dill and lemon pesto 125
  growing 21, 24, *24*, 25, 32, 33
  herb butter 122
  herb mayonnaise 122

knot gardens 18
  mixed herb pesto 126
  skin care 164
  spicy parsley sauce 123
  storing 118
  tomatoes and yellow peppers with herbs 130
parsley worms 30
pennyroyal (*Mentha pulegium*) 12, 34, **73**, *73*
peppermint (*Mentha* x *piperita*) **70–71**, *71*
  culinary uses 118
  essential oil 160, 161, 162
  growing in containers 24, *24*
  medicinal uses *143*, 144, 145, *146*, 147
peppers: tomatoes and yellow peppers with herbs 130
Peruvian bark (*Chinchona*) 14, 15
pestos 124–6
  basil 124
  basil and pecan 124
  cilantro and lime 124
  dill and lemon 125
  mint 125
  mint and ginger 126
  mixed herb 126
  pizza with herb pesto and goat cheese 126, 133
pests 29–30
Petroselinum crispum see parsley
pH values, soil 27
"physic" gardens 11–12, *12*
pillows 158–59, *159*
Pimpinella anisum see anise
pine nuts: mint pesto 125
pizza with herb pesto and goat cheese 126, 133
Plantago afra see psyllium
  P. major see plantain, broadleaf
  P. ovata see psyllium, blonde
  P. scabra see psyllium, black
plantain, broadleaf (*Plantago major*) 13, 82, 147–8
Pliny the Elder 10
pomanders 13
poppy, opium (*Papaver somniferum*) 15, *15*, **109–10**, *109*
pork: roast pork with *herbes de Provence* 134

Potentilla anserina see silverweed
  P. erecta see tormentil
potpourri 154, 155–57, *156*, *157*
Potter, Beatrix 144
potting mix 24–25
poultices 141
powdery mildew 31
preserving herbs 37
Prevost, Jean-Louis *15*
Primula veris see cowslip
propagation 32–35, *33–35*
pruning 28
Psychotria ipecacuanha see ipecac
psyllium (*Plantago afra*) 81–82, 142, *142*, *143*
psyllium, black (*Plantago scabra*) 82
psyllium, blonde (*Plantago ovata*) 82

Q
Al Qanum fi Tibb 11
quinine 14, 15

R
raised beds 25, *25*, 27
rashes 147–48
raspberry (*Rubus idaeus*) **87**, *87*, *143*
respiratory tract problems 145–47
Rheum palmatum see rhubarb, Chinese
rhubarb, Chinese (*Rheum palmatum*) 22, **83**
  growing 21
  medicinal uses 142, *143*
rice: basil risotto 133
  brown rice with bay leaves 134
Ricinus communis see castor oil plant
rings, herb 155
risotto, basil 133
Roman de la Rose 12
Roman Empire 10–11, 18
root rot 31
roots, drying 37
Rosa × *centifolia* 84, 147, 156
  R. × *damascena* 84, 156
  R. gallica 84, *84*, 147, 156
  R. moschata 156
  R. rugosa 84–85, *84*
rose (*Rosa*) **84–85**, *84–85*
  baths 163

drying 154, *154*
essential oil 160, 161, 162
flower-water skin toner 164
growing 21, 35
in the home 152, 153
medicinal uses 147
moisturizing cream 164–65
potpourri 156, *156*, 157, *157*
rose water 14
rosemary (*Rosmarinus officinalis*) 10, 12, 22, **86**, *86*
baths 163
drying 37
essential oil 160, 161, 162
growing 21, 24, 25, 35
hair rinse 165
harvesting 36
in the home 152, 154, 155, 159
knot gardens 18
medicinal uses *143*, 144, 145, 149
potpourri 156, *156*
storing 118
for wildlife 25
Rösslin *11*
Rubus fruticosus see blackberry
R. idaeus see raspberry
rue (*Ruta graveolens*) 12, 21, **110–11**, *110*
Rumex acetosa see sorrel
R. acetosella see sheep's sorrel
R. crispus see dock, yellow
R. scutatus see sorrel, French
rusts 31
Ruta graveolens see rue

S
sachets 158
sage (*Salvia officinalis*) 12, 22, **90–91**, *90*
baths 163
culinary uses 116, 118
drying 37
essential oil 161
growing 21, 24, 25, 34
harvesting 36
in the home 154, 158
medicinal uses 144, 147
potpourri 156
for wildlife 25
St. Gall 12
St.-John's-wort (*Hypericum perforatum*) **63**, *63*
growing 20
medicinal uses 15, 147, 148

salads 128–30
herbed salad 128–29
tomatoes and yellow peppers with herbs 130
unusual herbs with basil croutons 128
salicylic acid 15
Salix see willow
salsa, garlic, white bean, and sun-dried tomato 127
Salvia officinalis see sage
S. sclarea see clary, biennial
Sambucus caerulea see elder, blue
S. canadensis see elderberry
S. nigra see elder, European
sandalwood 157
Sanguinaria canadensis see bloodroot
sassafras (*Sassafras albidum*) **112**, *112*
Satureja hortensis see summer savory
S. montana see winter savory
sauces 122–23
cilantro and mint with almonds 122
pestos 124–26
sorrel 123
spicy parsley 123
savory *see* summer savory; winter savory
Saxons 11
scales 30
scented herbs 23, 153–54
candles 159
seasoning mixtures 119
seedlings 33, *33*
seeds: drying 37
harvesting 36, *36*
sowing 32–3, *33*
Shakers 14
shampoo 165
sheep's sorrel (*Rumex acetosella*) 88
shrimp with mustard and dill 134
Signatures, Doctrine of 13, 14
silica gel, drying herbs 154
silverweed (*Potentilla anserina*) 83
Silybum marianum see milk thistle
sinus congestion 145
skin care 163, 164–65
skin problems 147–48
sleep problems 149, 159
slugs 30

snails 30
soap, insecticidal 29
soil, growing herbs 25, 26, 27, 28
sorbet, minted melon 135
sorrel (*Rumex acetosa*) **88**, *88*
culinary uses 116, 118
growing 21, 26
medicinal uses 145, *146*
salad of unusual herbs 128
sorrel sauce 123
sorrel, French (*Rumex scutatus*) 88
soups 131–32
cucumber with mint 132
stinging nettle 131–32, *131*
vegetable with fresh herbs 132
southernwood (*Artemisia abrotanum*) **49**, *49*
growing 20
in the home 153, 158
sowing seeds 32–33, *33*
Spain 11
spearmint (*Mentha spicata*) 10, **72–73**, *72*
culinary uses 116
essential oil 162
medicinal uses 144
spider mites 30
spittlebugs 30
sprains 149
spreads 127
steam inhalations 145
Stellaria media see chickweed
stem rot 31
stinging nettle *see* nettle
storing herbs 37, 118
strawberries, herbed 135
summer savory (*Satureja hortensis*) 10, 12, **93**, *93*
drying 37
growing 19, 21, 24
sunburn 148
swamp valerian (*Valeriana uliginosa*) 102
Switzerland 12
Symphytum officinale see comfrey
syrups 37, 140

T
table decorations 155
tabouli 134
Tacuinum Sanitatis 10, 11
Tanacetum balsamita subsp. *balsamitoides see* costmary
T. parthenium see feverfew
T. vulgare see tansy

tansy (*Tanacetum vulgare*) 12, **112–13**, *112*
companion planting 31
growing 21
in the home 154, 158
pruning 28
for wildlife 25
Taraxacum officinale see dandelion
tarragon (*Artemisia dracunculus*) **48**, *48*
culinary uses 116
growing 20, 24, 32, 35
medicinal uses 144
Taxus see yew
tea tree (*Melaleuca alternifolia*) **69**, 161
tension 149
Teucrium chamaedrys see germander
Thompson, Samuel 14
thorn apple (*Datura stramonium*) **106–107**, *106*
throats, sore 147
thyme (*Thymus vulgaris*) 22, **98–99**, *98*
baths 163
drying 37
essential oil 162
growing 21, 24, 34
harvesting 36
in the home 152, 154
knot gardens 14, 18
medicinal uses 145, *146*, 147, 148, *148*
storing 118
for wildlife 25
thyme, wild (*Thymus serpyllum*) 98, 99
Thymus x *citriodorus see* lemon thyme
Tilia americana see basswood
T. cordata see linden
T. platyphyllos see linden, large-leaved
tinctures 140
tomatillo and avocado dip 127
tomatoes: garlic, white bean, and sun-dried tomato salsa 127
pizza with herb pesto and goat cheese *126*, 133
tomatoes and yellow peppers with herbs 130
tonka bean 157
"topiary" 155, *155*

tormentil (*Potentilla erecta*) **82–83**
  growing 21
  medicinal uses 142, 147
toxic herbs 104–13
Tropaeolum majus see nasturtium

U
UN Environment Program 6
Urtica dioica see nettle

V
valerian (*Valeriana officinalis*) **101–102**, *101*
  essential oil 160
  growing 21, 26
  medicinal uses 149
Valeriana sitchensis see mountain valerian
Valeriana uliginosa see swamp valerian
varicose veins 149
Vedas 10
vegetable soup with fresh herbs 132

veins, varicose 149
vervain (*Verbena officinalis*) **102–103**, *102*
  growing 21
  medicinal uses 147
vetiver root 157
vinaigrette 121
vinegars, herb-flavored 120, *121*
vitamins 118

W
walnuts: cilantro and lime pesto 124
  mixed herb pesto 126
warts 148
washes 141
watering herbs 28
weighing herbs 139
whiteflies 30
willow (*Salix*) 163
  black (*Salix nigra*) 89
  crack (*Salix fragilis*) 89
  purple (*Salix purpurea*) 89
  violet (*Salix daphnoides*) 89
  white (*Salix alba*) **89**

willow bark 15
wilts 31
winter protection 27, 28
winter savory (*Satureja montana*) 10, 12, **93**, *93*
  growing 21, 24, 25, 34
  knot gardens 14
Winthrop, John 14
"wise" men and women 11
witch hazel (*Hamamelis virginiana*) **60–61**, *60*
  growing 20
  medicinal uses 147, 148, 149
Withering, Dr. William 15
wormwood (*Artemisia absinthium*) 13, **104–105**, *104*
  companion planting 31
  in the home 155, 158
wormwood, Roman (*Artemisia pontica*) 49, *49*
wormwood, sweet (*Artemisia annua*) 49, *49*
wounds 148
wreaths 155

Y
yarrow (*Achillea millefolium*) 10, 22, **40**, *40*
  companion planting 31
  essential oil 160, 161
  growing 20
  in the home 152, 155
  medicinal uses *143*, 144, 149
  skin care 164
  for wildlife 25
yew 6
  English (*Taxus baccata*) **113**, *113*
  Pacific (*Taxus brevifolia*) **113**, *113*

Z
Zingiber officinale see ginger

PHOTOGRAPHIC ACKNOWLEDGMENTS

a=above, b=below, c=centre, l=left, r=right

AKG, London 10 (Erich Lessing), 11, 12, 13 (Erich Lessing)
Liz Artindale 1, 5, 8–9, 16–17, 25r, 38–39, 42a, 47ar, 53, 60l, 66, 82, 84l, 86, 94a, 96l, 105l, 109r, 113, 114–5, 116, 117, 119r, 121, 123, 124, 125, 126, 127, 129, 130, 131, 136–7, 139, 143 (all except 143acr), 144, 145, 146 (all except 146ar), 147, 148, 149, 150–1, 153, 154a, 155, 156a, 157, 158, 159, 160, 161, 163

Royal Horticultural Society, Lindley Library 15
Roger Tabor 2, 3, 7, 18, 19, 22, 23, 24, 25l, 26, 27, 34–35, 36, 40, 41, 42b, 43, 44, 45, 47al, 47ac, 48, 49, 50, 51, 52, 54, 55, 56, 57, 58, 59, 60r, 61, 62, 63, 64, 65, 67, 68, 70, 71, 72, 73, 74, 75, 76, 77, 79, 80, 81, 84r, 85, 87, 88, 90, 91, 92, 93, 94b, 95, 96r, 97, 98, 99, 100, 101, 102, 103, 105r, 106, 107, 108, 109l, 110, 111, 112, 118, 119al, 119bl, 122, 135, 142, 143acr, 146ar, 152, 154b, 156b